Happy 75th birthday, Pacific National Exhibition!

To help celebrate the 75th anniversary of the founding of the Vancouver Exhibition Association in 1907, this history of the PNE was produced in conjunction with the University of British Columbia Press.

Our thanks to Professor David Breen and historical researcher Ken Coates of U.B.C. for their excellent work on this project.

On behalf of the Board of Directors of the PNE, I sincerely hope you enjoy reading this enlightening document about the Pacific National Exhibition — a provincial institution which has served the people of British Columbia very well, and will continue to do so in the future.

Erwin M. Swangard

Erwin M. Swangard
President
Pacific National Exhibition

VANCOUVER'S FAIR

VANCOUVER'S FAIR

AN ADMINISTRATIVE AND POLITICAL HISTORY
OF THE PACIFIC NATIONAL EXHIBITION

DAVID BREEN AND KENNETH COATES

UNIVERSITY OF BRITISH COLUMBIA PRESS

VANCOUVER

VANCOUVER'S FAIR: AN ADMINISTRATIVE AND POLITICAL HISTORY

Canadian Cataloguing in Publication Data

Breen, David H.
    Vancouver's Fair

    Bibliography: p.
    Includes index.
    ISBN 0-7748-0161-1

    1. Pacific National Exhibition — History.
I. Coates, Kenneth, 1956-   II. Title.
S557.C22V353   607'.34'71133   C82-091210-7

INTERNATIONAL STANDARD BOOK NUMBER 0-7748-0161-1

Printed in Canada

Contents

Tables

Appendices

Illustrations

Maps

Plates

following p.102

Photographic Credits

All the photographs, with the exception of Plate 10 (courtesy of the Vancouver Public Library) and Plate 17 (courtesy of Allen Aerial Photos Ltd.), are reproduced with the kind permission of the Pacific National Exhibition.

Acknowledgements

Without the generous and helpful assistance of others this study would not have been possible. The archivists at the Public Archives of Canada and particularly those at Vancouver City Archives looked after our many requests with diligence and good humour. The Pacific National Exhibition allowed unrestricted access to contemporary board minutes, general mangers' and department files as well as all P.N.E. commissioned reports. For this, and for their constant support of this endeavour, we are especially grateful to P.N.E. President, Erwin Swangard, and Communications and Marketing Manager, Bill Joyner. Professor Robert McDonald helped us to better understand the political environment in Vancouver and Professor David Jones offered helpful comments upon the sociology of fairs. Jane Fredeman and the capable editorial staff at University of British Columbia Press helped us effect numerous improvements to the original manuscript. What merits this book may have owes much to the above mentioned; responsibility for what deficiencies remain rests with us.

To Derek, Stuart, Patrick, Bradley and Mark
who helped us better appreciate the essence
of the fair

1

Fairs and Exhibitions: an Historical Background

Fair and exhibition: these words instantly conjure up memories of candy floss, ferris wheels, roller coasters, livestock displays, the urgent cry of the operator of a game of chance, and the hustle and bustle of the carnival. Few people in North America have not been to a fair of some description, be it a small rural show, a major presentation such as Toronto's Canadian National Exhibition, or even an international "World's Fair" like Expo '67 in Montreal. To the people of Canada and the United States, the fair, large or small, is an institution that is at once familiar and nostalgic.

The fair is not, however, uniquely North American, although the institution has undergone some significant transformations on this continent. Fairs have been important social and economic factors in Europe since the Middle Ages. Although normally inspired by religious festivals, these early fairs had important commercial and entertainment components. Often serving as vital showplaces for local agricultural production, they quickly assumed an important marketing function for area farmers, particularly in France and England. Local craftsmen also took advantage of these regular assemblages to market their products, offering a variety of wares from clothing to household commodities. On the social side, fairs offered a break in the normal routine and drew people from a wide area to a central location. When jesters, musicians, and other entertainers began to follow the fair circuits, their performances generated a levity which provided a welcome respite from both the drudgery of everyday life and the commerce of the marketplace.[1]

As the agricultural revolution that accompanied the development of commercial agriculture swept across Europe in the eighteenth century, it became clear to some that many farmers were not aware of new farming technology or improved livestock breeding methods and therefore were not able to operate at maximum efficiency. Progressive farmers in England, often members of the old land-holding aristocracy, with a vested interest in improving tenant production, took an active interest in the dissemination of the newly acquired knowledge. To that end, they organized agricultural societies, offering prizes for new experiments and rewarding examples of agricultural excellence, from prize bulls to sheaves of wheat. The various societies quickly realized that the rural fairs provided a unique opportunity to promote the advancement of agriculture by comparing crops and livestock and spreading information on new techniques and practices. The rise of "progressive" agriculture, therefore, gave the British fair a new component, and, in time, the various contests for produce, cattle, and poultry came to serve as the focus for many annual gatherings.[2]

The concept and practices of the agricultural society and, through such organizations, the idea of the competitive agricultural fair soon spread to North America and was well established by the beginning of the nineteenth century. Societies were formed in Philadelphia, Pennsylvania, and Charleston, South Carolina, in 1795, and through the efforts of such men as Elkanel Watson, the "Father of the American Agricultural Fair," similar organizations were soon to be found scattered along the eastern seaboard of the United States.[3] British North America was not left behind, with the Agricultural Society of Upper Canada being formed in 1792. By 1854 more than fifty separate agricultural organizations were recorded in the Province of Upper Canada (Ontario), and under their aegis the development of agricultural fairs continued apace. The government of Upper Canada, recognizing the value of such events, even sponsored a provincial exhibition in 1846, offering 400 pounds sterling in prizes to try to attract competitors from throughout the colony.[4]

Newly arriving settlers brought this heritage to the Canadian prairies and Pacific coast in the last half of the nineteenth century. The first fair in the West was held near Victoria, on Vancouver Island, in 1861. Other communities quickly followed with their own. Winnipeg staged a fair in 1871, and the following year Portage la Prairie opened its first exhibition. The government of Manitoba took an active role in the development of both agricultural societies and fairs, establishing a prize fund for agricultural competitions in 1871 and sponsoring a provincial exhibition, held for the first time at Portage la Prairie in 1883. From these beginnings, fairs multiplied across the prairies, and by 1890 every self-respecting community in Manitoba and the Northwest Territories (Alberta and Saskatchewan) staged an annual show. The major centres clambered to jump on the bandwagon, with Edmonton (1879), Brandon (1882), Regina (1884), and Calgary (1888) heading the growing list of prairie fairs.[5]

Communities in British Columbia were actually ahead of their prairie counterparts. Following Victoria, Cowichan and Saanich presented their first shows in 1866, New Westminster in 1869, and Chilliwack in 1874. Interior fairs came somewhat later, reflecting the fact that only limited agricultural development occurred before the completion of the Canadian Pacific Railway in 1886. Kamloops joined the growing ranks of B.C. fairs in 1895 while Armstrong, later to offer the most important interior exhibition, did not commence fair activities until 1900.[6]

While these early fairs were largely agricultural, industry and manufacturing were soon vying with livestock and farm produce for the fair spotlight. This development, like the evolution of the agricultural fair, can also be traced to England and the formation of the urban-based industrial exhibition. Presentations of this type go back to 1756, when a national exhibition of manufacturing wares was held in London. A century later, in 1851, London's renowned Crystal Palace was the site of the first major international exposition. Industrial exhibitors, recognizing the tremendous advertising potential of the fair, used the occasion to reach potential markets throughout Europe. Other such expositions followed as both cities and nations became aware of the publicity and commercial benefits attending a world class exhibition. Paris in 1889, Chicago in 1893, St. Louis in 1904 are but three of the many cities which adapted the concept developed by the great London exposition.[7] While most fairs in North America stopped far short of copying the presentations of the international exposition, their development had a striking impact on the Canadian and American exhibitions. Recently settled regions and expanding urban centres both recognized the potential marketing value of the exhibition and quickly adapted the agricultural fair to the area's or city's needs.

After 1900, boosterism, regional pride coupled with unabashed salesmanship, became an increasingly important ingredient. It was crucial, promoters of this type of fair argued, not only to acknowledge superior produce, but also to identify it with a particular region. In Calgary, this development actually preceded the establishment of an agricultural fair, since the local agricultural society was more intent upon exhibiting the potential of their area to the Ontario business community than it was in promoting an annual fair. Samples of Calgary-area farm produce were gathered and sent for display at the Toronto exhibition.[8] Individuals who wanted to use fairs for this purpose felt it necessary to turn the events into publicity extravaganzas. Displays of mineral resources and local industrial output competed with agricultural products, as the organizers strove to exhibit their area's potential for future development and prosperity. To this end, fairs were not approached in a haphazard or indifferent fashion, but rather were organized with considerable urgency. Promotors saw the presentation as an excellent means of encouraging development, which would eventually have as a by-product enhanced regional real estate values. Not surprisingly, therefore, many land speculators and local boosters encouraged the development of exhibitions and argued vigorously that the agricultural components of the fair should be downplayed in favour of industrial and natural resource displays.

The organizers of an exhibition were therefore confronted right from the beginning with the need for a balance between boosterism and agriculture. This in itself would be a difficult task, but the problem was compounded by the existence of a third element — entertainment. Indeed, to many the fair was simply a carnival, a collection of games and amusements designed solely to entertain. The conflict between these three components began in the Middle Ages when jesters, criminals, and merchants first recognized the potential profit in joining with a fair, and it continues to the present day, where multi-million dollar amusement complexes vie with livestock shows and industrial exhibits for the attention of the fairgoer.

These components — agriculture, boosterism, and entertainment — can be found in virtually every North American fair. There are, of course, other activities which form integral parts of all fairs, including hobby and craft competitions, horticultural shows, presentations of "Women's Work," athletic events, and horse-racing, but it is the three key elements, or more correctly the balance between them, which determines the structure and content of an individual fair. Any exhibition placing particular emphasis on the "booster" component, as Vancouver's fair did in the first years, ran the risk of becoming more of an industrial showcase than a true exhibition. A more agriculturally oriented fair, such as the one in New Westminster, typically devoted less attention to entertainment, and in consequence sometimes experienced difficulty attracting a sufficiently large urban audience to ensure financial viability. The balance ultimately achieved by any particular fair reflects not just the aspirations of the exhibition association, but also and more importantly, it indicates the preferences of the host community. For this reason, the content of the fair, the emphasis on agriculture, boosterism, or entertainment, provides a useful image of the setting in which the fair functioned.

As Wayne Neely, one of the few scholars who has examined American agricultural fairs, noted years ago: "It is evident that fairs are the creation of the society underlying them, and that they are established, shaped and sometimes abolished in response to the processes that change that society."[9] But while fairs and exhibitions are such a prominent feature of urban and rural environments, and though the study of an individual North American fair seems an attractive perspective from which to view a particular community, to this point historians and others have shown little interest. Though discussion of fairs and exhibitions turns up in a remarkably diverse range of studies, in very few of these does the fair appear as other than a representative sidelight to a larger theme or issue before it is quickly absorbed into the larger topic under consideration.[10]

Convinced that "the fair" makes a worthy topic in its own right, we have directed our attention to the origins and development of the Pacific National Exhibition (P.N.E.), held annually in Vancouver, British Columbia, since 1910. The P.N.E.'s first purpose was to organize a yearly fair, and to do so, it always had to pay close attention to and function within the setting of civic politics. For this reason and because we have had access to board minutes that are uninterrupted from 1907, we felt it was appropriate that the central focus of this study should be on the fair's political and administrative history. We seek to address the politics of the fair, to examine guiding principles and forces that determined the character of each year's fair as well as the management of exhibition facilities, and to understand how these changed over time. The very important, but more elusive, social dimension of the fair and what it reveals about the urban community is not an explicit part of this study. This dimension we have left to a companion volume, an illustrated history. In all, our purpose will be largely served if in shedding some light upon the nature of the Pacific National Exhibition and upon the dynamics of the relationships between the fair and the city, we lead others to similar and perhaps more wide-ranging endeavours.

2

Origins of the Vancouver Exhibition Association, 1907-1910

Compared to other North American and western Canadian communities, Vancouver was late to establish an exhibition. The city was incorporated in 1886, only one year before the Canadian Pacific Railway extended its main line from Port Moody to the western end of Burrard Inlet. The extension ensured the future growth and development of what had been, until that time, a small lumbering community. In this early period, the city's boosters knew few limits, with businessmen and less savoury speculators alike extolling the economic prospects and the "guaranteed" future prosperity of Canada's "Gateway to the Pacific."[1]

As had happened elsewhere, a number of Vancouverites quickly struck upon the idea of an exhibition, believing that it could serve as more than simply an entertainment for local residents and a forum for the display of agricultural excellence. These men believed that the show could help advertise the agricultural and natural resource potential of British Columbia and the crucial role Vancouver was destined to play in exploiting this potential. The first serious proposal that such a fair be held was made in 1890 during negotiations between the Vancouver City Council and the B.C. Jockey Club concerning the development of a small corner of Hastings Park. Mayor David Oppenheimer favoured the establishment of an exhibition to utilize the park in conjunction with the Jockey Club. At his urging, a joint committee of the City Council and the Jockey Club was formed, but nothing materialized and two years later the B.C. Jockey Club proceeded on its own, constructing a small race track with the assistance of a $10,000 civic grant.[2]

Throughout the next seventeen years, there were various suggestions calling for an agricultural exhibition in Vancouver. A 1902 proposal recommended the construction of exhibition buildings and the holding of a fair on the south side of

False Creek.³ Like those before it, this idea died quickly, never going beyond the stage of minor public debate. The failure to develop an exhibition for Vancouver in this period was not for want of public spirit or boosterism among the citizenry, for both qualities were to be found in considerable supply. Nor was the inactivity owing to a lack of interest in the development of agriculture and other resource industries, for many Vancouverites were interested in the expansion of all economic activity in the province. Vancouver's major problem in attempting to get beyond the proposal stage and into the planning phase was the existence of the nearby New Westminster Exhibition, an annual fair presented since 1869 by that community's Royal Agricultural and Industrial Society. This exhibition was by far the largest in the province, and it had ample funding from both the dominion and provincial governments. Its size and the largesse of its prize lists ensured that it attracted agricultural exhibitors from throughout British Columbia, the Pacific Northwest, and the Canadian prairies and that it served as the focus for exhibition activities in the Lower Mainland. Most local agricultural societies, pet and livestock societies, hobby and craft groups were already committed to working with it. Vancouver was to find it very difficult to attract these organizations away from the R.A.I.S. fair. As well, the fact that much of the agricultural activity of the Fraser River Valley centred on the river rather than on Burrard Inlet made New Westminster appear a far more logical site than Vancouver for a rural-oriented exhibition.

In addition to the Royal Agricultural and Industrial Society's annual exhibition, a number of other agricultural societies in the Lower Mainland had been holding regular fairs. In 1910, the first year an exhibition was held in Vancouver, there was a total of twelve other fairs held west of Hope. With the exception of the New Westminster exhibition, which ran for five days, these shows were one- or two-day affairs. Dates for the various exhibitions were arranged to allow exhibitors to travel from one fair to another in succession, competing in as many as five exhibitions in a little over a week.⁴ It was clear, therefore, that the fairs of the Lower Mainland, and especially the New Westminster exhibition, were serving the needs of the local agricultural community. This made it difficult for supporters of a Vancouver exhibition to garner the widespread organizational assistance necessary for the successful development of an additional agricultural fair.

New Westminster and the other local exhibitions were not, however, meeting all of the specific demands of Vancouverites, and, ironically, it was the R.A.I.S.'s failure to respond to the requests of several Vancouver animal clubs which indirectly led to the founding of an exhibitor association for Vancouver. Henry S. Rolston, an early member of the Vancouver Exhibition Association and later manager of the fair, claimed that he decided to join the Vancouver fair organization when the New Westminster Exhibition refused to meet the demands of the Vancouver Poultry and Pet Stock Association, the Vancouver Kennel Club, and several other similar groups.⁵ The dissatisfaction of these people with the treatment they received from the R.A.I.S. and with the facilities available at New

Westminster seems to have provided the spark required to launch an organizational drive to form an exhibition association in Vancouver.

Equally important was the fact that a number of real estate promoters and Vancouver boosters recognized the potential advertising benefits attending a major civic exposition. It was the amalgamation of the boosters and those who wanted to show small animals and pets which led to the formation of the Vancouver Exhibition Association (V.E.A.) in 1907.

The man usually credited with being the most important force in the establishment of the association is J.C.V. Field-Johnson, an English newspaper-man whose enthusiasm for the concept originated with his earlier involvement with the exhibition in Winnipeg.[6] Field-Johnson arranged a preliminary meeting, which was held in the real estate office of Thomas Duke on 31 May 1907. The meeting, chaired by financial agent Edward Odlum, was a small gathering, comprising only twelve men. In calling for a general public meeting to discuss the formation of an association, the group declared that:

> in the opinion of this meeting the time has arrived for the establishment of an Exhibition Association for Vancouver to embrace Fat Stock, horses, dogs, poultry, also Horticultural, Agricultural and industrial interests and also for the object of maintaining the City of Vancouver in that leading position she by rights should occupy.[7]

This statement, exhibiting a combination of agricultural and "booster" interests, suggests the split personality with which the exhibition association would ultimately emerge.

The motivation of the founding members can be revealed in some measure through an examination of their economic and social backgrounds. The dozen men who gathered in Thomas Duke's office, while all established businessmen, could not, with few exceptions, be ranked among Vancouver's entrepreneurial and social elite. Of the twelve, not one was a member of the exclusive and prestigious Vancouver Club, the hallmark of social prominence in the city.[8] Several of the men, Odlum, Thomas Duke, and Charles Woodward, did have substantial business standing in the community. Odlum had extensive real estate and promotional interests, Duke was active in retailing in addition to his involvement in real estate, and Woodward was a prominent local merchant, who founded what became the Woodward's department store chain.

Looking more broadly at the 1907 V.E.A., this time including the first executive and the twenty elected committee members, several interesting patterns emerge. With the exception of R.H.S. Sperling, the general manager of the B.C. Electric Railway Company, none of these twenty-six men could claim upper level social prominence in the city. Interestingly, while only Sperling belonged to the Vancouver Club, at least six of the other men were members of the Terminal City

Club, which catered to the broader business community and lacked the exclusiveness of the haughty Vancouver Club. There were a number of prominent businessmen in the association, in addition to the four men discussed above; among them were L. D. Taylor, a local publisher and later mayor, Harold Clarke, also a publisher, Alderman E. H. Heaps, who was active in the timber industry, and P. N. Smith of the B.C. Leather Company. While the motives of the early leaders were not entirely self-serving, it seems clear that some members saw the V.E.A. not only as a vehicle for promoting the interests of the City of Vancouver but also as a means of furthering their own long-term personal interests. For example, four of them, J. J. Miller, Odlum, Duke, and Field-Johnson were primarily involved in the sale or promotion of real estate, as were several other members of that first committee. In addition, H. S. Rolston, a member of the initial executive, was a retailer of farm implements, while W. E. Flumerfelt, first secretary of the organization, was secretary of the Vancouver Tourist Association and consequently had particular interest and expertise in the promotion of the city. If the men constituting the first board of the Vancouver Exhibition had anything in common, it was the attachment of their financial interests to the growth and prosperity of Vancouver. The larger businessmen, with only one exception, were involved in urban-based activities which depended for their development on the expansion of the city. Less economically prominent individuals on the board, including Mayor Alexander Bethune and three aldermen, held similar attachments to the urban centre and undoubtedly saw in the V.E.A. a means of increasing the importance of Vancouver.[9]

The Vancouver Exhibition Association was, therefore, founded by essentially middle-rank businessmen whose financial interests were tied not to provincial, national, or international markets, but to the City of Vancouver. There is no evidence to suggest that any of these men saw the association as a device that might bring them direct economic benefit. Rather, there was a general feeling that an annual fair offered a very desirable means of promoting Vancouver's growth and development. But this was an objective with which city-centred businessmen could especially identify. In short, despite some rhetoric to the contrary, boosterism was at least as important to the early association as was the development of agriculture. This was to lead shortly to considerable and often acrimonious debate within the V.E.A. and among the wider community, with proponents of agricultural fairs criticizing the economic orientation of some of the V.E.A.'s activities, while supporters of an industrial, or booster-type, fair complained that agricultural exhibitions should be left to rural areas while Vancouver focused its endeavours on a more urban-oriented show. This dilemma was to haunt the Vancouver Exhibition throughout its history.

The first constitution of the V.E.A. demonstrates the organization's attempt to rationalize these conflicting positions into a statement of purposes and intentions for the fledgling association. The document stated that:

The objects of the Association are for the good of our country and our people to organize and conduct exhibitions for:

(a) The promotion of practical and scientific husbandry in all its branches.
(b) The improvement of the breed of horses, cattle, sheep, pigs, dogs, poultry, and other barn and domestic animals.
(c) The development of the industrial resources of the country.
(d) The dissemination of mechanical and scientific knowledge.
(e) The encouragement of the cultivation of the beautiful in nature and art.
(f) The stimulation of healthy rivalry for supremacy and excellence in the minds of the rising generation.
(g) The promotion of trade and commerce.
(h) The development of the rich mineral, fishing and lumbering resources of the country.[10]

According to the stated objectives, the V.E.A. intended to produce an omnibus exhibition, incorporating something for everyone under the general rubric of an agricultural fair. While the position sounded plausible and sensible in draft, it proved difficult to attain in practice. In many ways, the evolution of Vancouver's exhibition can be seen as an attempt to reconcile the disparate aims and ambitions of its founders, to select the appropriate level of integration between agriculture and industry, booster and country fair, local development and regional expansion. If the objectives and intentions were set so broadly as to capture the support of every interest group, so too was there general agreement that the first exhibition should be staged as soon as possible, with the fall of 1908 touted as a likely start-up date.

With charter in hand, founding members of the Vancouver Exhibition Association began immediately to expand the organization and to give substance to the constitutional framework. Setting the annual membership fee at two dollars (a fee subsequently raised to five dollars), the association moved to expand "public" involvement and raise money for administrative purposes. The twenty-six-man committee and executive was then divided into groups of two, with each group assigned to a section of the city to canvass for members. The search for recruits was not, however, as widespread as it might appear on the surface. It was in essence a canvass of the business community. The search was not intended solely to recruit additional manpower, although volunteers of suitable background and expertise were not turned away. The main thrust was directed towards the solicitation of funds, particularly through the sale of a special category of membership, the $100 life subscription.[11]

To further the aims of the association and, in particular, to make the financial, legal, and other arrangements necessary to hold an annual exhibition, the initial members next elected an executive and established a committee-based administrative structure. The first committees included Finance, Works and Grounds, Publicity and Advertising, and Scheduling. A fifth, the Transportation Committee, was added shortly thereafter. The committee structure was revised twice more before the first exhibition, with Sports and Attractions being added in 1909, then dropped early in 1910, with a committee of Prize Lists replacing it on the roster.[12] The expansion of the association's activities as the fair approached made it obvious that the limited committee structure could not accommodate the increasing workload. To prepare the individual events for the exhibition, a series of departments was established, and the V.E.A. drew heavily on existing organizations in the city to man them, allowing horticultural societies to organize the flower show, sheep breeders' groups to operate the sheep show and so on. An examination of the departmental structure suggests that in the balance between agricultural and industrial exhibits, the former had tipped the scale, with far more departments devoted to agricultural pursuits than urban concerns. The agricultural departments, however, drew heavily upon the outside organizations, leaving the core membership of the association free to apply its efforts to the larger direction of the exhibition. Each of the eighteen departments listed below was chaired by a director of the V.E.A.

Departmental Structure of the V.E.A., 1910[13]

Speed (racing)	Natural History
Dogs	Floriculture
Poultry and Pet Stock	Fine Arts
Educational	Harness and Hunting
Women's Work	Agricultural Products
Cattle	Attractions
Breeding Classes	Sheep and Swine
Machinery	Grounds and Buildings
Dairy Produce and Honey	Concessions

While the Board of Management (Control) retained considerable control over the association's activities, it was soon apparent that the board could not scrutinize the daily affairs of the organization in detail, particularly after the preparation of grounds for the exhibition began. As a result, they decided to hire an organizing secretary to supervise the association's affairs on a part-time basis. The position was advertised in early 1909, and from among the six who applied, W. E. Flumerfelt, former secretary of the Vancouver Tourist Association and the only member of the V.E.A. to apply for the post, was given the $100 a month job. Flumerfelt unfortunately fell ill shortly thereafter, and in July of that year he was forced to resign. Just as Flumerfelt was stepping down, the association decided to hire James Roy as manager of the exhibition. He was initially allocated a salary of

$250 per month, but with the rather interesting proviso that he was responsible for raising the money himself. Roy's appointment is important because he was the first full-time employee of the association. To save money and rationalize the management, Roy was also named to the recently vacated position of secretary, and his post was redesignated as secretary-manager.[14]

Once the Vancouver Exhibition Association had been established as a functioning organization, the group turned quickly to the two most important matters at hand, funding the exhibition and gaining control over the selected site. Financial arrangements were uppermost in the minds of the early directors, and they turned in some haste to various sources. The dominion government, which provided some assistance to most major western Canadian fairs by subsidizing prize money given for agricultural competitions (called prize lists), loans for building projects, and grants to specific fairs designated as Dominion Exhibitions, appeared the most likely source for funds. When it became known in 1909 that the funding for a dominion exhibition was to be granted to British Columbia the following year, the V.E.A. launched a series of written and personal representations to the federal minister of agriculture, Sidney Fisher, in an attempt to secure the show and the attending $50,000 grant. But to the association's chagrin, the decision was made in favour of the already well-established New Westminster fair where logic dictated the grant belonged.[15]

The association's luck with the provincial government was not much better. Knowing that Victoria was accustomed to providing financial support for British Columbia fairs and exhibitions, the Vancouver Exhibition Association set out to ask for an initial grant of $25,000, a request later raised to $50,000. Using examples of regional government aid for exhibitions in other provinces and even in B.C. to support their case, the association was relatively confident that the grant would be forthcoming. The directors were, therefore, more than a little perturbed when the provincial government turned down their request, arguing that the Lower Mainland was being well served by the New Westminster exhibition. The province did not, however, reject the V.E.A. appeal outright, offering $10,000 to be applied to the prize lists instead of the "no strings attached" grant requested by the association.[16]

Association directors should not have been entirely unprepared for the rebuffs they had received from Victoria and Ottawa, for even though they had approached the senior levels of government with the assurance that they had the support of Vancouver citizens, the struggle to gain widespread public backing had had its ups and downs and had nearly destroyed the V.E.A. before a single exhibition had been staged. One of the first actions of the executive was to approach City Council to ask for permission to submit a by-law to the ratepayers, asking for $50,000 to initiate the development of exhibition facilities.[17] Council allowed the proposal to be presented, scheduling the vote for January 1908. Trying to ensure passage of the by-law, the V.E.A. wrote to all aldermanic candidates soliciting their support and appointed a special committee to advertise the association's plans and address public meetings.

The Vancouver Exhibition Association was not particularly successful in capturing the imagination of the electorate. While there was some specific criticism of the concept of Vancouver exhibition, the popular feeling appeared to be one of caution rather than opposition. One commentator writing on the eve of the vote reflected the general mood:

> A sum of $50,000 is asked for as a loan to a proposed exhibition. A loan of this kind means practically a grant to a scheme of which the success is highly problematical. The amount is not very large but in view of present financial conditions, it might, perhaps, not be unwise to postpone the matter.[18]

Three-fifths of the total vote was required for a money by-law to pass. Much to the dismay of the V.E.A., the association lost by a mere 43 votes. Of the total vote, the by-law was supported by 58 per cent, only 2 per cent below the required margin.

Vancouver was at this time operating under a ward system, with the city divided into six districts for election purposes. As Table 1 illustrates, support for the by-law was strongest in the wards closest to the proposed Hastings Park exhibition. This region was, in 1908, less densely populated than the remainder of the city. Property owners in these underdeveloped wards probably saw the exhibition as a means of encouraging expansion in the city's East End which would, in turn, increase land and house values and stimulate the extension of civic services. The downtown districts were far less supportive. Nevertheless, with the exception of the downtown core, Ward 2, the by-law received a majority in each district.

TABLE 1: V.E.A. BY-LAW RESULTS, 1908-1910[19]
(Per cent in favour)

Ward #	West End		East Side		Other		City-wide
	1	2	3	4	5	6	
1908	53	45	70	65	63	55	59
1909	55	49	80	65	65	56	61
1910	65	60	79	75	67	62	68

Temporarily rocked by the defeat, the V.E.A. rallied in the aftermath of the rejection by the ratepayers. Taking some solace in the fact that a majority had favoured the by-law, the membership declared unanimously shortly thereafter that it was "the opinion of this Association that we should continue to carry on the work of the exhibition to a finish."[20] They turned immediately to City Council and asked for permission to resubmit the by-law the following year, counting on the close decision to ensure council's agreement. The council, however, turned down the request. Angered by the lack of assistance from the civic government, the

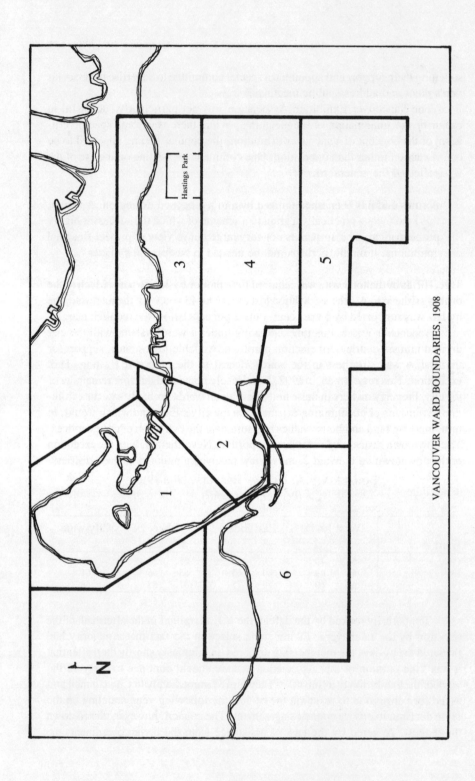

VANCOUVER WARD BOUNDARIES, 1908

association charged that the move was "calculated to retard the progress of the City" and was "not a reflection of the public spirit of the people."[21] Unable to rely on council for support, the V.E.A.'s Executive Council decided to take matters into their own hands, stating rather bitterly,

> that the time has arrived when public opinion should be awakened to the interests they possess in that splendid property — the Hastings Park which for twenty years has been totally neglected and abandoned by the Park Authorities and has been monopolized by and for racing purposes.[22]

The association struck a responsive chord and, through public meetings and by lobbying the mayor and the aldermen, succeeded in having the $50,000 by-law placed before the ratepayers a second time.[23]

The 1909 ballot was a virtual re-run of the previous year's vote, this time resulting in a narrow victory for the Vancouver Exhibition Association. The tables tipped ever so slightly, and the association emerged with twenty-five votes more than the requisite 60 per cent. Once again, support was divided, with the heaviest favourable vote coming from east-side wards and the strongest opposition from the central city district. The victory, however narrow, gave the V.E.A. the public funding required to commence the physical development of the exhibition grounds and the planning for Vancouver's first fair.[24] (See Table 1.)

Even with the $50,000 boost from the ratepayers, the association was far from ready to begin with the first exhibition. The first civic loan provided little more than seed money for clearing some sections of land in Hastings Park and erecting rudimentary fencing.[25] As plans for the physical development of the Park were finalized, the V.E.A.'s financial needs became more acute. While at this time they still hoped for assistance from both the federal and provincial governments, the V.E.A. was conscious that previous approaches had not proven fruitful and there was little reason to expect the position of either government to change, particularly as the New Westminster exhibition continued to flourish. The one major recourse, therefore, was the city; they would have to ask council once again to allow the association to place a by-law before the ratepayers.

In October of 1909, the V.E.A. asked council for $125,000 for the construction of a grandstand with exhibition halls underneath ($50,000), clearing of land ($10,000), fencing ($5,000), drainage and sewage ($10,000), and sundry other developments. The V.E.A.'s $50,000 appropriation was all but exhausted, and there were few other sources of income in sight. It was with some trepidation, therefore, that the association approached council for the third successive year. In the interval, through the effective lobbying of Aldermen McSpadden, a member of the V.E.A., the council had been swung around squarely behind the exhibition, and while they did not pass on the association's request verbatim, they did allow a by-law request for $85,000. The vote, held on 13 January 1910, indicated that the ratepayers, like council, had at last been convinced not only of the value of an exhibition for Vancouver but, equally important, that the Vancouver Exhibition Association was capable of organizing one. More than three-quarters of the ratepayers favoured the by-law with even such formerly recalcitrant areas as Ward 2, the downtown district, voting upwards of 60 per cent in support of the exhibition. The two wards closest to the Hastings Park grounds, Wards 3 and 4, once again displayed their solid support for the development of the park. (See Table 1.) The V.E.A. had, it seemed, gained a public vote of confidence with this victory and could now proceed with the development of Vancouver's first exhibition.[26]

This turnaround in the by-law fortunes of the V.E.A. was not solely the result of the organization's status within the city. Vancouver, British Columbia, and the Canadian West in general were moving into an era of unprecedented expansion and prosperity. As the economy continued to improve, the ratepayers of Vancouver became increasingly generous. Also, the exhibition was well suited to the city's growing boosterism, and as Vancouver expanded and prospered, it seemed only fitting that an urban fair reflecting the growth and development of the area be well funded.

Still, the Vancouver Exhibition Association had not relied entirely upon public munificence to finance the operations of the organization. After the rejection of the 1908 by-law, the association recognized that they would always be financially vulnerable if they depended upon public grants and so they tried to find ways to reduce this dependence. The one major avenue left open was voluntary subscriptions. Initially, the $5 annual and $100 life memberships had provided little income to the association, serving primarily to pay for administrative costs. By 1910, however, after several successful canvasses of the city's business district, the V.E.A. was able to claim revenue of $17,125 from the sale of life memberships, representing 170 new members, and dues of $1,945 from over 380 annual members.[27] While such amounts were substantial and of obvious benefit to the association, the timing of the subscriptions was such that they were of little help to the association in its years of financial distress. The majority of the memberships came, not from 1907 to 1909, when the V.E.A. was in real danger of being dragged down by a lack of funds, but in 1910, when the association was in a more stable financial position and was on the verge of launching its first exhibition.

Simultaneous with the attempts to secure funding, the V.E.A. had moved to acquire a property on which to develop exhibition facilities. Shortly after the association had been formed, in July 1907, the directors had voted to hold their exhibitions at Hastings Park and to approach the civic government for a lease of the land. Hastings Park, the city's second largest after Stanley Park, had been transferred to Vancouver by the British Columbia government in 1889 after the local government had asked for a grant of land in the eastern section of the city in order to stimulate its development. As part of a winter works programme, the city

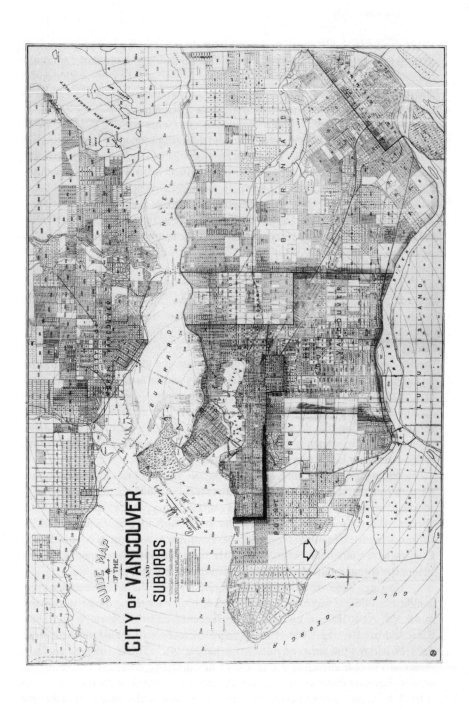

GUIDE MAP
—OF THE—

CITY OF VANCOUVER
AND
SUBURBS

fathers wanted to build a road to the east from the city centre and it seemed logical to them that the road should have a suitable destination. A major park, not unlike Stanley Park on the western flank of Vancouver, appeared to be a reasonable choice and the province agreed. Indeed, the final 160-acre land grant finally awarded the city was actually larger than City Council's original request.[28]

At the time there was some confusion as to what purpose the park was to serve. Mayor David Oppenheimer is quoted as saying soon after the land transfer that "This Park will no doubt become a pleasant pleasure resort in the near future, having many equal advantages with Stanley Park. This Park must eventually become a constant resort for all lovers of romantic woodland scenery and lovely groves."[29] While Oppenheimer appeared to believe that the park would be left in a natural state, City Council was not similarly disposed. Indeed, with limited access to the area, there was little rush to utilize the park and few ideas about what to do with it.

Importantly, and rather surprisingly, Hastings Park was not turned over to the Board of Park Commissioners, an elected body responsible for the administration of civic parks, but rather remained under the control of City Council. The motive for council's action was simple. Hastings Park was not to remain as another natural park, but rather was to be developed to serve the amusement and sporting interests of the citizens of Vancouver. The first project suggested for the park was the development of facilities for an exhibition, but that idea died quickly. Indeed, lack of a neighbourhood population (the densely settled area was still a considerable distance to the west) meant that there were initially no demands to develop the land or even requests to improve access to the heavily forested property. The first serious suggestion that development of the grounds take place was made a year after the transfer, when a local horse-racing club approached council with a request that land be provided for the construction of a race track.[30]

While the Jockey Club was granted the use of approximately fifteen acres of the park in 1890, the lease was held in abeyance until 1892. In that year, the B.C. Jockey Club was formed, and the new organization bought the original race track charter. Although a small race track and grandstand were prepared, the racing facilities hardly constituted a major development.[31] Nevertheless, the Jockey Club's area remained the only section of Hastings Park to be developed in any way before the formation of the Vancouver Exhibition Association.

Hastings Park was, in many ways, an unusual location for a major urban exhibition. While it was civic property, which suggested that it might be available to the V.E.A. at little or no cost, it was far removed from the city's population base. Additionally, there was virtually no public access to the park, since the street car lines had not yet been extended to the park in 1907. Those using the grounds, principally people attending B.C. Jockey Club meetings, came to the park by train or boat. Remembering the real estate backgrounds of many of the early members of the V.E.A. and, more importantly, the booster philosophy which permeated the entire organization, it seems that the selection of Hastings Park for the erection of fair facilities was made very much with a view towards the long-term development of Vancouver.

The V.E.A. moved quickly to secure a lease to Hastings Park, sending a delegation to wait on City Council in 1907 to discuss the transfer of the land. After more than a year's agitation, City Council finally approved the Vancouver Exhibition Association's request in December of 1908, offering the organization sixty acres in the northwest corner of the park for $1 a year, the lease to run for five years.[32]

The granting of the lease was not greeted with equanimity throughout the city, although the vote for the 1909 by-law, held only one month later, suggests that the majority of the ratepayers favoured the development of the park for exhibition purposes. Two groups in particular, the B.C. Jockey Club and the Parks Board, took umbrage at council's actions and protested the lease. The Jockey Club, the original tenant at Hastings Park, stood to lose substantially from the transaction since the proposed lease incorporated the race track into the V.E.A.'s grounds. A series of meetings were held between the exhibition association, the Jockey Club, and City Council in an attempt to reach an amicable solution, but on each occasion the discussion broke off without a resolution of the matter. The V.E.A. had initially adopted a fairly conciliatory attitude towards the Jockey Club, offering the racing interests a lease for the race track, stables and grandstand rent free for five years, with the club obliged to maintain all facilities in good order. With this tentative agreement in place, the V.E.A. experienced considerable difficulty in getting their own lease for Hastings Park past City Council. The council's hesitation in this instance was caused by mounting opposition to racing in a public park, led by such groups as the Mount Pleasant Council of the Royal Templars of Temperance. Reacting to growing public pressure and anxious to conclude lease negotiations, the V.E.A. withdrew from the tentative agreement with the Jockey Club. The result was that horse-racing was forced out of Hastings Park, much to the chagrin of the racing fraternity and the delight of the growing number of opponents of the sport.[33]

The second major opponent of the V.E.A., while not enjoying any wider support than the Jockey Club had, was to haunt the association for a number of years. The Parks Board publicly declared that it was "opposed to leasing of any park or portion of park to any person or corporation."[34] The board was, it seems, attempting to stop short two potentially damaging precedents, the alienation of lands from the parks system for development and the leasing of park lands to private interests. Although the Parks Board received some support for its position, including a minor petition from residents of Hastings Townsite (then not a part of the city) and the city's East End calling for the handing over of Hastings Park to the Parks Board, its representations went virtually unheeded. The minor regional assistance received by the board was more than cancelled by the strong support for

an exhibition given by the Ratepayers' Central Executive and the East End
Ratepayer's Association, both of whom criticized council not for leasing the land
to the V.E.A., but for not doing so quickly enough. Supporters of the retention of
Hastings Park in its natural state were few and far between. For the most part,
Vancouverites supported the development of a major exhibition on the site, and as
the date of the first exhibition approached that support intensified.[35]

Firmly in control of Hastings Park, with grandiose plans for the development of the property and, after 1909, with sufficient capital to finance construction, the Vancouver Exhibition Association could finally proceed with the
preparation of the grounds for the first fair. After arranging for the transfer of the
$50,000 from the city to the V.E.A., the association called for tenders to clear 10.5
acres in the northwest corner of the park and also advertised for design and
estimate submissions for a main exhibition building. Simultaneously, the British
Columbia Electric Railway Company was approached with a request that streetcar
lines be extended from the existing urban grid to reach Hastings Park.[36]

The site preparation and construction of exhibition facilities were not
accomplished without some unanticipated difficulties. A contract for grading was
given to A. Rhodes, but he surrendered it in mid-June 1909, forcing the association to hire W. H. Grendell Smith to complete the work. The latter contractor took
until mid-October to complete the initial section, and then only after the V.E.A.
had given a severe reprimand and issued an ultimatum requiring that the property
be developed as specified or the work would be completed by the association and
charged to the contractor. The second major project undertaken by the Vancouver
Exhibition Association before the first exhibition was the erection of a main
exhibition hall. The association had called for tenders for the structure early in
April 1909, and by the end of May had accepted the submission of Hayfield and
Williams. Designed by an architect named Watson, the structure was estimated at
a cost of $31,700, which obviously took a large bite out of the V.E.A.'s limited
budget. The actual construction was delayed by a series of controversies, involving architect Watson, who was replaced by S. M. Everleigh in August 1909. The
building was ready for the first exhibition, but not before both City Council and
the V.E.A. had hired engineers to survey it and report on its structural deficiencies. Foreshadowing problems that were to plague the association in decades to
come, one such report placed much of the blame on the original architect while a
second, more comprehensive examination found that the difficulties with the
exhibition hall could have been avoided had there been more co-operation between
the architect, the V.E.A., and City Council. After a year of attempting to meet the
numerous, often contradictory requests from the various groups involved, con-
tractors Hayfield and Williams finally renounced control of the building in July of
1910. After all the problems over financing, design, and construction, the Vancouver Exhibition Association was left with one of the more imposing structures
in the city, and the structural defects and other apparently minor problems were, in

the euphoria surrounding the first exhibition, dismissed rather lightly, an oversight which was to be regretted in later years.[37]

Crucial to the success of V.E.A. in this formative period was the maintenance of amicable relations with the City Council. Relying heavily on civic loans as a means of financing its operations and requiring a civic lease to use Hastings Park, the organization would probably have never got off the ground had it not enjoyed close and generally harmonious contacts with council. Council saw the V.E.A. as a convenient tool for advertising the city and offered strong, if not unwavering, support for the association. This allegiance was assisted by the fact that civic officials, including Mayor Bethune, Aldermen McSpadden, Bird, and Heaps, and City Comptroller Baldwin, had been among the first twenty-six members of the executive and committee of the V.E.A. in 1908. There were several strained moments as the association seemed to flounder on its way towards the successful prosecution of its aims, particularly in the aftermath of the by-law defeat of 1908, but for the most part City Council was supportive.[38]

Under the terms of the lease between the city and the Vancouver Exhibition Association, Hastings Park and all developments within the boundaries of the park remained the property of the city. As a result, council felt obliged to keep a watchful, if not a vigilant, eye upon the activities of the association. Council was also required to oversee the dispersal of funds allocated under the 1909 and 1910 by-laws, making it necessary for the V.E.A. to have all expenditures approved by council for payment. As the activities of the association expanded and council's supervisory duties became more onerous, the mayor and aldermen decided to establish a separate committee, the Exhibition Committee, which was charged with overseeing all work on the grounds and the payment of any monies voted by the taxpayers.[39] Under this arrangement, as long as the aims of council and the V.E.A. meshed, there was little likelihood of strained relations. On those occasions when the two groups diverged in either action or plan, and there were to be many such down the road, there existed the possibility of considerable and serious conflict. At this time, however, the primary aim of both the Vancouver Exhibition Association and council's Exhibition Committee was to get on with the business of establishing a fair for Vancouver and the two managed to work in considerable harmony towards that goal.

When the association was formed, the group was hesitant to make any ringing declaration about the date of the first fair, deciding instead to finalize arrangements for land and funding before making a public announcement. Indeed, the first official V.E.A. statement referring to the holding of an exhibition came in January 1908, on the heels of the rejection of the first by-law submission. The passing of a resolution calling for an autumn exhibition was more of an attempt to present a strong and unified front in the face of what was potentially a fatal blow. More rational heads prevailed, however, doubtless spurred on by the fact that the association had very limited funding and that the grounds were still in a virgin state.[40]

It was a much more confident association which began to plan for a fall exhibition in the spring of 1909. With coffers swollen by the $50,000 loan proffered by the ratepayers and with construction underway on a major exhibition building, it seemed not only possible but even probable that a fair would finally take place. By July of that year, the Attractions Committee had arranged for a series of events to coincide with what was to be an October exhibition. The attractions were to include bronco busting, band competitions, the display of an airship and a major marathon race. One prominent event, a series of concerts by a popular American group, the Ellery's Band, hired at a cost of $2,500, promised to be the highlight of the show. It soon became apparent, however, that the grounds would not be prepared in time and, with considerable reluctance, the V.E.A. decided on 13 October 1909 that it was impossible to use the grounds for public purposes. Given the precarious financial position of the Association, it was a major setback, costing the organization over $2,500 just to settle with the Ellery's Band. To cover the losses, the V.E.A.'s directors were required to sign personal promissory notes.[41]

Somewhat hesitant and embarrassed, the Vancouver Exhibition Association, declared for the third time on 30 December 1909 that an exhibition would be held the following year. But things brightened early in the new year with passage of the $85,000 by-law. With the strain on finances relieved and spurred on by what was taken as a vote of confidence, the directors threw themselves wholeheartedly into the task of organizing the 1910 fair, the first major exhibition to be held in the City of Vancouver.

3

First Years, 1910-1914

The decision finally made, Vancouver's first exhibition was now scheduled for 1910. Through two substantial loans from the city's ratepayers and monies raised through the sale of memberships, the Vancouver Exhibition Association was at last financially capable of proceeding with the final preparations for a fall fair. The main exhibition building had recently been completed, and the clearing and grading of the grounds had proceeded to the point where the space necessary for an exhibition was available. A full three years after the founding of the V.E.A. and despite a series of setbacks which threatened the existence of the youthful organization, the association was finally on the verge of achieving its primary objective, the organization and presentation of an industrial and agricultural exhibition for the City of Vancouver.

The first issue to be settled in order to set the organizational machinery in motion was the matter of selecting the precise date for the first fair. The debate over the dates indicates once again the conflict within the association between the proponents of an agriculturally oriented fair and those other members who emphasized other aspects of the exhibition's programme, including horse shows and industrial displays. It was obvious to anyone even minimally connected with agriculture that the best dates for an agricultural show were in the fall, especially late September and early October. At that time crops had been harvested, farming produce was readily available for display, and, perhaps most importantly, the farmers themselves had sufficient leisure time to attend fairs and display the fruits of their labours. The two major British Columbian agricultural shows, Victoria and New Westminster, held their fairs in this period, with the former usually hosting an exhibition in the last week of September while the Royal Agricultural and Industrial Society staged their show in the first week of October. Holding a fair at this time was, to most exhibition associations, a fitting and obvious way of meeting the needs and demands of the farming community.

There was, however, an argument supported by some within the V.E.A. for hosting an exhibition earlier in the year, either in July or August. Aware that autumn in Vancouver was often a season of rain and generally cloudy weather, some members argued that the association could not afford a fall exhibition. A mid or late summer date, they maintained, would ensure that the fair enjoyed good attendance and that the fiscal results of the exhibition would likely be favourable. This position, not surprisingly, met with considerable opposition, primarily from those supporting an agriculturally based fair. The conflict was not, however, solely between the financially and the agriculturally minded. A third group, men involved in the showing and racing of horses, also joined the fray. These individuals saw little benefit in a fall fair, particularly since their activities were scheduled to take place out-of-doors, and they came down solidly in favour of a summer exhibition. The horse owners had gained considerable power within the association in 1910, with four of their number joining the Board of Control in that year. Their enhanced position within the organization, when coupled with those members supporting an August show for fiscal reasons, was enough to ensure the defeat of the agriculturalists' representations. The first exhibition, it was decided, would be held in the middle of August, 1910.[1]

The non-agricultural orientation of the Vancouver exhibition made it something of an anomaly among British Columbia's fairs. Of the thirty-three fairs constituting the B.C. Agricultural Fairs Association (B.C.A.F.A.) in 1910, the Vancouver Exhibition Association was the only one to schedule a summer show. The majority of the exhibitions, twenty-five out of thirty-three, were staged in September, while seven others including the New Westminster and Richmond fairs, were not held until October. Vancouver's refusal to join in the apparently preferred range of dates meant that it functioned outside of the fair circuits then operating in the province. To organize a coherent exhibition schedule, the member fairs of the B.C.A.F.A. had been divided into five separate units, with dates arranged to avoid conflict within the individual circuits. This agreement on dates enabled exhibitors and spectators to follow the "circuit," attending one fair after another in succession, with the farmers able to compete with their produce in a whole series of shows. Organized geographically, the circuits included Vancouver Island, Upper Fraser River Valley, Lower Fraser River Valley, Okanagan and Shuswap, and the Kootenays. A glance at the dates for the fourth circuit which, nominally at least, incorporated the V.E.A.'s show indicates just how much Vancouver's fair was removed from the flow of agricultural fairs in the province.[2]

LOWER MAINLAND FAIR CIRCUIT, 1910

Vancouver	August 15 to 20
North Vancouver	September 9 and 10
Central Park, Vancouver	September 21 and 22
Delta (Ladner)	September 23 and 24
Surrey	September 27
Langley	September 28
New Westminster	October 4 and 8
Richmond (Eburne)	October 11 and 12

SOURCE: B.C. Agricultural Fairs Association, Report on First Annual Convention, *B.C. Sessional Papers*, 1910, p. N17.

On this, the first occasion when the Vancouver Exhibition Association had a major public opportunity to determine the direction of its fair, it had rejected agriculture in favour of attendance and profits. This is not to suggest that agriculture and farming displays did not form an important component of the association's programme, but more that the V.E.A. had decided that its first priority was not agriculture but attendance.

With physical preparations more or less under control, the V.E.A. could direct its attention elsewhere. The question of fair dates and exhibition priorities notwithstanding, it was necessary that the exhibition work to gain credibility within the agricultural community, a task made difficult after the decision on the dates. Blocked by their own actions from appealing to individual farmers and agricultural exhibitors, the association found somewhat unexpected support from a number of broadly based agricultural organizations. Much to their delight, the V.E.A. found that several prominent groups had selected Vancouver as the site for their 1910 conventions and that they were willing to hold their meetings in conjunction with the exhibition. The most prestigious organization agreeing to meet at the fair was the United Farmers of Alberta, who saw their convention as a means of discussing the contentious issue of national freight rates with representatives of the B.C. agricultural community. Other groups indicating their intention to hold their annual gatherings at Hastings Park were the Retail Grocers' Association of B.C., Stockbreeders Association of B.C., Dairymen's Association of B.C., and the Poultry Association of B.C. The groups attending the exhibition reflected the livestock orientation of the Vancouver Exhibition Association. Noticeable by their absence were the local farmers' associations, organizations which would be expected to support a regional agricultural fair.[3]

It seems clear that livestock interests had won out over farming concerns in the battle for control of the agricultural component of the fair, just as agriculture had lost out to industry as the focus of the entire exhibition. Although livestock and farming displays contributed a large number of exhibits to the show, as is evidenced by the construction of two new stables and two new cattle barns to handle anticipated entrants, it is apparent that the principal emphasis was on advertising the industrial potential of Vancouver and British Columbia. The main exhibit hall was aptly named the Industrial Building and was slated to house most of the manufacturing displays during the fair. In addition, a $12,000 Machinery Building had been erected and was similarly scheduled to be a repository for industrial exhibits. That the exhibition was primarily oriented towards the promotion of industry was widely evident, and the Vancouver Exhibition Association, far from hiding the fact, highlighted it. They saw their fair not merely as an agricultural show or an industrial display, but rather as a combination of the two, an amalgamation reflecting the unique position of Vancouver and the diverse potential of the city's hinterland. In public discussion, the agricultural aspects of the fair received limited attention, with the fair being generally referred to as the "Industrial Exhibition."[4]

By the early summer of 1910, the physical development of the Hastings Park grounds was well advanced. The Industrial and Machinery buildings were nearly complete, although the latter was not opened until virtually the eve of the exhibition. Stables and barns had been provided for race horses and livestock, and areas had been developed for the "Skid Road" carnival and for a concessionaires' row. Ever vigilant for the opportunity to turn a profit, and confident that horse racing would prove to be a popular fair-time activity, the association also proceeded with the erection of a major new grandstand, slated to be over 250 feet long. Construction delays hampered the project, however, and by the time the exhibition opened, only 150 feet capable of holding three thousand spectators had been built. Additional improvements to the grounds included a perimeter fence for crowd control, an Administrative Building, a band stand, and a variety of personal service facilities, including telephone booths, lavatories, and park benches. As well, a restaurant was completed underneath the grandstand.[5] The various buildings, race track and accoutrements, V.E.A. President J. J. Miller was quick to point out, were not to be used exclusively for fair-time activities. "The gates," he stated on the eve of the exhibition, "will be ever open and it [Hastings Park] will be kept as a beautiful park, such as will be greatly appreciated by the people, particularly those in the East side of the city."[6] Even as the first fair approached, the association was looking to the future, planning the further development of Hastings Park. Such dreams, which included an aquarium, a forestry building, an art gallery and an improved race track, however, hinged directly on the success of the first fair.

With dates set, physical developments underway, important conventions lined up, and an exhibition schedule clearly outlined, final preparations could proceed. The most important item still outstanding was the vexing question of transportation. In 1910, Hastings Park and the exhibition grounds were still not within the urban streetcar grid, and the road system provided only rudimentary access to the park. In order to ensure that both spectators and exhibitors could reach the grounds, the V.E.A. was required to negotiate with a number of transportation companies to arrange either special rates or an extension of services. Concluding arrangements for the handling of exhibitors' livestock and produce was the easiest of the problems to solve. The Canadian Pacific Railway had a longstanding policy of subsidizing exhibitors' transportation to agricultural fairs, offering a roundtrip ticket for the cost of a one-way fare. It required only a formal application to the C.P.R. to have that arrangement applied to Vancouver's exhibition. Passenger traffic to the exhibition was considerably more troublesome. Two existing facilities were capable of bringing spectators from the city to the grounds, the C.P.R. train and boats running between the Vancouver docks and the Brighton wharves. An agreement was reached with the owners of the *S.S. Hamelin* calling for regular trips from the city to the exhibition throughout the week of the fair. In addition, individuals were encouraged to make use of the docking facilities and thereby provide their own transportation. Although the C.P.R. was initially reluctant to expand its normal operations to meet the needs of the fair, it was eventually agreed that the railway company would run eight trains daily, charging 25 cents per passenger for the fifteen-minute ride. More important, however, was the fact that the V.E.A.'s directors were finally able to convince the British Columbia Electric Railway Company to extend the streetcar lines to the exhibition. Although the association was more than a little concerned about the level of service promised by the B.C.E.R.C., the streetcar operators assured the directors that they could cope with whatever demands were placed on the system. With the V.E.A. highlighting the province-wide nature of the fair, efforts were also directed towards attracting visitors from outside the city. Special excursion rates were negotiated with railway and steamship lines, thus opening up relatively low cost access to the exhibition to people from the B.C. interior and from Vancouver Island.[7]

The stage was almost completely set, and only window dressing was required to complete the preparations. The necessary extra frills were provided when Sir Wilfrid Laurier, prime minister of Canada, agreed to open the exhibition officially and when plans were finalized for Sir Robert Baden-Powell, founder of the Boy Scout movement, to review a massed rally of his charges during the fair. Three years of planning had finally reached fruition, and the directors waited with both anticipation and apprehension for Vancouver's response to the presentation. Signs were abundant that the city was prepared to support the fair to the fullest. Glowing representations of the trials and tribulations of the Vancouver Exhibition Association filled the newspaper columns, their extremely laudatory character being largely explained by the fact that most were written by members of the association. Equally positive editorials appeared, praising the efforts of the membership and calling for "a determined effort on the part of all and sundry to make this initiation of new enterprise an overwhelming success."[8]

Although the official opening was scheduled for 16 August, the fair gates were thrown open for the first time on the preceding day. The highlight of the day (Preparation Day) was Baden-Powell's appearance; he reviewed a large rally of Boy Scouts assembled for the occasion in front of the grandstand. Slightly over four thousand people paid the fifty-cent general admission charge to pass through the gates.

The prime minister's visit, part of a larger tour of Western Canada designed to improve the Liberal Party's fortunes in the four western provinces, was attended with all manner of difficulties. Addressing a grandstand crowd reported to be over five thousand, Laurier had his speech interrupted frequently by members of the audience who were more intent upon watching the horse races continuing in the background than they were in hearing a politician's harangue. At the same time, a large mob, denied the opportunity to purchase tickets for the grandstand to hear Laurier, formed outside the entrance gates and began to press eagerly forward. Admission facilities proved woefully inadequate on this occasion and in a short time the surging crowd overwhelmed the ticket-takers. Observing the impending chaos, a number of the V.E.A. directors rushed to the gates, more intent upon preserving the exhibition's financial return than on restoring order. Unable to control the crowd, they resorted to taking what admissions they could grab from the surging mass, stuffing their pockets with money as the mob passed them.[9] The fiasco did not generate widespread concern, with one writer noting somewhat impassively, "At different times, women and children were forced beneath the feet of the crowd, but were extricated with no worse damage than a fright and some bruises."[10] The situation was as comic as it was potentially dangerous. On at least this one occasion the crowds were considerably larger than anticipated, and neither the facilities nor the management of the exhibition had been up to the task. At this point, however, all such errors were tacked up to inexperience, and the euphoria of the moment carried the day.

While they were obviously highlights, Laurier and Baden-Powell constituted only a small segment of the fair-time activities at Hastings Park. A major attraction for Vancouverites was the daily entertainment staged on the grounds. Bands were a particularly popular feature, with the V.E.A. bringing in a series of groups to play for the assembled crowds. Indian bands from Sechelt and Squamish, the Kilties Band, and a Regimental Band were among the acts providing free shows throughout the park. A series of vaudeville presentations, including a gymnastic troup, comedians Ramza and Arno, acrobats Frank and True Rice, and the triple bar act of the Marlo Trio also drew spectators. In addition, specialty acts that included a high dive which saw a "daredevil" plummet from a height of seventy-five feet into a small pool covered with flaming gasoline were also provided free of charge. These various entertainments, bands, and acts proved to be extremely popular and were responsible for attracting many people to the exhibition.[11]

The second part of the V.E.A.'s programme of attractions was the "Skid

Road," an extravaganza of games, sideshows, and rides. The diversity of the carnival was at once appealing and overwhelming. Burlesque shows of every description, boxing and wrestling matches, dances, games of chance, palmists, a horse "with a human brain," and a "petrified" woman from Arizona vied with hucksters and salesmen of a wide variety of wares of dubious quality for the attention, and more importantly, the money of the fairgoer. As one newsman wrote, "Everything new and novel in the amusement line, every means that human mind can devise to gather in the spare nickel, dime or quarters of the amusement seeker, is now in operation."[12] To many the carnival served as the focal point for the exhibition, for it was the Skid Road more than any other display, attraction, or event which drew them to the grounds and which enticed them to return. The fact that many of the shows were run by charlatans, that many of the games provided little if any chance of winning deterred few of the spectators, and the carnival remained one of the most popular features of the exhibition.

While bands, vaudeville acts and the carnival atmosphere generated by the Skid Road may have helped generate public interest in the Industrial Exhibition, they could not disguise agriculture's secondary role in the fair. Although free entertainment was a major and irreplaceable feature of the fair, it was, supposedly, secondary to the primary purposes of the show, promoting the agricultural and industrial potential of Vancouver and British Columbia. Agricultural exhibits obviously suffered from the selection of dates for the fair, and no one was surprised that the number of entrants in the "farmers' classes" was low. There was a smattering of produce displays and only a limited selection of entrants in the livestock competitions.[13] Horse departments, as expected, fared much better, with major racing and display competitions taking place in all categories. Racing proved particularly successful, drawing large crowds to the grandstands and serving as a valuable source of entertainment for the fairgoers. The comparatively poor showing in the agricultural programme, however, seriously hampered the V.E.A.'s claim to major agricultural fair status. This first exhibition demonstrated that the promotion of agriculture had a low priority and reinforced in the minds of many the belief that New Westminster was and would continue to be the major farming show in the Lower Mainland and British Columbia.

The other side of the V.E.A.'s promotional activities, the encouragement of industry, proceeded much more successfully. Both the Industrial Building and the Machinery Pavilion were filled to capacity with manufacturing exhibits. The displays in the first building were directed towards personal consumption and included exhibits by a stationery firm, furniture companies, clothes and silk manufacturers, and a sewing machine company. The upstairs of the structure, somewhat removed from the main flow of traffic, housed a major display of knitting, sewing, and cooking organized by the Local Council of Women and designed to demonstrate the products of the "woman's sphere," an art exhibit, and a taxidermy show. An exhibit prepared by schoolchildren from throughout the

Vancouver area displayed the best work from industrial and technical classes, "proving" to the fairgoers that the education system was training the city's children for the tasks which lay ahead. The Machinery Building, similarly, was devoted to showing the products of individual firms, although this facility was restricted primarily to larger items such as carriages, farm implements, gas engines, and a unique display of automobiles.[14] Although space in the two buildings was completely sold out, the industrial component of the V.E.A.'s programme was not viewed as a complete or even a partial success. The displays, obviously, had focused almost exclusively upon individual businesses and included not a single major exhibit centred upon the natural resources of the province. While the V.E.A. was keenly interested in encouraging local retailing and manufacturing, they did not see the exhibition solely as a corporate advertising tool. The association had much larger ambitions. What was desired in addition was a series of displays exhibiting the resource potential of the region, focusing on fishing, lumbering, and mining. But time constraints, the fact that the organization's management was busy elsewhere and, most importantly, the fact that most of the larger industrial concerns in the province were adopting a "hands-off" attitude towards the V.E.A. until its success was ensured, meant that no such exhibits were prepared for the first fair. In the two primary areas, agriculture and industry, the Vancouver Exhibition Association's first show had fallen short of expectations and intentions.

This first fair, a curious amalgam of vaudeville, agriculture, industry and hucksterism, provides evidence not only of the association's attempts to stage a successful exhibition, but it says something also about the character of Vancouver society at the beginning of the century's second decade. The city was at a transition stage in its development, exhibiting the characteristics of a comparatively new frontier settlement while at the same time there was evidence of a more settled community with metropolitan pretensions. Gambling, horse racing, and the carnival atmosphere of the Hastings Park show were clearly directed towards the baser instincts of the frontier community, a city that was still rough around the edges. At the same time, however, the fair also contained elements attractive to the more staid and conservative members of society. The "booster" aspects of the show, industrial and agricultural displays and competitions, appealed to those seeking evidence of Vancouver's emerging status as a major North American city. The 1910 exhibition and the subsequent fairs, therefore, were not just in Vancouver, they were of Vancouver, with the structure and content of the show reflecting the aspirations and interests of the city's divergent population.

That the association was given the opportunity to remedy the deficiencies of the first fair was primarily the result of the financial returns of the first exhibition. The six-day fair had proven to be both publicly acceptable and financially rewarding. Almost 68,000 people were reputed to have passed through the turnstiles, with total gate receipts reaching almost $18,000. Interestingly, this figure suggests that either the V.E.A. was granting an abnormally high number of free passes or that it had woefully inadequate gate counts. Even if it is assumed that one-third of the people attending paid only the twenty-five-cent children's admission while the rest paid the full fifty-cent fee, gate returns should have been over $28,000. Association directors and their immediate families were accorded free entrance, but it is obvious that, if the gate count is at all reliable, thousands of others also passed onto the grounds without charge. In total, however, the exhibition proved financially acceptable, with final receipts from all sources reaching over $40,000.

The V.E.A.'s returns were swollen dramatically by an eleventh hour contribution of $10,000 from the provincial government for the agricultural prize lists. In addition, the association raised more than $8,000 from the rental of space to concessionaires and entry fees for the various competitive classes. Expenses were kept to a minimum, although over $4,300 was spent on the various fair-time attractions, and over $3,000 was allocated for advertising. Of the more than $16,000 that the V.E.A. paid out in prize money, most went to the "speed," or horse racing, events. Although the amount may seem large, its impact was softened by the timely $10,000 provincial grant. When the final results were tabulated, the association had emerged from its first exhibition with a healthy $7,430 surplus, not enough to pay for future expansion of facilities, but a sum which indicated the financial viability of the Vancouver exhibition and which could form the basis for later appeals to civic, provincial, and dominion governments for additional funding.[15]

Generally the first exhibition had proven both a financial and a public success. While warning of a tendency towards blatant materialism, one columnist nonetheless found much to praise in the fair, commenting that: "It speaks of a people who are accomplishing much, but looking forward to vastly greater achievements, who are making vast material progress but do not altogether overlook the grapes and refinements which long possessed wealth, leisure and study."[16] The exhibition was not without its critics, with the skid road carnival and the horse racing being singled out for attack. Gambling on the games of chance and betting on the races were decried as assaults on public morals, and opponents of this aspect of the fair called for a complete cessation of all such activities. J. J. Miller and the association's directors, caught in the euphoria of a successful fair, made light of the complaints, with Miller claiming during an address to the association that "Even the church people had crowded the grandstand to see the races, while some were talking about buying horses."[17] The comment delighted his audience and was greeted with profuse laughter, but such levity hid the fact that an identifiable civic minority was strongly opposed to part of the exhibition programme. For the most part, criticism of the exhibition was muted by resounding commendations.

With one exhibition under their belts, the association members turned to the problems of preparing for future fairs. The most obvious difficulty encountered during the 1910 show was the lack of administrative expertise, as the manager James Roy, and even the directors themselves, had displayed a rather remarkable lack of foresight and planning. Although the directors were quick to absolve Roy of any personal blame for the setbacks encountered, they nonetheless eagerly accepted his resignation and began the search for a new exhibition manager. The position was advertised in a number of newspapers and trade journals across Canada and the Pacific Northwest, with the campaign eventually gathering a total of twenty-six applicants. Two men in particular caught the directors' collective eye, H. P. Good of Toronto, who offered his services for $1,200 a year, the lowest in the competition, and J. W. Pace of North Yakima, Washington whose $3,200 bid was at the opposite end of the scale. Although Pace was clearly better qualified for the post, the V.E.A. at first decided to go with thrift and recommended that Good be offered the position. A number of directors, however, were not happy with the appointment of an outsider, and they approached H. S. Rolston, secretary of the association, with a request that he allow his name to stand in the competition. Rolston apparently required little persuasion, especially when it was decided that the appointment would carry a $3,600 a year salary. On 25 November 1910, he formally accepted the position. Rolston, who had previously held a similar post with a Winnipeg fair, now became a leading figure in the Vancouver Exhibition Association and, together with president J. J. Miller, was primarily responsible for determining the scope and direction of the exhibition over the following decade.[18]

The three years before the outbreak of World War I in the autumn of 1914 saw the V.E.A. consolidating gains won through the first exhibition and expanding the fair to serve the stated goals of the organization more adequately. The physical development of the Hastings Park grounds, hampered somewhat by the ever-present funding difficulties, continued apace. A Stock Judging Pavilion was erected in time for the 1911 exhibition, although other buildings planned for that year were deferred owing to a lack of funds. 1913 saw a flurry of construction activity as a 300-foot-long Transportation Building, slated to serve as an exhibition hall for machinery and automobiles, was completed and work commenced on a major Forestry Building, to be constructed entirely from local timber and to serve as a showcase for that important industry.[19]

The development of facilities, while obviously important in allowing the association to expand its activities, did not of itself bring the V.E.A.'s presentation more in line with its objectives. This same three-year period, however, saw a marked change in the composition of the exhibition programme, with ever-increasing importance being placed on agricultural contests and the province's natural resources. A mineral exhibit was added in 1911, as was an international egg-laying contest. Further developments included a small forestry display, a Fisheries Building designed to house an aquarium and an exhibit of the ocean resources of British Columbia, and the beginnings of a small zoological collec-

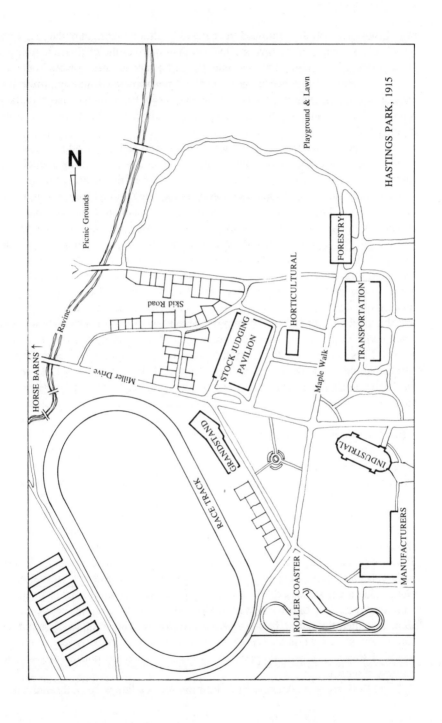

HASTINGS PARK, 1915

N

Picnic Grounds

Ravine

HORSE BARNS

Miller Drive

Skid Road

Playground & Lawn

FORESTRY

HORTICULTURAL

TRANSPORTATION

Maple Walk

STOCK JUDGING PAVILION

GRANDSTAND

RACE TRACK

INDUSTRIAL

MANUFACTURERS

ROLLER COASTER

tion. Livestock exhibits continued to be the agricultural highlight of the fair, with the directors continuing to favour a late summer date for the exhibition. An auto show, immodestly claimed by the manager to be second only to New York's in North America, maintained its hold on the Transportation Building, while the Industrial Building continued to house the products of local and national manufacturers.[20] Such developments notwithstanding, industrial exhibits remained the highlight of the fair.

A wide and diverse range of acts, games, and shows providing entertainment throughout the grounds continued to serve as the highlight of the fair for many and perhaps most fairgoers. The V.E.A., still referring to horse racing as its "Speed Department," attempted to cloak this major attraction under its agricultural programme, but it was obviously serving more as entertainment than as a display of horse breeding or training expertise. An important addition to the amusement package after 1910 was the incorporation of sports, both amateur and professional, into the schedule. Lacrosse matches, athletic meets, and motorcycle races, among others, served as popular attractions. In this period as well, the V.E.A. expended considerable effort on the improvement of the racetrack oval, making it available for a variety of sporting and entertainment features. The fact that this oval was set in front of the grandstand meant that the association could stage major events on the site, recouping their investment by the sale of admissions.[21] These additions to the programme, focusing on active organized entertainment, marked the beginning of an important trend. Hereafter, the V.E.A. would put forth increasing effort on providing large-scale attractions at Hastings Park to supplement what for many were the less exciting agricultural and industrial displays. This adaptation, clearly designed to lure more people through the turnstiles, was to prove very popular in subsequent years.

As before, both the skid road and the vaudeville acts continued to be prime attractions. Evidence of the increasing importance being placed on attractions and vaudeville acts as a means of drawing people to the grounds is provided by the V.E.A.'s expenditures on such displays through the first four fairs. Both 1910 and 1911 saw spending on this aspect of the programme remain comparatively light, totalling $2,600 and $2,500 respectively. The year following, when the Astorino Dancing Girls, two nights of fireworks, and a series of acts staged by the Parker Shows provided the main entertainment, expenditures rose to over $8,400. Although that figure declined to $6,300 in 1913, the sum was still substantially higher than the first two exhibitions. The V.E.A. was not altering its programme without reason, but rather it was expanding and improving those sections of its show to which the public had responded favourably. The addition of organized entertainment and the increased expenditures on vaudeville acts were primarily intended to suit community preferences and, as an important by-product, to improve attendance.[22]

The efforts of the Vancouver Exhibition Association were well rewarded in these formative years, with attendance increasing from 68,000 in 1910 to over 93,000 in 1913. Interestingly, however, gate revenues rose far less rapidly, from $18,500 for the first fair to only $20,400 for the 1913 exhibition. The management of the exhibition was apparently either engaging in some judicious gate "padding" for promotional purposes or continuing to allow large numbers of people onto the grounds free of charge. Despite the seemingly low returns from the gate, the association continued to show a surplus. Profit from the 1911 fair exceeded $13,800, although the following two years saw the surplus drop precipitously to $3,074 in 1912 and only a meagre $251 the following year.[23]

Two other developments are particularly worthy of note. First, despite the poor receipts in 1912 and 1913, the V.E.A.'s ability to turn any kind of a profit made it something of an anomaly among agricultural fairs. Many exhibitions across Canada operated with considerable annual deficits, requiring government largesse to maintain their operations. The "poor" financial situation did not deter the association's management, and they found justification for their grandiose plans in the markedly increased attendance, however contrived. J. J. Miller's optimism, in particular, knew few bounds, and in 1913 he confidently stated that the exhibition needed and would soon get a major Agricultural Hall, a women's building, extra stables, improvements to the grounds, and a series of other minor additions. More crucial to the early planning for the fair itself was the idea that a major exhibition of world stature might be held in 1915 to coincide with the opening of the Panama Canal. Indeed, many of the construction and development plans were conceived with a view to what was anticipated would be a significant international show, a fair which would indicate not only the progress of the Vancouver Exhibition Association but, more importantly, the natural resources of British Columbia and the potential of the City of Vancouver in light of the opening up of many and varied vistas as a consequence of the completion of the canal. The association's enthusiastic projections called for between one-half and one million visitors to flow through the exhibition's gates in 1915, no doubt marking the V.E.A.'s presentation as a major world fair. World events conspired to ensure that an exhibition on this scale never took place, but much of the planning for Hastings Park between 1910 and 1914 was done with this anticipated show in mind.[24]

Throughout this early period, the Vancouver Exhibition Association maintained fairly cordial relations with City Council, with few tensions developing between the two organizations. One problem did emerge on the eve of the first exhibition, when council carelessly granted a licence to a travelling circus which allowed it to stage its show on the last day of the fair. The V.E.A. was upset with council's actions and appealed for a revocation of the permit. The association alleged that the granting of the licence cost them several thousand dollars in lost revenue. Even on this occasion, council was more than a little contrite over the error, and they publicly reiterated their support for the exhibition. The continued allegiance between council and the V.E.A. was illustrated in 1911, when the

Exhibition Committee of the City Council agreed to the association's request that a half-day civic holiday be declared to coincide with "Citizen's Day" at the fair. Although council retained a watchful and occasionally critical eye over the operations and plans of the V.E.A. through this formative period, it was generally consistent in its support of the exhibition.[25]

The solid backing of the association by the local government also was clearly demonstrated in its response to the V.E.A.'s request for a grant of additional land in Hastings Park. The whole thorny issue of the control of the park had resurfaced on the eve of the first exhibition when council decided to investigate the possibility of turning the park over to the Board of Park Commissioners "for the public use forever."[26]

On the heels of a successful first exhibition, the Vancouver Exhibition Association was hardly prepared to give up control of the sixty acres it held in the northwest corner of the park. Quite the contrary; in October of 1910 an appeal was made to City Council for an extension of the initial grant to include all park lands north of Hastings Street. When council agreed to the proposal, the Board of Park Commissioners protested vigorously, arguing that the entire park should be placed under their administration. Hoping to appease the park commissioners, the V.E.A. and City Council agreed that a section of Hastings Park bounded by Triumph, Pender, Rupert, and Renfrew Streets would be turned over for park purposes. Although the agreement cut into the V.E.A.'s newly granted lands, over half of Hastings Park remained for exhibition uses.[27]

Spurred on by the success of their 1911 and 1912 exhibitions, and eager to continue physical developments that would prepare the way for the projected major fair in 1915, the V.E.A. returned to council in 1912 with another request for additional land in the park.[28] The park commissioners again registered their "strong opposition" to any increased grant, but despite this representation council extended the V.E.A.'s holdings in the park south of Hastings Street in February, 1913.[29] This third land transfer also elicited the first serious suggestion that the lease of Hastings Park be granted only for fair-time activities, with control of the grounds for the remainder of the year revolving to the park commissioners. The arrangement was one which was used extensively throughout North America, and had served in many areas as a means of reconciling public opposition to the development of a park with the activities of an exhibition. The suggestion was never implemented, and indeed there was little public support or demand for such an arrangement. Apparently, few people in Vancouver opposed the V.E.A.'s lease of Hastings Park or were critical of the manner in which the park was being developed. Throughout the Hastings Park controversy, council had repeatedly backed the Vancouver Exhibition Association and had rejected the appeals of the Board of Park Commissioners.[30] Council obviously supported an exhibition over yet another natural park for the city and was prepared to acceed to the V.E.A.'s plans to turn Hastings Park, as V.E.A. President Miller put it, from a veritable "wasteland to one of the best public assets the city possesses."[31]

Through almost continuous contact with the Vancouver Exhibition Association, City Council was able to record its approval or disfavour with the exhibition or the association on a regular basis. The city's ratepayers were also offered opportunities, although less frequent, to register their opinion of the fair, apart from their support of the exhibition through their attendance. Three times before 1914 the V.E.A. approached the electors requesting the passage of a money by-law, and the results of these campaigns indicate something of the general and regional support for, and opposition to, the annual fair and its management. Basking in the success of the first exhibition, the V.E.A. requested that a by-law for $115,000 be submitted in January 1911. With over 75 per cent voting in favour, the results displayed widespread public approval of the fair and future plans. Support was uniformly high across the city, with the lowest percentage (70 per cent) not surprisingly coming from Ward 2, the central city district. The west end of the city, initially opposed to the development of the fair, swung heavily behind the V.E.A., voting 81 per cent for the proposition. Buoyed by the results of the 1911 vote and a second successful exhibition, a confident, even cocky, V.E.A. once again approached the electorate the following year, this time asking for an additional $85,000. To the surprise and dismay of the overconfident directorate, the by-law received only 58 per cent of the vote, falling short of the 60 per cent required for passage. The year was generally a poor one for by-law submissions, with fourteen out of the thirty-four going down to defeat, an unusually high proportion. Although the V.E.A. had maintained its traditional east side support, garnering 68 per cent from the four East and South East wards, it had failed to hold the city-wide backing it had won on the previous year's ballot (see Table 2).[32]

TABLE 2: V.E.A. BY-LAW RESULTS, 1911-1913[33]

| Ward # | Downtown | | East Side | | Other | | City- |
	1	2	3	4	5	6	Wide
1911	81	70	76	75	71	74	75

| Ward # | Downtown | | East Side | | | Other | | | City- |
	1	2	3	4	7	5	6	8	Wide
1912	48	47	69	59	87	52	51	63	58
1913	54	51	78	69	85	63	58	59	65

The Vancouver Exhibition Association was rocked by the defeat. Many construction and development plans were momentarily shelved, although the ever-confident directors refused to become overly pessimistic. The by-law did, however, ensure that the V.E.A. would no longer take the support of the electorate for granted. The overwhelming backing for the 1911 submission had given the

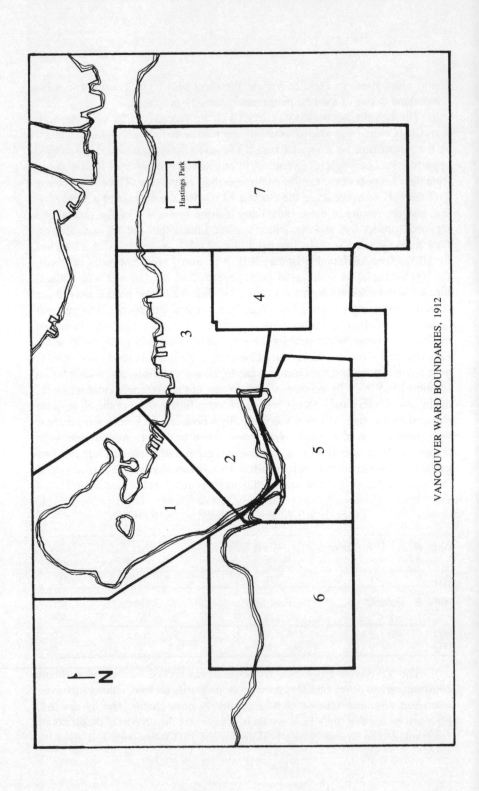

Hastings Park

VANCOUVER WARD BOUNDARIES, 1912

association considerable faith in the ratepayers, and it made virtually no attempts at publicity or public solicitation in conjunction with the 1912 vote. From this point on, the V.E.A. would take a more cautious approach to their by-laws, checking for probable public support, ensuring themselves of the backing of prominent local politicians, and conducting fairly extensive publicity campaigns. The love affair between the exhibition and Vancouver citizens, if indeed it ever existed, was over, and relations hereafter would be conducted on a more business-like level.

Smarting from the 1912 defeat, but still requiring a major loan in order to continue its development programmes, the V.E.A. approached council yet again in the fall of 1912 with a request for another by-law. A full slate of twenty-one by-laws was brought before the ratepayers on 9 January 1913, one of which was a $165,000 loan for exhibition purposes. Although the V.E.A. received over 65 per cent of the vote, passing the by-law by a healthy margin, they had failed to return to the heady heights of the 1911 ballot. The East End once again fell in solidly behind the association, with Wards 3, 4, 7, and 8 providing a 77 per cent favourable vote.[34] This side of the city, still comparatively underdeveloped, apparently saw the exhibition as a means of further expanding Vancouver's east side and also found much to support in the facilities being developed at Hastings Park. Although the grounds were being developed primarily with a view towards their utility at fair time, the improvements increased property values in the area, expanded part-time employment opportunities, and made the park a popular picnic and party site for east end residents, factors which go a long way towards explaining the region's solid and consistent support for the V.E.A.'s by-laws.

While the city had, on two out of three occasions, provided major funding for expansion, the association continued to cast around for other sources of capital. Though the federal government repeatedly turned a deaf ear to appeals for assistance, the provincial government maintained its support for the prize lists. The provincial grant, however, fell from $10,000 in 1910 to $6,000 in 1911 and declined even further to $5,000 for both 1912 and 1913.[35] The V.E.A. reacted with considerable bitterness to the government's action, commenting in 1912 that:

> In view of the usefulness of the Vancouver Exhibition Association to the Province as an educational and advertising institution and in encouraging the development of the industrial resources of the Province this meeting views with sincere regret the attitude of the Provincial Government towards this valuable public institution, and, the distinctive treatment meted out to it as compared with that accorded other kindred associations in the Province.[36]

Appeals for additional assistance went unheeded, however, forcing the association to look elsewhere for financing.

Another traditional source of funding, the sale of memberships, also dried

up considerably in this period. During the period between 1908 and 1910, when the
V.E.A. had relied heavily on the public for assistance, it sold in excess of $20,000
in memberships, most of which were $100 life-time subscriptions. After the rush
to hop on the exhibition bandwagon in 1910, however, the number of new members
dropped steadily. Obviously, most of those individuals and businesses holding life
memberships were reluctant and felt little obligation to provide additional financial assistance to the association. With life members excluded as a future source of
revenue, the Vancouver Exhibition Association turned instead to its annual
members to provide funds, with money garnered from this source earmarked for
year-round administrative costs. This source of supply proved anything but
lucrative between 1910 and 1913, providing only between $1,400 and $3,000 a
year.[37] The directors were concerned with the lack of direct public involvement in
the association and called repeatedly for a greater number of members to come
forward. J. J. Miller, appealing for an increased effort in the solicitation of new
members, wrote in 1912:

> The spirit of democracy pervades it, for under its auspices every man, woman
> and child in the community can find some individual interest, no matter
> whether it be agricultural, industrial, commercial, educational, inventive or
> sublime.
> Then let the people realize that at Hastings Park at their doorstep is slowly but
> steadily being accomplished and developed a people's gigantic public school
> and playground worthy of a progressive people, a progressive province and a
> progressive country.[38]

Despite the association's remonstrances, however, it was apparent that memberships were being solicited more with a view to their financial benefits than to their
democratizing impact.

The interests of the V.E.A. in this period were not entirely local and
organizational; they were occasionally diverted towards regional concerns. As
Vancouver's fair developed and expanded, it began to assume an increasingly
active role in the various fair associations of the Pacific Northwest. With aspirations as a major exhibition, the V.E.A., like the New Westminster exhibition
association, tended to disdain the local fair organization, the B.C. Agricultural
Fairs Association, in favour of groups representing the larger urban exhibitions
along the west coast. In 1912, to provide one example of the level of V.E.A.
involvement, Manager Rolston was the president of both the North Pacific Fairs
Association and the International Circuit Association, and a director of the
Western Canada Fair Managers Association, the Pacific Grand Circuit and Racing
Association, and the Congress of Festivals. The Vancouver Exhibition Association held memberships in all of these organizations and a number of others,
including the Western Canada Fairs Associations and the International Fairs

Association. These associations served a number of functions, including acting as a booking agent for attractions for member fairs, offering recognized lists of stock judges and race starters, and serving as freight bureaus to assist in the shipment of exhibits between fairs. As well, the various regional organizations arranged dates among the fairs, ensuring a minimum of conflict and easy passage of exhibitors and competitors throughout the circuits. Despite Rolston's prominent role, assumed largely on the basis of his long involvement with the horse-racing fraternity, the V.E.A. did not adopt an overly assertive position in these associations. As one of the newest of the west coast fairs and one, therefore, in a somewhat tenuous situation, the V.E.A. was not in a position to be overzealous in its demands. Vancouver's rather passive stance can also be attributed in part to the fact that its early dates normally precluded it from competition with other members of the regional circuits and hence prevented any serious conflicts from developing.[39]

While there was occasional conflict between member fairs over the question of dates, it is important to point out that there was an exceptional amount of co-operation between the exhibition associations. By banding together, a group of fairs could bring in major attractions that a single exhibition simply could not have afforded; it meant that exhibitors could be offered a series of shows and competitions, thus increasing the attractiveness of each individual fair. Nevertheless, by its choice of dates, Vancouver was normally excluded from joining in such benefits. In 1913, however, the fair was held just after the Western Canada Circuit (largely a prairie organization) was completed, thus enabling a number of important exhibits and entrants from the east to come to the coast.[40] With this one exception, and that rather more fortuitous than planned, Vancouver lost out on what was perhaps the major benefit of belonging to the fair associations.

While its principal interest was directed towards the larger urban fairs, the V.E.A. did maintain contact with the smaller local exhibitions. Annually, a number of directors from the V.E.A. would visit each fair in the Lower Mainland and on Vancouver Island, with especially large contingents travelling to Victoria and New Westminster. The purpose of these trips was threefold: to maintain cordial relations with other fair associations, to contact agricultural exhibitors and attempt to convince them to travel to the Hastings Park exhibition, and to observe recent improvements in layout, advertising, and attractions in order to develop ideas for the V.E.A.'s presentation. In addition to the directors' visits to local fairs, Manager Rolston was sent on extended trips to other major exhibitions throughout Canada and the United States. His particular purpose on these occasions was to observe the physical plants of the fairs, to compare funding arrangements, and to make notes on the financial affairs of the various exhibitions. Rolston's excursions were extensive, taking him in 1912 to the Canadian National Exhibition in Toronto, "the recognized greatest annual event of its kind in the world, and the one after which all others pattern," the Western Ontario Fair in London, the Eastern Ontario Fair in Ottawa, and a number of other smaller exhibitions.[41] In addition, he visited fairs in Oregon and Washington while he was in the United States attending the meetings of the various exhibition and circuit associations. Given the embryonic state of the Vancouver Exhibition Association and the lack of experience among the directorship, these visits and the subsequent reports proved highly enlightening and served to stimulate the development of Hastings Park and the expansion of fair-time activities.

As with any exhibition, the success or failure of Vancouver's fair did not rest essentially on its internal evolution, its funding arrangements, or its relations with various and sundry fair associations, but instead on the maintenance of a rapport with the residents of Vancouver and, increasingly, of British Columbia. Public image and acceptance, therefore, were crucial to the Vancouver Exhibition Association. In these formative years, from 1910 to 1914, criticism of the association was minimal. Occasional complaints were registered about the skid road gambling, about horse racing during the exhibition, and about the leasing of a public park for development.[42] Such criticism, however, was more than muted by widespread acclaim for the exhibition and the improvement of Hastings Park. During the first four exhibitons, the V.E.A. was able to establish and then maintain a cordial relationship with the citizens of Vancouver. The residents of the East End in particular supported the exhibition, and in return the directors of the association did their utmost to provide and encourage public access to the park facilities throughout the year. The development of the exhibition had resulted in the provision of a wide variety of picnicking, party, and sports facilities in the otherwise poorly served east side, and the area residents felt their interests to be closely allied with those of the exhibition association.

Although public acceptance of the Vancouver Exhibition Association declined somewhat from its high point in 1910-1911, it nonetheless remained substantial throughout this period. The V.E.A. not only provided a desired recreational outlet for the urban centre, but also developed much needed facilities and, perhaps most importantly, remained very aware of the close ties beween the exhibition and the City of Vancouver. The Industrial Exhibition was Vancouver's show, and although the programme incorporated wider regional concerns, its primary emphasis was on the local scene.

4

The War Years, 1914-1918

Plans had never been more advanced and expectations had never been higher for the Vancouver Exhibition Association than they were in the summer of 1914. This optimism was shown in the directors' decision to alter the fair dates, moving for the first time from the "safe" days of August to the first week of September, a choice which obviously favoured the agricultural departments.

On the eve of the 1914 exhibition, however, war broke out in Europe. Canada's participation in the war, supported by the nationalist and imperialist sentiments released by the outbreak of hostilities, resulted in a country-wide appeal for total devotion to the war effort. Virtually without hesitation, one exhibition association after another announced its decision to postpone all fair activities for the duration of the fighting. Many of these associations eventually turned their grounds and facilities over to the militia, while others merely decided to hold their exhibitions in abeyance until hostilities had ended. The cancellations took place for two basic reasons, a desire to participate fully in the national war effort, something many saw as impossible if energy and money was diverted towards an exhibition, and a belief that it was totally inappropriate to operate a fair, an activity based upon gaiety, frivolity, and amusements, while the country was at war. For most exhibition associations, it was not a difficult decision to make, and the 1914 fairs were cancelled soon after war was declared.

The Vancouver Exhibition Association, more than a little reluctant to risk the life of their new exhibition, refused to join the closure movement. With the grounds prepared, attractions contracted for, and advertising well under way, the association felt that it was too late to call off the 1914 exhibition. The decision was not simply a crass financial move. The directors took the position that the opening of the grounds and the holding of a fair was intended to inspire public confidence in Canada and in the country's ability to emerge successful from the war. It was to be "business as usual" at the exhibition.¹ Besides, the widely held belief that the conflict would be "over by Christmas" discouraged the V.E.A.'s directors from reacting to what was perceived to be a short-term confrontation.

It is difficult to completely understand the V.E.A.'s motives for continuing with the fair, particularly in light of the decision by New Westminster and Victoria to close their doors for 1914. They were flying in the face of public and provincial government opinion and, indeed, faced considerable opposition within their own organization over the issue. Financial concerns and the fear that the young association could not weather an indefinite postponement certainly constituted part of the rationale, as did a genuine belief that staging an exhibition would improve public morale and confidence at a time when both were being severely tested. Some argued as well that agriculture and industry would certainly have to continue as before and indeed be accelerated to keep up with wartime demands. Therefore, if the stated aims of the V.E.A. had any validity at all, the exhibition should be indispensable during the war. If the association, as the constitution declared, was intended to spur the development of industry and agriculture and to stimulate innovation and excellence, then the fair not only should not, but emphatically could not, be shut down at a time of national crisis. It was this belief that the exhibition had a valued role to play in the preparation of Vancouver and British Columbia for wartime production that was probably the most important factor in the V.E.A.'s decision to continue operations.

This view, never adequately presented to either the public or the government, was seen by many as misguided and by others as merely a cover for the fiscal motives behind the association's decision. Regardless of the good intentions of many of the V.E.A. directors, and it is important to acknowledge that there were others who held to the cruder, purely economic rationale, the decision was hardly greeted with equanimity throughout the city and province. Although it continued the $5,000 grant previously promised for 1914, the provincial government withdrew further assistance for the exhibition since it opposed holding a fair at such a time. The Vancouver Board of Trade, an organization which had only reluctantly accepted the presence of an exhibition in Vancouver, similarly spoke out against the fair, despite the fact that they had been reassured by representatives of both the V.E.A. and the militia that holding the exhibition would not impede military training already underway at the Hastings Park grounds. A number of patriotic organizations joined in the opposition, but the protests were all to no avail and preparations proceeded on schedule.²

It is important to note that while there was considerable opposition to a wartime fair, there was simultaneously noticeable public support for the Vancouver Exhibition Association's action. The Local Council of Women, the B.C. Manufacturers' Association, Vancouver City Council, and a variety of agricultural associations all backed the V.E.A. Although newspapers were generally occupied with developments elsewhere, on the eve of the 1914 exhibition the *Vancouver*

Daily Province took the time to reflect upon the contribution of the fair during wartime. Reflecting the widespread belief that the war would be over in a short time, the commentators also assessed the post-conflict impact of the V.E.A.'s show.

> The exhibition is a timely reminder that the world still whirls through [sic] space in spite of the agony it is enduring. . . . The Vancouver Exhibition should give much food for thought. It will undoubtedly open the eyes of many to the possibilities which are at hand, did we but view them in a proper light. If it convinces us now is the time to prepare to take advantage of these possibilities, and organize so that when the money markets are right we are fully prepared to offer them excellent inducement for investment purposes, then the exhibition will have accomplished much for us all.[3]

The city and the province, therefore, were divided over the question of holding a wartime fair. The success or failure of the 1914 exhibition, as with all others, rested ultimately upon the level of support accorded by the citizens of Vancouver. Between 1910 and 1914, the Vancouver Exhibition Association had worked conscientiously towards building a rapport with area residents, adapting the fair to suit local needs and demands and making the grounds available year-round to any and all sporting, cultural, fraternal or other organizations. The effort had been well rewarded and the citizens had generally responded favourably to the first four exhibitions and to the association. With the decision to hold a fair in 1914, however, the V.E.A. provided a welcome opening to opponents of the fair. A group of critics was to coalesce around this issue of patriotism and contribution to the national war effort, and, in subsequent years, they used the V.E.A.'s actions as a springboard from which they would attack other of the association's endeavours. In the short term, however, the main concern was how the citizens of Vancouver would react to the 1914 exhibition.

Attendance at the exhibition fell by almost 50 per cent, with only 46,130 people passing through the gates, the lowest total in the five-year history of Vancouver's fair. The V.E.A. suffered financially as well, losing over $10,000 on the exhibition and ending the fiscal year with a net deficit of $14,700. The association found some solace in the fact that it had rained throughout much of the five-day fair and blamed the poor attendance and the declining returns on the decision to accommodate the farmers by holding a September exhibition.[4] While intemperate weather undoubtedly hastened and accentuated the decline in the exhibition's fortunes, it is apparent as well that public support for the fair had dropped substantially. Stark evidence of this decline is found in the Vancouver Exhibition Association's membership rolls. In 1914, with expectations high and plans well formulated, over 550 people held annual and life memberships. The following year, in the aftermath of the first wartime exhibition, the number of members fell dramatically to less than 50. Whereas public support and confidence in the exhibition had been on the rise before 1914, the V.E.A.'s standing within the community showed signs of sharp reduction thereafter. It was hardly an auspicious turn of events for the association, but they nonetheless declared their intention to continue.

There was one further unfavourable consequence of the decision to hold the 1914 fair that was to have a long-term effect on the attitudes and actions of the Vancouver Exhibition Association. Along with most of the Canadian fairs, some American fairs cancelled their 1914 operations after the war broke out even though the United States was not yet involved. In the Pacific Northwest, all the other major exhibitions including New Westminster, Victoria, and Seattle, which apparently felt it could not operate properly with other regional fairs shut down, closed their gates, with unexpectedly grim consequences for Vancouver's fair. It was estimated that as a direct result of these closures the V.E.A. lost over $7,000 in exhibit and racing fees and concession rentals. Located in the midst of a thriving west coast fair circuit, Vancouver had gained significant benefits from its position in the area. Exhibitors, concessionaires, and attraction operators would come west only if there was an opportunity to participate in a series of major exhibitions. The 1914 closures highlighted the V.E.A.'s reliance on other exhibitions and indicated the value, indeed the necessity, of functioning within co-ordinated fair circuits. Henceforth, the Vancouver Exhibition Association was to direct more time and effort towards stabilizing its position within the exhibition circuits of the Pacific Northwest.[5]

In the aftermath of the disastrous 1914 exhibition, the V.E.A. engaged in a greater than normal amount of introspection. President Miller reiterated the value and function of the Vancouver fair, claiming that "it is a publicity bureau, an exemplifier of possibilities, possessions and resources, and it is a playground and a health-giver."[6] Such grandiose statements rang a little hollow in the face of the poor response to the first wartime exhibition. Building plans were postponed indefinitely, forcing a re-examination of the use of existing facilities and a reordering of exhibition arrangements. The hoary question of date was once again raised, with the September dates of the 1914 show being held up by the association as an important reason for the financial distress. Two suggestions were made for a new starting date for the exhibition, July 1 or mid-October, with the directors oddly claiming that the former date was most beneficial to the farmers. The following year, the fair was moved back to what was seen as the more fiscally responsible date of mid-August. Even more remarkable was the suggestion made in all seriousness by one director that owing to the unstable fiscal position of the V.E.A., the association should attempt to secure a rebate of 50 per cent on all prize monies won at the fair. Wisely, the directors did not accede to the request, which would have further weakened the already strained credibility of the exhibition within the agricultural community.[7]

In the four years following the 1914 fair matters returned somewhat closer to normal. Most of the other major exhibitions in the area reopened after a year's hiatus, enabling the Vancouver Exhibition Association to draw in a greater number of exhibitors, concessionaires, and attractions. Criticism of the exhibition and of the V.E.A., however, continued throughout the war years. While much of this criticism was directed towards specific aspects of the fair, it is important to recognize that the origins of much of this civic hostility can be traced primarily to the decision to hold an exhibition in 1914. That decision and the resulting outcry had essentially knocked the V.E.A. off the pedestal it had previously occupied. Whereas earlier attacks on the exhibition were often viewed as attacks on the city itself, residents were less defensive about criticism of the V.E.A. after 1914. Groups who had previously backed the association were now prepared to take a more questioning, even hostile stance. In 1915, for instance, the Exhibition Committee of City Council, long a staunch defender of exhibition interests, recommended:

> that the Vancouver Exhibition Association be given six months notice of cancellation of the lease entered into between the City and the Association on May 20, 1913 of Suburban Lot 90 Hastings Townsite, and that the City will take over the Buildings and Grounds on the expiry of such notice.[8]

No reason was given in the minutes for the unexpected move, but the resolution was laid over shortly thereafter, and no action was taken to revoke the association's lease.[9] Still, the fact that the committee made such a recommendation does suggest that the V.E.A. had lost its former "blank cheque" for the use of Hastings Park and that the activities of the exhibition were being subjected to ever closer scrutiny by the City Council.

Public criticism, similarly, became more widespread. The amusements staged by the Great Worthen Shows aroused the sensibilities of many people who viewed the "fat" girl, the Siamese twins, and the other human aberrations as "freaks." The Vancouver Board of Trade protested the continuing displays of gambling at the exhibition and the presentation of "unsatisfactory" skid road shows.[10] The most severe complaint, and the most telling, came in a 1917 petition from the Ratepayers' Central Association, an omnibus group claiming to represent taxpayers throughout the city. The petition enumerated nine specific points and requests. They asked that City Council cancel the lease and that Hastings Park be turned over to the Board of Park Commissioners. If the exhibition was to be allowed to remain, they argued, then the V.E.A. should be forced to pay rentals for the use of the land and facilities. The R.C.A. joined with the Women's Christian Temperance Union in declaring that "public morality was violated at the last annual show" and suggested further that council should stop the exhibition association from spending any further funds as it was a self-appointed and therefore irresponsible organization.[11] It was a biting criticism and condemnation from one of the largest citizen's groups in the city, revealing once again that the V.E.A. had fallen from favour in some circles at least, and now served as a ready target for social critics.

The Vancouver Exhibition Association could not sit back passively as the critics railed on. The directors responded in kind to the Ratepayer's Central Executive, pointing out among other things that the exhibition was flourishing as a family show, that the V.E.A. hired the same carnival companies as other major exhibitions, that admission prices were the lowest in Western Canada, and, most importantly, that the association consistently showed a profit despite a virtual lack of government aid and without revenue from horse-racing.[12] The following year, President Miller reacted even more firmly to criticism of the exhibition and the skid road, claiming that the association would pay no heed to "some Pharisaical[s] who sit in condemnation of the exhibition because of the presence of this form of entertainment." The skid road, Miller maintained, was a "rollicking, carefree, semi-theatrical entertainment," and the Vancouver Exhibition Association was not about to give in to a "social purity party."[13]

Miller's protestations notwithstanding, public criticisms were not without effect and some attempts were actually made to meet the public demands for a cleansing of the skid road, including enlisting assistance from the police to control gambling and allowing a committee of citizens appointed by the Ratepayer's Association to approve the contents of the Hastings Park carnival. In 1918, following a rather severe condemnation of the fair by the W.C.T.U., the V.E.A. solemnly resolved to co-operate with that organization to provide a series of special amusements for children and families, including concerts, musical presentations, educational contests and physical competitions for young people. The V.E.A.'s actions did not, however, keep pace with their promises and there were few additions to the following year's programme along the lines suggested.[14]

Throughout this period, the V.E.A. increasingly saw itself made the focus for public debate, and its frequent, vocal replies to criticism usually lengthened and intensified the controversies. Their many and varied activities left the V.E.A. open to attack from innumerable angles. The exhibition directorate, however, had not yet acquired the thick skins that often go with such positions and instead responded vigorously to each and every public criticism of the fair.

Too much should not be made out of these specific criticisms of the exhibition programme. Although the existence of such strong opposition was of considerable concern to the V.E.A., the fair continued to enjoy fairly widespread backing throughout the war, with such diverse groups as the Ward 3 Ratepayers, the *Vancouver Sun,* Vancouver Rabbit Breeders, and the B.C. Dairymen among others urging the association to maintain its level of activities. The general attitude of the citizens of Vancouver towards the wartime exhibitions seems to be somewhere between these two extremes, a position best exemplified by the actions of the Vancouver Board of Trade. The Board of Trade's concern over the propriety of hosting a wartime fair, first evident in 1914, resurfaced in 1918, when they approached the military authorities concerning the advisability of holding an exhibition that year.[15] After considerable debate and after hearing submissions from both the militia and the V.E.A., the special committee formed to investigate declared that:

> in the opinion of this Committee it would be advisable in the interests of conservation of manpower and transportation as well as on general economic grounds that all Exhibitions throughout Canada should be suspended during the continuance of the War.
>
> If, however, the Federal Government does not adopt such policy then this Committee recommends that no exception should be made with respect to Exhibitions being held in British Columbia.[16]

The attitude of the special committee of the Vancouver Board of Trade appears to be a fairly accurate representation of the general feeling in Vancouver. There was limited enthusiasm for the exhibition, except in agricultural circles, but there was also a recognition that as long as the federal government did not object, the fair should be allowed to operate.

Fortunately for the Vancouver Exhibition Association and for agricultural fairs across Canada, the dominion authorities not only allowed the exhibitions to proceed, but provided tangible evidence of their support for them. In 1915, at a time when many agricultural fairs faced financial ruin, the government decided to step in with some timely financial assistance, offering to subsidize the agricultural prize lists of the various fairs. In Vancouver's case, this largesse amounted to almost $5,000 in 1915, $2,500 in both 1916 and 1917, and $4,875 in the last year of the war. More important, perhaps, than the limited financial aid was the fact that by its actions the dominion government was acknowledging the value of the V.E.A.'s show and was encouraging the organization to continue its efforts. Ottawa was quick to recognize the fair's potential as a morale booster and publicist for the war effort. The government's official recognition proved to be a powerful weapon in the arsenal of the V.E.A., and it was trotted out whenever the decision to continue operations during wartime elicited public comment.[17]

Impelled by declining revenues and more vociferous opposition in some quarters, the Vancouver Exhibition Association took renewed interest in the activities of the fair associations of the Pacific Northwest. The 1914 exhibition graphically demonstrated the vulnerability of Vancouver's exhibition and also revealed that its success was closely tied to the success of other regional fairs. As well, the various exhibitions in the area were rapidly realizing that isolation from the major exhibition centres of North America, particularly the American Midwest and central Canada, virtually shut the individual west coast fairs out of the market for first-class entertainment and exhibits. Members of the North Pacific Fairs Association decided in 1916, for example, to establish a uniform contract for carnival companies hired by regional fairs, and to draw up a blacklist of carnival operators, concessionaires, and entertainers who had run into trouble with any of the member exhibitions. Two years later, the same organization extended its regional activities even more, establishing a uniform race programme and registering all horses and jockeys active in the area. By instituting standard contracts and providing uniform conditions throughout the Pacific Northwest, the organization hoped to make member fairs more attractive and consequently to increase the number and variety of exhibitors, raise the quality of entertainment and attractions, and place west coast fairs in general in a more advantageous position. As well, by working out a circuit within the N.P.F.A., the association ensured a smooth flow of exhibits between fairs and minimized competition.[18]

The Vancouver Exhibition Association did not restrict its activities with other fairs to such formal ties, but also relied on more informal connections as a means of improving its exhibition. The V.E.A. decided, for example, to unite with other local exhibitions to hire one carnival company for the entire area, offering that firm a series of fairs instead of the normal single exhibition. They expected that working in unison would make a better quality of carnival available to British Columbia. Owing to the war and the high costs of transportation to the Coast, few quality carnivals were available, and in 1918, the V.E.A. and associated fairs were forced to accept what they regarded as the "second-rate" programme offered by H. Meyerhoff of New York.[19]

In this period, the Vancouver Exhibition Association exhibited an increasing awareness of its own place within the larger universe of west coast and Canadian fairs. Besides taking a more active role in the various fair associations, the V.E.A. began to consider its development and funding arrangements in the context of the evolution of other Canadian exhibitions. Although the V.E.A. was not yet chauvinistic enough to claim that it hosted the most important exhibition in Western Canada, the association did take pride in comparing its progress to that of other regional fairs. Self-esteem, however, was not the sole reason for placing Vancouver's exhibition alongside others. The V.E.A. found that a judicious comparison with similar sized Canadian fairs provided a useful argument when appealing to either the federal or provincial government for increased assistance.[20]

The government's involvement with the V.E.A. during the war was much more than just assistance with prize lists for agricultural displays. With the war came the military occupation of Hastings Park. When war was declared, local militia organizations went in search of suitable parade and muster facilities. Not surprisingly, their eyes quickly fell on the excellent buildings and grounds at Hastings Park, almost tailor-made for military use. Having the militia ensconced in the exhibition's backyard, while an imposition in many ways, had its compensations, not the least of which was the $8,000 rental charged the militia for the use of the grounds in 1915.[21]

When it became clear that, contrary to initial expectations, the war was likely to continue for several years, more formal arrangements were concluded between the V.E.A. and the military administrators. This done, the grounds quickly came to serve as the major manning depot for the Canadian armed forces in the Vancouver area, often having more than 3,000 soldiers encamped on the property at a time. Most of the mobilization for British Columbia occurred at Hastings Park, and even in the midst of the annual exhibition, soldiers' tents filled the racetrack oval and much of the cleared land in the park.[22]

The militia continued to occupy portions of the V.E.A.'s facilities throughout the war and even when the conflict ended late in 1918, the army maintained its hold on the premises, using the grounds for demobilization purposes. It was not until this final phase of occupancy that relations between the V.E.A. and the militia became strained. Colonel Harvey, who was in charge of demobilization, repeatedly claimed that Hastings Park would not be returned to the Vancouver Exhibition Association in time for the August 1919 exhibition. An appeal to Harvey's commanding officer, General R. G. Leckie, soothed the troubled waters, and Leckie stated that every endeavour would be made to vacate the grounds in time.[23] This debate at war's end reveals the V.E.A.'s vigilant approach to the military use of the grounds. As long as their occupation did not interfere with the exhibition and provided the dominion government paid for the inconvenience caused by the military presence, the association was only too pleased to do its patriotic duty. At the suggestion that fulfilling that duty would imperil the annual fair, however, the V.E.A.'s directors drew the line. To them, the exhibition was serving a national purpose just as important as turning over Hastings Park for exclusive military use would be.

Thus, the war had a varied effect on the Vancouver Exhibition Association. Perhaps of more importance in the long run, was the effect of the war on the structure of the exhibition itself. With Canada embroiled in a major international conflict, with many of the young men of Vancouver and British Columbia engaged in overseas combat, with severe restrictions on the availability of certain commodities, and with women assuming a greater and more visible role in the economy, the V.E.A. was required to adapt the fair to conform more closely to the new realities. Women's work, in particular, became a major focus of the wartime fair. Patriotic organizations such as the Red Cross, the Imperial Order of the Daughters of the Empire, and others were encouraged to use the grounds during the exhibition to raise funds for their overseas work. Yet the attempt to solicit greater female participation in the annual show ran into difficulties in the latter stages of the war, and the V.E.A. found that the space allocated for women's displays often stood half empty. Apparently many of the longstanding contributors to the fair, when faced with the option of arranging a suitable exhibit or volunteering their energies to one of the many wartime assistance agencies, chose the latter course.[24]

One of the most popular programmes throughout the war was the Better Babies Contest. Founded in 1913, the contest assumed a new life and importance following the commencement of hostilities. For a fifty-cent registration fee, a mother could bring her family to the exhibition grounds, have the children examined by a team of physicians and nurses, have them rated according to a standardized scoring system, and depending upon the health of the baby either receive medical advice and treatment or win prizes and recognition. Originally operating under the auspices of the Local Council of Women, the contest was taken over by the Child Welfare Committee of the V.E.A. in 1918 when it was in danger of being cancelled owing to lack of organizational support. The show was consistently successful, attracting 600 entrants in 1914, a high of 1,100 two years later, and 800 in 1918. The contest was credited with many achievements in the amelioration of child health problems, including improving maternal awareness of medical problems, selecting sick or diseased children and directing them to a hospital, and even creating such a demand for better medical facilities for children that 20 beds for youths were added to the Vancouver General Hospital.[25]

Other special programmes were developed in response to the demographic and economic conditions of the war. With the number of farmers and young men participating in the exhibition declining annually, the association decided in 1917 to direct special attention towards increasing enthusiasm for agriculture among the boys of the province. In that year, a Boy's Guest programme was instituted. The Vancouver Exhibition Association sponsored competitions in various school districts throughout the province to select boys with interest and expertise in agriculture to represent their regions at the fair. The programme soon ran into difficulties, however, as a number of districts resented the regional distribution of representatives. Because there was such a strong focus on the Vancouver area, other school boards saw the entire enterprise as an advertising gimmick and refused to participate. The boys who eventually attended (32 that first year, of whom 16 were from Vancouver) were treated royally while they were at the exhibition. They were given guided tours of the city and immediate environs, boat rides through the harbour, special agricultural lectures and demonstrations, formal luncheons and other events, all at the expense of the V.E.A.[26]

The onset of the war and changes in attendance forced additional alterations in the basic content of the presentation. In addition to the changes discussed above, existing features such as school exhibits and home economy displays, shows which drew on women and children as both spectators and participants, were expanded, while other features, including livestock and horticultural competitions, were cut back. Despite these cosmetic changes, however, the core of the fair remained remarkably constant; industrial and manufacturing exhibits again filled the main halls, with mining and forestry displays assuming ever more prominent positions, and with horse-racing, livestock shows and agricultural displays still assuming their customary secondary role in the annual fair. The V.E.A. attempted as much as possible to soften the impact of the war on the exhibition and to retain some measure of continuity through the five fairs held under the shadow of the conflict. At the same time, the association did not miss an opportunity to publicize the war effort or its contribution thereto, holding an annual Veteran's Day and requesting that the militia leave some of their heavy armaments on the grounds during the exhibition to serve not only as a reminder of the overseas battle, but also as a popular addition to the V.E.A.'s collection of attractions.

The exhibitions held between 1915 and 1918 saw a steady return to prosperity by the V.E.A. After 1914, when public resentment and poor weather conspired to force down attendance, the number of people attending the exhibition rose steadily, reaching a reported 73,000 the next year, 81,000 in both 1916 and 1917, and topping 94,000 in the last year of the war. Profits from the annual fair also climbed consistently, recovering from the 1914 deficit to a bare profit of $460 in 1915 and a total of more than $17,000 by 1918. Although the attendance figures cannot be taken at face value, it does appear that the citizens of Vancouver were gradually reconciling themselves to the concept of a wartime exhibition. They had come to accept that the European conflict was not going to be of short duration and thus moved towards the V.E.A.'s position that it should be "business as usual."

Despite the revival of the association's fiscal fortunes, it is clear that the war had serious ramifications for Vancouver's exhibition. In addition to the weakening in support for the fair from council, the agricultural community, and the citizenry at large at the beginning of the war years, other problems were developing. For example, building plans, in full gear when the conflict began, were shelved for four years, and there was a consequent overuse and in some instances misuse of existing structures, hastening their deterioration. While it is difficult to gauge the depth of antagonism towards the V.E.A. and the exhibition, the important factor here is that public outcry against the content of the show and the V.E.A.'s management had begun. The grains of future controversy and opposition had been sown.

As the Vancouver Exhibition Association turned its attention towards planning for a "Peace and Victory" exhibition for 1919, the organization could only hope for better things to come. As the European war drew to a close, President J. J. Miller wrote:

Five times since the outbreak of war have we carried out an exhibition. A false idea at one time took possession of many minds that exhibitions should be closed during war time. This view was not taken by the Imperial and Dominion Government, who saw in them an influential means of educating and inspiring the people to devote their best energies to greater and better production, besides being an important factor in maintaining the commercial and social equilibrium of communities in times of danger and unrest.[27]

The V.E.A. emerged from the war with its spirit unbroken and confidence intact, firm in the belief that the fair had served a valuable function in assisting with the prosecution of the war. Some Vancouverites were not as sure.

Plate 1 J. J. Miller, first president of the Vancouver Exhibition Association, 1908 to 1922.

Plate 2 H. S. Rolston, manager of the V.E.A. from 1911 to 1925.

Plate 3 Parking was always a problem at Hastings Park. Renfrew Street was often the sight of traffic congestion as people double-parked their cars in their haste to get to the fair.

Plate 4   The Industrial Building was built in 1910 with great haste and little caution, and deteriorated rapidly. It was finally demolished in 1936.

Plate 5   Built in 1913, entirely of local wood products, the Forestry Building succumbed to dry rot and had to be torn down in the 1930's.

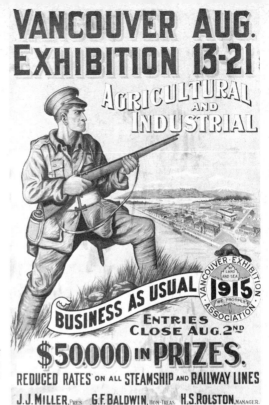

Plate 6   In the face of public debate on the propriety of holding a fair in wartime, the V.E.A. adopted a **Business as Usual** campaign, and continued to promote the annual exhibition.

Plate 7   Hastings Park was pressed into service during World War I and many soldiers camped in battalion tents such as these before going Overseas.

Plate 8   With the collapse of the New Westminster Exhibition in 1930, following a fire which destroyed the buildings at Queen's Park, Vancouver's show became the major agricultural event in the province.

Plate 9   The Shoot-the-Chutes, foreground, and the Big Dipper, background, were popular features of the amusement area in the 1930's.

Plate 10   The Pure Foods "Sample House" was a favourite of fairgoers as exhibitors freely dispensed samples of their food products.

Plate 11   During World War II, various branches of the Canadian Armed Forces established fair time displays, hoping to attract young men to join in the war effort.

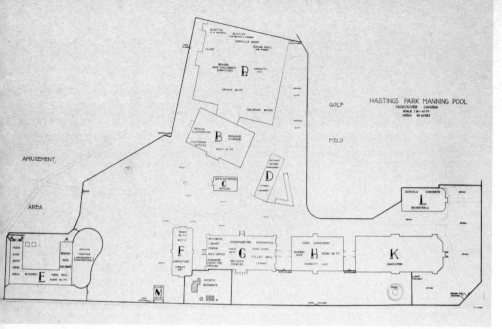

Plate 12 This plan of Hastings Park shows the variety of services established on the fair grounds for the evacuation of Japanese Canadians

Plate 13 More than eight thousand persons of Japanese descent passed through Hastings Park between March and September of 1942. This massive collection of bunk beds was the dormitory for all the men and older boys.

John Landy
3:59.6

Rogr Bannister
3:58.8

Plate 14 Dubbed the Miracle Mile, the Bannister-Landy Race was the highlight of the British Empire and Commonwealth Games in 1954.

Plate 15 Public response to the Timber Show held in 1960 was very positive, and by 1966 the show had become a regular feature of the annual fair.

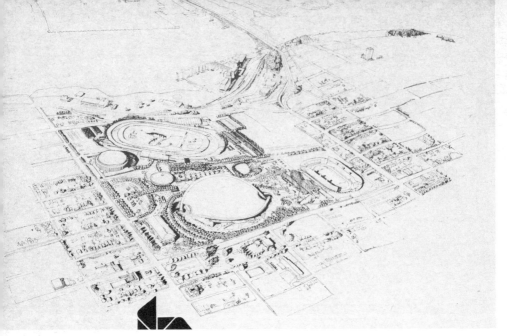

Plate 16   In 1977, the P.N.E. formulated plans for the construction of a 60,000 seat stadium, however the Multiplex plan lost out to a counter proposal for a stadium in downtown Vancouver.

Plate 17   The P.N.E. has undergone massive changes since the first fair was held in 1910, and in 1982 it stands as one of North America's great exhibitions.

5

Controversy, Defiance and Expansion, 1918-1930

The war is over. Peace is established. It will take time for rehabilitation, for a return to normal. Our natural resources are great and varied. The influx of population from other lands is reasonably expected. It is in the power of our association to make known to the world the wonderful possibilities of the country, and to be of even greater service in exploiting the rich natural resources in which the country abounds, and in encouraging the production and manufacturing of the best.[1]

With these words in 1919, President J. J. Miller attempted to close the book on the war years and delineate yet again the goals and aspirations of the Vancouver Exhibition Association. The war and all the attending internal and external difficulties behind them, the directors now wanted to press ahead, to hold a massive "peace and victory" celebration in conjunction with the 1919 exhibition and then to establish the position of Vancouver's fair as the greatest in the Pacific Northwest.

Several major changes had been made in anticipation of the first post-war show, including the adoption of September dates. The decision, representing only the second attempt by the association to hold a true fall fair, was made primarily as a result of the vigorous representations of the Livestock Committee. This group correctly pointed out that "the agricultural people have never been thoroughly in sympathy with the Vancouver exhibition, because it is held at the wrong season to ever make it truly an agricultural exhibition."[2] If Vancouver was ever to achieve real status as a major agricultural fair, with all the attending provincial and federal financial support, it was clear to many that later dates were required to boost the number of exhibitors. With this rationale, the exhibition's opening date was pushed back to 8 September 1919. Another significant change in the programme was the addition of a horse show, claimed to be "the second largest event of its kind in America."[3] The horse show turned out to be a hastily arranged enterprise, since the organizers had to scramble to find suitable facilities, but a show was eventually staged. Physical developments, suspended by the war for four years, began again with a small campsite being prepared on the grounds for tourists, and a major renovation of the Women's Building, formerly the Industrial Building.[4] Additional improvements to the grounds were postponed until after the 1919 exhibition since the militia did not vacate the property soon enough to allow for anything other than emergency construction or repairs before the fair.

In the end, the show was an organizational and financial success. The weather co-operated and over 120,000 people were reported to have passed through the turnstiles, a jump of almost 26,000 over the previous record. The faith placed in the agricultural community proved well founded; the farmers and livestock breeders responded to the September dates by entering a record number of exhibits. Many departments enjoyed a significant increase in the number of competitors or displays, and, with the exception of the Horticultural Department, they all agreed that the new dates had injected a fresh breath of life into their section of the fair. The association as well found considerable solace in the fact that the total number of exhibits at the Vancouver fair far outstripped New Westminster's exhibition, its most important rival and supposedly the premier agricultural show in British Columbia. The only significant negative vote was sounded by supporters of horse-racing since the September dates had meant that Vancouver had had to drop out of its traditional place in the Pacific Coast racing circuit.[5]

With agriculture leading the way for the first time, participants generally agreed that the 1919 show was the Vancouver Exhibition Association's finest. Financially, the 1919 fair was a resounding success; the association realized a record profit of $23,630. Importantly, the 1919 exhibition also heralded the return of provincial government funding, with Victoria offering a $5,000 grant towards the prize lists. Similarly, the dominion government continued to subsidize the agricultural competitions, giving the association a sum of $2,680 as payment of an agreed upon percentage of the prizes allocated for utility class events.[6] Recognition of the exhibition's success also drew a larger number of citizens into the V.E.A. fold; the annual memberships rose from a low of 44 in 1919 to more than 450 following the first post-war fair.

As had now become commonplace, however, the exhibition still had to face its critics. Soon after the fair closed a minor debate erupted once again over the matter of gambling on the Hastings Park grounds. In October, deputations from the Child Welfare Association, Vancouver Board of Trade, Parent Teacher Association, the Ministerial Association of Vancouver met with the V.E.A. Board of Control to discuss the issue. Criticism rained on the fair from all the sides. One man in the party complained about the manner of selling tickets, claiming that there were "gestures and remarks not nice to hear," while Reverend Sovereign from Mount Pleasant remarked that "as a result of the wheels [gambling devices] at the Exhibition, the children all over that district were operating small wheels, and, in order to get the necessary money to manipulate them, were in the habit of breaking into stores, and stealing." The Civic Bureau of the local Board of Trade joined the growing chorus of displeasure, arguing in particular that the "Hula-Hula show was both immoral and disgraceful and should not be tolerated in the community." Pragmatically aware of the potential ramifications of widespread criticism, the association agreed to set up a committee, including a representative from the deputation, to resolve the matter.[7] Even if the Vancouver Exhibition Association had wanted to eliminate all gambling from the fair, and evidence suggests that this was not the case, there was actually little that could have been done. The skid-road games were operated by individual carnival companies who contracted with the V.E.A. for the use of the grounds during the fair. Because Vancouver was so isolated from the primary carnival circuits, the association was forced to rely on what were clearly second-rate productions. Provided the individual shows and games were not violating the law, in this instance by allowing children to gamble, the V.E.A. had little recourse. Regardless, the fact that the association lacked the desire to eliminate gambling and other vaudeville acts found offensive by some ensured that little was done in response to the criticism. The association's refusal to move on this matter was based on a simple premise. Despite the fact that a vocal minority continued to protest about the nature of the exhibition programme, it was apparent that most of the fairgoers, far from protesting about the carnival atmosphere, welcomed it, and many actually saw the gambling and vaudeville acts as the principal attractions of the fair. Evidence of continued support for the fair by the "silent majority" is provided by the steadily mounting attendance through the 1920's.

The 1919 exhibition launched the Vancouver Exhibition Association on what proved to be a decade of tremendous growth and development, years which saw the Vancouver fair emerge as the sole major exhibition in British Columbia and one of the most important in Canada. At first it did not seem that way, for the next few presentations had disappointing results. The attendance declined to 90,000 in 1920 and climbed only slightly to 96,000 in 1921. The low attendance in 1920 was attributed to a return of Vancouver's wet September weather, since rain fell during all but the final two days of the exhibition. Despite President Miller's argument that a return to August dates would be "at the expense of the primary objects of the Association,"[8] it was decided to abandon the fall in favour of a late summer show. Ironically, after a summer of fine weather the clouds opened on the second day of the August 1921 fair, and once again attendance was poor. Nevertheless the association concluded that the August scheduling would be more advantageous for the exhibition in the long run and the fair eventually became firmly entrenched in that month.

For the remainder of the decade, attendance mounted steadily. In 1922, 110,000 patrons visited the grounds. By 1925, the annual attendance had reached 197,000, and by the end of the 1920's, as many as 288,000 people were to pass through the gates in a single year. Somewhat surprisingly the V.E.A. did not enjoy a similar surge in profits from the fair, recording a loss of $380 in 1922 and averaging $16,900 profit a season between 1920 and 1929. While this was a major improvement on the annual return from the exhibition's first decade, when profits averaged only $6,900, the rise in income was not keeping pace with the attendance. Although profits provide a reasonably accurate reflection of the fair's fiscal success, the V.E.A. was not in business to make a profit. The association was established to organize a yearly exhibition and to provide the necessary facilities. Any profit derived from a year's efforts was either used as seed money for the following exhibition or channelled into the V.E.A.'s ever-expanding budget for capital expenditures. One reason for the somewhat sluggish revenues was that the association was distributing increasing amounts of money in prizes for the various competitions. The V.E.A.'s prize list averaged over $26,000 a year, compared to $19,600 for the first decade, marking it as one of the most generous exhibitions in Western Canada. Indeed, the V.E.A. noted with considerable glee that "both of the Associations [Victoria and New Westminster] are repeatedly complaining to us that we are too extravagant in the amount of money offered as premiums."[9]

This was unquestionably a decade of growth, but it was achieved only at considerable cost and effort. Oddly, during this period when the V.E.A. appeared to be coming of age there were at least three occasions when the future of the Hastings Park exhibition was seriously in doubt and when the Vancouver Exhibition Association stood on the verge of losing control over either the park or the annual fair.

Flushed by continued support for the post-war exhibitions, the V.E.A. began to press for an early renewal of the Hastings Park lease in 1923. Since the original lease was not yet up for revision, the directors' move was obviously calculated to take advantage of the fact that public support was at its peak, which in turn suggested that resistance to an expanded lease would be at a low ebb. The association hoped, in effect, to push the issue through City Council without going through the tedious and potentially dangerous procedure of opening up the operation of the fair to general public scrutiny. After a meeting with city aldermen in March 1923, it soon became clear, however, that passage would not be easy. The aldermen took turns pointing out what they saw to be the deficiencies in the V.E.A.'s operation and called for a re-orientation of activities at Hastings Park.[10] It was hardly an auspicious start to the association's attempt to have the lease re-examined, and it was decided to proceed much more cautiously with the negotiations.

With the issue of control of Hastings Park once again thrown open for debate, opponents of the exhibition association lined up to call for a revision in the administration of the park. District 5 Ratepayers and the Vancouver Ratepayers Association both approached the Board of Park Commissioners with the suggestion that the board attempt to gain command of the property. The former group in particular pressed its request, declaring that it was circulating a "monster petition" in the east end of the city "in an endeavour to have the present lease terminated."[11] Recognizing that public opposition to the use of the park for the annual fair, while not yet widespread, was mounting, the Vancouver Exhibition Association adopted a very conciliatory stance.

At the same time, the association was not about to leave anything to chance in its negotiations with the city. An informal poll of the aldermen revealed that while four aldermen were likely to support a ten-year lease, a like number were opposed to such a tenure, and three of them even argued for a city-wide plebiscite to determine the future of Hastings Park. Aware of the attitude of the councillors and wanting to have the lease signed quickly, the V.E.A. restructured its request, initially dropping the demand for a ten-year lease in favour of a five-year agreement and later exhibiting an unusual willingness to accede to certain of council's requests. As the question moved closer to a resolution, the V.E.A. found itself facing a formidable array of opponents, including Ward 5 Ratepayers, Central Ratepayers' Association, Grandview Chamber of Commerce, New Era League, Retail Merchants Association, Franklin Parent and Teachers Association, and District 6 Ratepayers, with many of these groups and several of the aldermen in favour of turning the property over to the Parks Board. At the same time, however, the V.E.A. was not alone in its fight, finding welcome support from such groups as the Trades and Labour Council, Chilliwack Board of Trade, and a plethora of agricultural organizations.[12]

The Vancouver Exhibition Association martialled its support carefully, and when the lease came up in City Council, the aldermen voted five to three in favour of a new accord. The association found much to be pleased with in the new lease, particularly since council had even been moved to sign a ten-year agreement. Though the document altered little from the lease that had been in effect since 1908, the aldermen had secured some concessions from the exhibition association. The V.E.A. was now required, as an on-going condition of the lease, to erect and maintain a Tourist Auto Camp and to improve and operate a golf course on the property, the construction of which had begun in 1921, to pay the civic scale of wages to all employees, and to spend 50 per cent of all the gross receipts from any sublease granted for amusement devices on the improvement of the grounds facilities. Council also asked, unofficially, that the association agree to open up its directorate to public election, a request that was never met. For their part, the V.E.A. received the security of a much desired ten-year lease and control over all subleases of facilities and grounds. It was, in retrospect, all or more than the

Vancouver Exhibition Association had expected, and they were more than a little pleased that the matter had finally been settled.[13]

Their success notwithstanding, the V.E.A. did not lose sight of the hostility generated by the debate over the lease, and they worked assiduously to calm public outcry. Directors attended a series of meetings held by groups expressing an interest in Hastings Park, explaining the purposes of the exhibition and plans for future development. In response to sustained public interest and criticism, the association held a special meeting early in June to discuss the lease and to answer questions raised about the fair. Most of those attending, including representatives from the Local Council of Women, Society of Friends, Child Welfare Association, the Trades and Labour Council, and a number of individual citizens, voiced the traditional objections to the holding of horse-racing at the park and to gambling during the exhibition. Comments were directed towards the "indecent and disgusting sideshows" along skid road, but several participants rose to voice their support for the fair and the events held at Hastings Park. Despite the largely hostile tone of the debate, the meeting ended on a positive note with the passage of a resolution thanking the V.E.A. for participating in a public forum and pledging those still in attendance, only about one-half of the original number, to work together to eliminate all the objectionable features in the exhibition.[14] The holding of the public discussion on the future of the fair appears to have gone some way towards tempering public opposition, and the long debated question of the control of Hastings Park seemed finally laid to rest. Almost forty years were to pass before the lease issue would again become the focus for public debate.

The second major controversy in this period, one which eventually led to a wide-ranging civic investigation of the annual fair and the association, developed in the year following the debate over the lease. In the late summer of 1924, public criticism of the V.E.A., led by the *Vancouver Star* newspaper, reached new heights.[15] For once, the mounting opposition did not focus on the exhibition programme, but rather was directed at the association management. Aiming their attack at Manager H. S. Rolston in particular, critics claimed that the V.E.A. was acting as a private body and not as a civic institution. It was insinuated that the association's financial affairs were not entirely above board, and some argued that neglect of the Hastings Park facilities had resulted in the serious deterioration of buildings, stables, and barns. Organizations which had only shortly before attacked the association during the lease controversy eagerly joined in with the new opposition. Responding to growing complaints and, in particular, to petitions organized by the Grandview Ratepayers' Association and the Vancouver Property Owners' Association, City Council decided in late December to commission a special committee to investigate "all phases of the Exhibition question."[16] A committee of five was formed with Alderman Bennett serving as chairman and W. R. Carmichael and Norman McLean of the V.P.O.A., C. C. Delbridge of the G.R.A., and President W. C. Brown and Manager H. S. Rolston of the V.E.A.

rounding out the group. The composition of the committee shifted considerably over the next four months, with Lt.-Col. Victor Spencer replacing McLean as the V.P.O.A. representative and R. P. McLennan sitting in for President Brown of the exhibition association on several occasions.[17]

The committee was armed with an extensive mandate and was instructed to investigate questions of financing, profitability, facilities, and, most importantly, management. In order to conduct its investigations, the Special Joint Committee appealed far and wide for information on the exhibition, calling for public submissions on any and all aspects of the fair. The financial records of the V.E.A. were also scrutinized, and the committee delved into the complex issue of government grants for buildings and exhibition purposes, conducted an extensive examination of the Hastings Park facilities, and prepared and circulated a questionnaire in order to solicit the opinions of agricultural and industrial exhibitors about the fair.[18]

The investigation was a remarkably thorough, if not always equitable, affair and touched on virtually all aspects of the operation of the exhibition from public response to sinking fund investments. The grounds were given a complete going over by representatives of the special committee, and the results were far from favourable. They labelled the stock-judging ring as "nothing less than a quagmire," recommended barns for demolition, stated that horse-racing facilities "apparently received little or no attention in the way of repair," questioned the stability of the grandstand, called the Women's Building "unsafe," and regarded sanitation and fire protection throughout the grounds as woefully inadequate.[19] The debate quickly spilled outside the confines of the civic inquiry, inciting a lively discussion in the letters to the editor and editorial columns of the local press.[20] The sorry condition of the facilities did not auger well for the future results of the investigation.

Two public meetings of the Special Committee were held to hear submissions and to provide the Vancouver Exhibition Association with a public opportunity to defend itself. Sentiments expressed ran consistently against the association; the general tone of the meetings can be summarized in the words of one individual who charged that "costs are too high, stables dirty, side shows a great detriment, gambling a disgrace, all of which should be abandoned and the fair brought to sound financial standing under proper management."[21] Debate at the two meetings centered in part on the handling of questionnaires. Feeling that the committee was not providing an adequate representation of the association's position, the V.E.A. had decided to circulate a questionnaire of its own to individuals on the association's mailing list. Alderman Bennett, chairman of the Special Joint Committee, refused to acknowledge the results of the V.E.A.'s poll, however, and the results were never entered as evidence.[22] Both public sessions proved inconclusive and ended without a satisfactory resolution of the outstanding issues.

Far from surrendering acquiescently to the investigation, the association maintained a vigorous defence throughout the hearings. A series of exhibits were entered in support of the exhibition, including an official declaration of the progress made by the V.E.A. from its inception, and a point-by-point refutation of the Special Joint Committee's survey of the Hastings Park facilities. As well, the association circulated the results of its questionnaire, although it is not surprising that is gained little public credibility.[23]

Although it provided a public forum for criticism of the Vancouver Exhibition Association, the Joint Committee was unable to come to any final conclusions regarding the exhibition and the entire issue was passed on to the City Council. Council's interest in the matter revolved primarily around the question of control of the association. Responding to the aldermen's request for adequate and ensured representation on the Board of the Control, the V.E.A. had amended its constitution in January 1925 to allow a specified number of aldermen to sit on the board.[24] The new arrangement only served to whet council's appetite, and they clamored to secure full control over the management of the fair. As the debate progressed, the focus began to shift more squarely onto Rolston, who had managed the fair since 1911. E. S. Knowlton, a V.E.A. director, indicated that the association was not going to sink or swim on Rolston's coattails and publicly declared that "the present manager has exceeded his authority and has lost the capability of obtaining and retaining public confidence."[25] Anxious to rid the exhibition of Rolston, council brought forward a candidate of its own for the manager's position, and Mayor L. D. Taylor, going one step further, indicated his support for placing the exhibition under complete civic control and operating it as a city department.[26]

Reacting to the public criticism of Rolston and of the exhibition in general, the Board of Control decided to assume the management of the 1925 fair, with each member of that board pledging to devote more attention and effort to his individual department.[27] As pressure on the association continued to mount and as council became increasingly assertive in its intent to control the exhibition, the Board of Control hit upon a clever strategy designed to call the council's bluff. With just a little more than two months to go until fairtime, the entire board tendered their resignations, throwing the management of the fair directly into the hands of the aldermen. Council was forced to respond to the precipitous action and hastily called a special "in camera" meeting with the Vancouver Exhibition Association. The final resolution clearly favoured the V.E.A., and the council agreed to limit their demands for representation and control. Well pleased that their action had brought a quick and favourable end to the controversy, the directors withdrew their resignations and declared their willingness "to carry on to make the Exhibition a success."[28]

Public assessment of the association was not limited to City Hall and the Joint Committee investigation. The preceding fall, City Council had approved the V.E.A.'s request that a by-law asking for a $25,000 loan be submitted to the ratepayers. Unfortunately for the association, the civic investigation broke in the midst of the campaign. With the V.E.A. embroiled in a major civic controversy and with the future of the exhibition very much in doubt, the association expected their ill-timed request to go down to defeat. They had not, however, anticipated that the request would be so overwhelmingly rejected. In contrast to earlier appeals, barely one-third of the electors, 37 per cent, voted in favour of the proposition, with only one of the eight wards even giving the by-law a simple majority. Ward 7, the district in which Hastings Park was located and an area of traditional support for the V.E.A., proved to be the sole ally (See Table 3). Outside of the Hastings Park ward, the strong east-side support for the exhibition had finally broken down. A defeat had been expected and the public inquiry had virtually guaranteed that the required 60 per cent vote would not be achieved. The magnitude of the rejection was, however, totally unanticipated. The amount of money lost was not large, and the potential economic impact was therefore reduced. Psychologically, however, the defeat was shattering, and two years passed before the Vancouver Exhibition Association risked another submission.[29]

The Vancouver Exhibition Association obviously did not emerge from the conflict unscathed. Despite V.E.A. remarks to the contrary, public opinion towards the association and the exhibition fell as a result of the Special Joint Committee's revelations, and the association was hard pressed to regain its former stature. The V.E.A. recognized its weaknesses as a result of the controversy and began to exert considerable effort to solve the problem. Public support, once again, had been seriously strained by the 1925 controversy, and the association was forcibly reminded that its civic standing was always precarious. For the first time, City Council had attempted to involve itself in the management of the exhibition, and it had come out of the contest badly bruised. Nonetheless, the long-term result of the debate was a widening of public and civic scrutiny of the operations of the V.E.A.

The V.E.A. therefore was not prepared to let matters rest with the end of the public controversy and was deeply concerned that an attempt be made to regain public confidence. The most important move in this direction came in the form of an attempt by the directors to deflect criticism from themselves or the entire association onto one individual. A ready and obvious scapegoat could be found in manager H. S. Rolston. He had ruled the exhibition in an often dictatorial manner and incurred the wrath of many civic officials for his independence. The directors pressured him into resigning and softened the blow somewhat by providing a generous separation allowance that included six months' salary, permission to purchase the manager's car, and a blanket letter of recommendation thanking him for his long service to the organization. This matter was not easily laid to rest, for like the entire inquiry the decision to fire Rolston touched off another public debate. Rolston and his supporters waged a vigorous battle to gain his re-instatement, but as one editorial writer noted, "The Fair itself is more important

than the saving of the face or position of any man connected with it." For the
Vancouver Exhibition Association the stakes were indeed high, and since sacrificing the general manager appeared to satisfy many of the exhibition's critics, the
decision was accepted as final.[30] J. K. Matheson was named to replace Rolston,
although he was given only a temporary appointment. Matheson's future status
was made dependent upon his performance during the 1925 exhibition, leaving the
V.E.A. with a safe "out" should he prove unsatisfactory.[31]

The special committee's investigation and the attending public furore had
momentarily weakened the association, but the resulting agreement with the city
inspired a certain degree of organizational confidence. The return to stability was
not to last long, however. Following swiftly on the heels of the 1925 controversy
was yet another major issue which again called into question the propriety of
holding an annual exhibition in Vancouver. This third conflict of the decade
centered on suggestions made by many individuals, organizations, and government officials that the two lower mainland fairs, Vancouver and New Westminster,
amalgamate their operations on one site. Indeed, as the debate progressed, it
became increasingly evident that such a union was inevitable and that the sole
outstanding issue was whether the new exhibition should be staged at Hastings
Park, at Queen's Park in New Westminster, or at some alternative location.

The first public indication that an amalgamation was being considered came
soon after the 1925 fair. In October of that year, the Board of Control of the V.E.A.
wrote to the Royal Agricultural and Industrial Society of New Westminster
suggesting that a preliminary meeting be held to discuss the matter. The association clearly felt that it was dealing from a position of strength, for one of the major
conditions of the meeting was that any agreed amalgamation would result in a fair
based in Hastings Park. Organizational matters were treated much more liberally.
The V.E.A. offered to split representation on the new board equally between the
two cities and suggested that the presidency of the larger organization should be
held alternately by individuals from the two societies. Not surprisingly, the offer
was greeted with little enthusiasm by the R.A.I.S., and the suggestion was firmly
but politely rejected.[32]

Once it was brought out into open discussion, the issue would not lie down.
Central Park in Burnaby was suggested as a compromise location the following
year, with supporters of the site arguing not only that was it equidistant from the
competing fairs, but also that it was directly in line with the way in which Greater
Vancouver was expanding. The V.E.A. harshly criticized the proposal, comparing
the size of Hastings Park, buildings, financing, amusements, and transportation
facilities with the suggested locale and concluding that the Vancouver site was
superior in every possible regard. "As to amalgamation itself," the V.E.A. brief
went on to say, "this is easy of accomplishment, if New Westminster will
recognize Hastings Park as the logical place, which undoubtedly it is from every
conceivable angle. . . . In a word: what objection has New Westminster to

amalgamating at Hastings Park."[33] The V.E.A. was clearly not about to move, and the matter was laid aside for a time. Two years after the original proposal, the Vancouver Exhibition Association decided to make one "final offer" to the R.A.I.S. Although they were still wary of the V.E.A.'s suggestion, the New Westminster directors were not unwilling to consider a rationalization of exhibition affairs in the Lower Mainland and asked to have the matter postponed for several months' examination.[34]

Delays continued to be the order of the day, however, and the issue was again deferred until 1929. By this time, however, it was clear that the question had to be settled forthwith. New Westminster's fair was running into ever more serious financial difficulties, while the Vancouver exhibition was becoming increasingly industrially oriented and many argued that it was not serving the needs of the agricultural community adequately. At the same time, the federal government was forced to divide its attention, funding, and exhibits between the two fairs, and it was especially eager to see an amalgamation. The federal director of agriculture summed up the feeling within that department when he commented:

> Is it not too bad that some Federal influence cannot induce Vancouver and New Westminster Shows to get together and put on one really good show with facilities for a winter fair, rather than have these two competing expensive exhibitions so close to each other, one developing more along industrial lines and the other with healthy deficits attempting to feature agriculture. Needless to say, we are called upon to support both of these with our exhibits and it is quite a bill of expense from our appropriation, which would be halved and with much more beneficial results were there one consolidated fair.[35]

During 1928 and early 1929, lines were clearly drawn on the matter, with location serving as the single stumbling block. British Columbia's premier, S. F. Tolmie came out solidly in favour of the principle of amalgamation. This was a crucial development, and it was now necessary to secure the premier's backing for the Hastings Park site. Failure to achieve his support could mean that the V.E.A. would have great difficulty raising any provincial funds for additional building projects. As well, the association wanted the help of Vancouver City Council for their stance, which could not be considered automatic in the aftermath of the 1925 controversy. The council-elect of 1928 indicated their willingness to support the retention of the Hastings Park fair, a fact noted with considerable relief by the Vancouver Exhibition Association. While a final decision had yet to be made, it was apparent that a resolution of the matter was in the offing.[36]

The complexion of the debate was altered dramatically in the summer of 1929 when fire swept through the exhibition buildings at Queen's Park, leaving the R.A.I.S. homeless on the eve of its Diamond Jubilee fair. Overcoming considerable adversity and at considerable expense, the New Westminster association proceeded with the exhibition, staging the entire event under large tents. While the show was held as scheduled, with Winston Churchill and Premier Tolmie attending the opening ceremonies, the destruction of the fairground facilities seriously weakened the hand of the R.A.I.S. in its negotiations regarding the site for a consolidated exhibition.[37]

New Westminister's major advantage, its fine set of agricultural exhibit facilities, was wiped out. The R.A.I.S. was not altogether eager to, nor for that matter financially capable of, rebuilding at Queen's Park. Like Hastings Park, the property was city owned and subject to dual control, and the society preferred a privately owned site.[38] As the R.A.I.S. cast about for a new plot of land which it hoped would house an amalgamated exhibition, it found an unexpected benefactor. At this juncture the Corporation of Burnaby, a large, sparsely inhabited district between the two cities, entered the fray and offered a significant parcel of land surrounding Burnaby Lake as an alternative site.

Burnaby City Council put considerable effort into the proposal, drawing up comprehensive maps and plans, eliciting support from civic, provincial, and federal politicians, and even adding a parcel of land picked up in tax auctions to the original grant in order to sweeten the package. The Royal Agricultural and Industrial Society jumped at the offer and tried once again to convince the V.E.A. to reconsider its opposition to an alternate site and to join with them in the development of a provincial exhibition at the new location. Vancouver's association continued to turn a cold shoulder to all appeals, indicating no willingness to even consider abandoning Hastings Park.[39]

Lacking funds, facility, and a future, the New Westminster directors became even more desperate. An appeal to the federal government secured the following response from J. H. Grisdale, deputy minister of the Department of Agriculture:

> In reply I may say that the Minister and in fact all the officers of the Department who are interested in Fairs are keenly interested in the situation in Vancouver and New Westminster and we would really like to see a Fair established at some intermediate point between the two cities, say at Burnaby Lake. Of course it is very difficult for us to take a very prominent part in any effort to amalgamate the two Fairs.[40]

Grisdale did offer to send a government representative to discuss the matter, but it was already too late.

The appeals and protestations of the R.A.I.S. began to ring hollow as the organization's plight became ever more apparent. The Burnaby Lake scheme never got beyond the proposal stage, and the R.A.I.S. settled into the ashes of its burned facilities, marking the end of sixty years as the major agricultural fair in British Columbia.[41] The smugness of the Vancouver Exhibition Association when the amalgamation issue finally died was, however, tinged with the realization that the disaster at Queen's Park had been very fortuitous for Vancouver's fair. It is of course impossible to know what the final resolution would have been had the New Westminster Exhibition remained in operation. However, since both the provincial and dominion authorities were leaning towards an amalgamation at a neutral site, it is debatable whether or not the V.E.A. could have maintained its hold on Hastings Park without the not inconsiderable backing of these two bodies.

While these three issues, lease renewal, the 1925 Joint Committee investigation, and the negotiations over amalgamation, were the major hurdles for the Vancouver Exhibition Association in this decade, financing was a constant additional difficulty throughout the 1920's. Although the exhibition had proven to be financially viable on a short-term basis, profits from the annual fair were quickly plowed back into the Hastings Park infrastructure. The returns from V.E.A. events, therefore, did little more than allow the association to maintain a set level of activities. Any expansion, either physical or organizational, depended on outside funding. The association called repeatedly upon federal and provincial authorities for assistance, and in the 1920's three separate bylaws were placed before the ratepayers of Vancouver. The V.E.A.'s indifferent success in attempts to raise funds indicates a great deal about the status of the Vancouver fair in the city, province, and country.

Playing up the agricultural aspects of the exhibition, the V.E.A. continued to receive almost $10,000 a year from provincial and federal subsidies for the prize lists. The grants were not, however, obtained without difficulty, since both governments began to exercise fiscal restraint in the early 1920's. The provincial government decided in 1921 to cut its annual grant of 50 per cent of all monies spent on prize lists for agricultural products and utility classes of livestock and poultry to 40 per cent. The following year, the government moved to reduce it even further. A meeting between the V.E.A. and the B.C. minister of agriculture, E. D. Barrow, lessened the proposed additional cutback, although the minister would not commit himself to more than a 37 per cent subsidy. As a result, the provincial grant dropped from $7,700 in 1922 to $5,600 the following year. The system instituted for 1923 remained in effect with few modifications until 1930, when the government dropped the percentage arrangement in favour of a straight cash grant of $5,000 per annum.[42]

The federal funding formula, which was much more complex, also underwent significant revisions in this decade, although the changes basically concerned the designation of fairs rather than a decrease or increase in the annual allotments. W. R. Motherwell, federal minister of agriculture, decided in 1922 to reduce federal assistance to agricultural fairs substantially. Explaining his decision in the context of a general cutback of federal disbursements, he wrote, "I know of no vote or expenditure that we could possibly curtail, without sacrificing the public service, unless it were the vote for Exhibitions."[43] Fair associations throughout the country protested the government's high-handed action, and after

Motherwell had received a report on the situation from a departmental assistant, it was decided that rather than reducing the grants by 75 per cent as originally planned, the subsidies would be cut by only 25 per cent.[44]

The furore over the federal grant in 1922 made the Department of Agriculture realize it needed to rationalize its ad hoc method of providing subsidies, and in 1923 a new formula was introduced. The larger fairs were accorded either a class "A" or "B" status, largely in terms of the size of the prize lists. The number of class "A" fairs allowed in each province was restricted, with two allocated for British Columbia, Alberta, Saskatchewan, and Manitoba, three for Ontario and Quebec, and one for each of the three Maritime provinces. In order to secure this grant, the various fairs were required to meet certain conditions, including restricting competition in various livestock classes, following set judging and display procedures, and using a prize scale which was graded according to the number of entries received. The major fairs, the Class "A" presentations, received approximately $5,000 a year, with the final grant dependent upon the amount of money expended on prize lists. The smaller Class "B" exhibitions, offering less than $5,000 in prizes, were restricted to a maximum subsidy of $1,500 a year.[45]

Allocating the grants soon became highly political, especially in British Columbia where three exhibitions, Vancouver, Victoria, and New Westminster, were vying for the two Class "A" designations. The Vancouver Exhibition Association petitioned the federal government on the issue, arguing that offering only two top grants to B.C. was hardly equitable. The association was

> not arguing in our own interests in this respect as it is patent that if only two Fairs are to be recognized, Vancouver is pre-eminently entitled to first consideration and Victoria would, by all systems that could be adopted, be rejected and at the same time we feel that this would work a very great hardship to a valuable Fair representing quite an extended territory.[46]

To many others, however, it was not so "patent" that Vancouver would be one of the two designated fairs. The federal minister of public works, J. H. King, a member of Parliament from British Columbia, rejected the V.E.A.'s argument and claimed that "New Westminster and Victoria should have first consideration on account of their being more of the nature of Agricultural Fairs."[47]

Obviously, the issue concerned not only exhibition funding, but also, civic stature and pride. All three cities were unwilling to accept designation as a second-class fair and hence a second-class city. To prevent a public outcry, Motherwell decided to fund three Class "A" fairs for the province, although the arrangement was not made permanent. Granting special status to British Columbia was not acceptable in the long term, and the Department of Agriculture was forced to seek a new subsidy plan which would both satisfy federal fiscal requirements and would also quell any possible opposition in the province. The final decision was typical of those that seem to characterize the Liberal governments of Prime Minister William Lyon Mackenzie King. Under the new formula, first implemented in 1926, British Columbia was allocated two Class "A" and an additional Class "B" designation. The total grant for the three fairs was then lumped together and divided into three equal parts, with Vancouver, Victoria, and New Westminster each receiving $3,833. This system satisfied no one, but placated everyone. The arrangement came under attack again in 1928 when the federal government decided to eliminate Class "B" grants entirely and focus assistance on the larger exhibitions. In theory, the cancellation of this funding should have opened up the question of which of the three cities would receive Class "A" status once more. For the following two years, however, the old arrangement remained intact. The New Westminster fire in 1929, and the closing of its fair the following year ended the problem, and Vancouver was finally granted full status as a Class "A" exhibition.[48]

Over time, the federal government and the Vancouver Exhibition Association largely eschewed the consideration of agricultural fair policies, focusing instead upon matters of partisan politics. Indeed, the Department of Agriculture was generally critical of the fair, the widespread feeling among agriculturalists in Ottawa being that "the whole Vancouver Exhibition has gone ahead rapidly far more as an industrial than an agricultural show."[49] At the same time, however, the directorate of the V.E.A. had strong political ties with the federal government and counted among their 1926 directors the presidents of the Vancouver Centre Liberal Association, Burrard Liberal Association, Vancouver South Liberal Association, North Vancouver Liberal Association, an ex-Liberal candidate, and a Liberal member of the B.C. legislature.[50] The association never hesitated to use this not inconsiderable clout and arrangements eventually concluded with the federal government usually had less to do with the fair's agricultural content, than with the strong Liberal orientation of the Vancouver Exhibition Association. These political connections were of utmost importance when it came to secure federal funding for the development of Hastings Park facilities.

The reason the Vancouver Exhibition Association was forced to seek federal money to finance capital improvements was that the standard source of funds, ratepayer approved loans from the city, virtually dried up during the 1920's. After the V.E.A.'s 1925 request for $25,000 had been defeated, in 1927, the association again asked City Council to place a by-law before the ratepayers, on this occasion asking for $130,000 to construct a new series of buildings. Once again, the V.E.A. was rejected and for a second time failed to gain even a simple minority, let alone the required 60 per cent. Only 49 per cent of the ratepayers supported the proposition, with Ward 7 again providing the sole bright spot (see Table 3).[51] Twice the Vancouver Exhibition Association had placed itself before the electorate in what amounted to votes of confidence, and on both occasions had lost decisively. Obviously, the V.E.A. could not blame this second loss on the 1925 inquiry, but rather attributed it to the fact that its stock in the city had dropped considerably. Opposition to a V.E.A. by-law was not, of necessity, an attack on the exhibition or the association, and indeed many critics of the various submissions founded their criticism on questions of civic fiscal responsibility. The exhibition association, however, seldom saw matters in this light and viewed almost all opposition to the various by-laws as direct assaults on the Vancouver Exhibition Association. It was, therefore, the V.E.A. which turned each by-law campaign into a vote of confidence. Voters at large did not necessarily see the matter in this light.

TABLE 3: V.E.A. BY-LAW RESULTS, 1925-1930
(per cent in favour)

Ward #	Downtown		East Side			Other			City-Wide
	1	2	3	4	7	5	6	7	
1925	30	25	32	39	54	29	33	34	37
1927	47	47	43	47	62	37	53	49	49

Ward #	Downtown			East Side			Other						City-Wide
	1	2	3	4	5	6	7	8	9	10	11	12	
1930	63	60	55	75	71	70	67	65	65	67	69	70	68

After two consecutive defeats, the Vancouver Exhibition Association hesitated to approach the ratepayers again. No submission was made in either 1928 or 1929, and even the following year there was considerable trepidation within the organization as plans were formulated for another request. When the mayor approached the association with a request that the by-law be withdrawn so that public attention could be focused upon the passage of a major loan for a Burrard Street bridge, the V.E.A. initially deferred to council's wishes.[53] The association eventually decided to proceed, however, on this occasion asking for $300,000 to finance a series of new exhibit buildings.

Painfully aware that public support would have to be carefully cultivated, the Vancouver Exhibition Association approached the 1930 campaign in a somewhat different manner. Nothing was to be left to chance. All ratepayers' meetings were attended by a representative of the association, special canvasses were conducted throughout the city, advertising was placed in important urban newspapers, service clubs were visited to explain the V.E.A.'s submission, President Dunsmuir and Alderman Loat appeared on several radio shows, and an attempt was made to get election-day drivers for various local political organizations to carry publicity for the exhibition association's cause.[54]

Publicity paid off with a resounding victory. A full 68 per cent of the electorate favoured the proposition, with all but one of the twelve wards (the number had been enlarged in 1928 to accomodate expanded city boundaries) providing 60 per cent for the by-law. Once again, the city's east side provided the largest measure of support; the district encompasing Hastings Park (Ward 4) voted

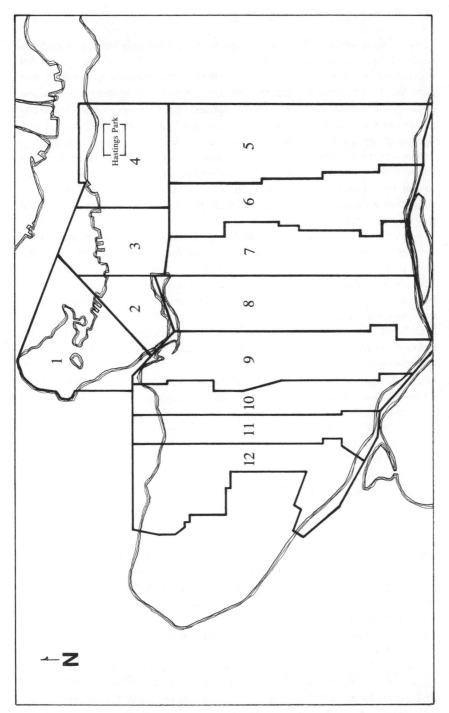

VANCOUVER WARD BOUNDARIES, 1928

75 per cent in favour.[55] The victory was important not only because it ended a string of losses and launched the V.E.A. into the 1930's with an important declaration of public support. It also indicated that attention to publicity had guaranteed the success and that the previous method of submitting a by-law and allowing the matter to run its course unaided was no longer satisfactory. The success of the V.E.A.'s submission is remarkable not only in the context of a decade of by-law losses, but also in light of the national and international economic climate. The stock market collapse the previous year portended future financial difficulties, and indeed a "depression mentality" was already beginning to fall over North America. In a time of increasing economic distress, the exhibition association had succeeded in having its largest ever by-law request passed by the electorate.

Primarily as a result of the V.E.A.'s inability to secure civic funding, little development occurred at Hastings Park during the 1920's. Working under the terms of the 1923 lease, the V.E.A. did undertake to prepare and maintain a tourist auto camp. The association spent over $20,000 on the development of the camp between 1923 and 1925, installing stoves and other equipment and generally improving the facilities. Still, it is apparent that the exhibition association always considered the camp as an imposition, simply one of the concessions made to City Council in order to secure an early lease renewal. Although the required funds were provided, no serious attempt was made to operate it or to integrate it into the larger activities at Hastings Park. In 1925, the future of the camp was thrown in doubt when the V.E.A. declared its intention to cease the operation that year, citing economic difficulties. At the request of the Vancouver Publicity Bureau, which argued that the space was urgently needed for tourists, the camp was kept open until October of that year when it was permanently shut down. Council did not press the matter, despite the fact that the association was legally obliged to maintain the facility under the terms of the 1923 lease. Another of the obligations was the construction and operation of a public golf course. The association had a more positive attitude to this project and had actually started clearing land for such a course two years earlier. By 1924, the golf links had been completed at a cost of less than $18,000. They were not open to the public that season owing to consistently dry weather, but the next golfing year saw the commencement of operations at Vancouver's first public golf course. While golf was far from being a game for the masses the construction of the Hastings Park course certainly fit well with the V.E.A.'s accepted mandate of providing public recreational facilities. The V.E.A. saw the golf course as more than just for the city's golfers. It was also an effective means of justifying the continued encroachment on the forests of Hastings Park. From this point on, the shape of the course was altered regularly, as it was in 1930 when it was expanded from its original nine-hole layout to a full eighteen-hole course. Lands that were initially cleared for golf were then expropriated for exhibition facilities. More land would then be cleared for the golf course.

The course, therefore, served as a useful vehicle for the physical expansion of the exhibition.[56]

The most significant development of the fairgrounds in this period was the addition of a permanent amusement complex. In face of continuous criticism of the Skid Road, the V.E.A. began early in the decade to look towards the construction of a central amusement area. While several permanent devices, including a "Scenic Railway," dancing pavilion, and merry-go-round, were in operation on the grounds for the exhibition, the association had to contract with a travelling carnival to provide additional rides and games. Because the carnivals in the West were substandard, the V.E.A. decided that a permanent amusement area should be planned, with a core of devices serving as a year-round attraction at Hastings Park. The contract to begin developing the site was given to the British Columbia Amusement Company, and by 1926 the additions were estimated to be worth half a million dollars. On special occasions, such as the 1930 "Coming of Age" exhibition, the B.C.A.C.'s facilities were supplemented with additional features. In that year, a major attraction consisting of eight rides and nine shows was set up on the grounds apart from the permanent attractions, and the carnival operators were required to pay a percentage of their profits to the B.C. Amusement Company.[57]

Physical development, other than the auto camp, golf course, and amusement area, was very limited. On the urging of the Board of Parks Commissioners, the Hastings Park oval was converted from a lawn into a standard playing field, thus providing much needed athletic grounds for the east side. The most important development came in 1920 when City Council decided to widen and pave Hastings Street. Before that time, all facilities had been aligned towards the north-west and the Powell Street entrance where transportation was available. Improvement of Hastings Street and the development of a street-car line along that route made it essential that the association not only erect a new archway facing onto the corner of Hastings and Renfrew, but also that all future development of the grounds be oriented towards Hastings Street.[58]

The only significant structure erected in this period was the new livestock building, which was not planned for the annual summer exhibition, but rather as a part of a new yearly Winter Fair. This Winter Fair was the single most important expansion of activities by the Vancouver Exhibition Association in this decade as well. The show was designed exclusively as an agricultural event, with virtually no attempt made to add carnival-type activities and no expectation of a profitable return from the venture. Focusing on the display and sale of Fat Stock (cattle ready for slaughter), the Winter Fair was intended to serve as a marketing outlet for the province's livestock breeders, providing them with a ready forum for the sale of their animals under prime market conditions. Local slaughterhouses and butchers would attend the show and auctions would be held to sell the cattle. The V.E.A. saw this fair as an excellent means of bringing farmer and city dweller together, to the benefit of all concerned. The federal Department of Agriculture, aware that such fairs provided an excellent marketing tool for the farmer and that the sponsoring exhibition association was almost certain to suffer considerable financial losses as a result of staging the event, was very active in subsidizing such shows, offering both prize list assistance and aid in the financing of livestock facilities.

The first Winter Fair at Hastings Park was held in 1925, with over 3,000 entries (1,600 in poultry classes) on display. Wanting to encourage the V.E.A. in this direction, the federal government provided a $2,500 grant, even though their initial promise to pay one-half of the value of the prize list committed them to only $1,500. The government, however, was not entirely pleased with the presentation, observing that the Winter Fair was "very largely a duplication of your Fall Show." The principle behind the Winter Fair, Deputy Minister Grisdale reminded the association, was to encourage the utility grade displays and not, as the V.E.A. had done, to emphasize breeding classes.[59]

Because the financial return from the Winter Fair was so poor, federal funding remained crucial. When it was learned that the Royal Winter Fair in Toronto had received a guaranteed grant of $35,000 a year for twenty years, the Vancouver Exhibition Association immediately appealed for similar consideration. "The British Columbia Winter Fair," it was argued, "is destined to become a Pacific Royal and as such can do immense good work in the development of the agricultural policies of the Dominion government."[60] The request, submitted in 1926, asked for $25,000 annually for ten years. The Department of Agriculture was scarcely prepared to commit itself to such a venture, even though the V.E.A. show had shown a marked improvement in its second year of operation. The standard funding formula remained intact, with the federal government paying one-half of the monies granted as prizes in the utility classes of livestock and poultry, to a maximum of $5,000. In Vancouver's case, the department agreed to waive the requirement that a minimum of $2,500 in prizes be granted in the stated classes, offering instead to match the V.E.A. dollar for dollar up to the maximum.[61]

Although the Winter Fair consistently operated with financial shortfalls, the Vancouver Exhibition Association maintained and expanded the show throughout the remainder of the decade, adding such features as an industry and province sponsored National Apple Show in 1927. The major development, however, resulted from the recognition that the Winter Fair might be used as a means of securing federal and provincial assistance for the construction of improved livestock facilities. After extensive negotiations following a meeting with W. R. Motherwell, minister of agriculture, in January 1928, the V.E.A. managed to elicit a promise of $33,000 from the dominion government provided the city and the province offered like amounts. Acting on the basis of the association's promise to continue the Winter Fair, the three levels of government ratified the agreement in

October 1929. All the contributors were to spread their grants over a number of years, paying $4,500 a year until capital costs and amortization charges were paid up. Importantly, such federal assistance was available only for Winter Fair facilities and would not have been offered to the V.E.A. for the expansion of the summer exhibition.[62]

While the Winter Fair was the major addition to the V.E.A.'s activities in the 1920's, considerable development of the annual summer exhibition took place as well. A Horse Show, featuring jumping and riding competitions, was established, but poor attendance and heavy losses forced its cancellation after a trial of only two years. Just as persistent criticism of gambling on the fair grounds was an important factor in the decision to create a permanent amusement complex, it also led to some new departures in the entertainment area. First there were attempts to remove the "unfavourable" characters from Skid Road. The association hired a man from the Child Welfare Department to circulate through the grounds to ensure that young boys did not participate in any of the games. They also realized that alternative amusements should be provided, attracting attention away from Skid Road. In 1926, the association embarked on a programme of placing "first class" entertainment in front of the grandstand and charging admission to see the shows. This entertainment, later to become a main feature of the fair, gradually replaced wandering bands, free attractions, and, importantly, Skid Road, as a major drawing card of the exhibition.[63]

The grandstand also served as the centre of another prime attraction, horse-racing. Recognizing that horse-racing was a favoured activity in the city, the V.E.A. moved in 1920 to expand the competitive horse-racing on the grounds. The first attempt to lease the facilities to the B.C. Thoroughbred Association, an arrangement calling for two seven-day meets each year which would have netted the association $10,000 per annum, was rejected by the Market and Exhibition Committee of City Council. The V.E.A.'s continuing attempts to negotiate a sub-lease with the racing interests met sustained opposition. Such groups as the Y.M.C.A., Women's Christian Temperance Union, Mothers' Pension Association, Vancouver Child Welfare Association, and representatives of the Methodist, Baptist and Presbyterian churches were always ready to protest the association's plans before City Council. So long as City Council retained the right to veto any V.E.A. sub-leases, no long-term horse-racing arrangement was worked out. After 1923, when the new lease gave the association complete freedom regarding sub-leases, the situation changed dramatically. Despite opposition from many quarters, the association granted the Westminster Thoroughbred Association a five-year lease at a basic rental of $1,000 per racing day. In addition, they were to pay an immediate bonus of $10,000. Although there were problems in 1925, and the V.E.A. attempted to secure a surrender of the lease, the agreement remained in place until its 1928 expiry date. At that time the W.T.A., renamed the Ascot Racing Association, was granted a renewal of the lease, with the new arrangement tentative until the V.E.A.'s own lease expired in 1938. In the agreement the A.R.A. offered a $5,000 signing bonus, and $9,000 annually for the first five years, with negotiations to revise that figure upwards to start in 1930.[64]

These various racing leases did not apply during the exhibition, and the V.E.A. continued to offer its own race card providing prize purses, but without on-track betting. The Ascot Racing Association and its predecessors owned a federal charter which granted them the right to operate races on a set number of dates and which permitted the operation of parimutuel betting. The V.E.A. attempted to break into the field in 1930, approaching the federal government with a request for a charter for seven days of racing. A seventy-five-cent admission would be charged to view what was to be a "B.C. horses only" competition, and all parimutuels were to be retained for the development of the exhibition and the Winter Fair.[65] It would have been an ideal arrangement for the association, but it never got passed beyond the proposal stage.

While the expansion of exhibition attractions such as horse-racing proved effective in encouraging attendance at the annual fair, the V.E.A. continued to be plagued by rain. Virtually every year, showers cut several days out of the week-long fair. A clever solution was found. Picking up on an idea employed effectively elsewhere, the V.E.A. arranged an advance sale of exhibition tickets in 1926, whereby the association began selling them several months early with special prizes offered to entice purchasers. In the first year of operation, three Oldsmobile automobiles were offered as prizes to lucky ticket holders. Tickets sold for the standard entrance fee of fifty cents each, or three for a dollar. The system worked effectively as "rain insurance" and provided financial backing against Vancouver's unpredictable climate. City Council attempted to limit the sale of tickets in 1927, arguing that the sale was interfering with other civic celebrations in Canada's jubilee year, but the association's remonstrances that the money so acquired was essential to the fair's survival carried the day.[66]

Neither the advance ticket sales or the expansion of horse-racing represented a unique departure for the Vancouver Exhibition Association; they were ideas culled from the experience of other North American fairs. Indeed, as the 1920's progressed the association assumed an ever more active role in various organizations of fairs and exhibitions from Western Canada and the Pacific Northwest. These associations proved useful not only as a vehicle for the dissemination of new ideas, but also in a pragmatic way. Fair circuits became increasingly important as the V.E.A. joined with other exhibitions in arranging scheduling, horse races, carnival contracts and tours by entertainers. The V.E.A. also joined with other fairs, principally those from New Westminster and Victoria, to share publicity and printing costs and to make united representations to the federal government for increased funding.[67] The excellent Hastings Park facilities, the size and generosity of the prize lists, and the consistently large number of spectators ensured that Vancouver's fair would quickly rise in status. By the end of the decade, it was clearly the most important in British Columbia and among the largest on the west coast. Other fairs in the province relied heavily upon Vancouver's attractiveness to exhibitors, concessionaires, and entertainers and were beginning to ride on the V.E.A.'s coattails. Even though the Vancouver Exhibition Association had encountered increasing difficulty at home and had been subjected to serious criticisms, the organization's stature within exhibition circles was well established.

The directors of the V.E.A. had become hardened to local criticism in the 1920's and, before the resounding by-law victory just as the decade ended promised more amenable relations with Vancouverites and local politicians, found considerable solace in the steadily improving international prestige of the fair. While the V.E.A. retained the basic ambition of developing the exhibition as "the great show room, the sample house, the great publicity bureau, the great educator and exponent of the wonderful God-given resources of the country," a major change had occurred within the association.[68] Local roots were being severed, largely because the city had shown signs of turning its back on the fair, and the organization was placing increasing attention on its role as a British Columbian and Western Canadian institution. Although the name of the fair was not officially changed, "Canada's Pacific Exhibition" replaced the "Vancouver Exhibition" as the title of the annual show. The aspirations of the association clearly had evolved from predominantly local concerns to a desire to become the "Toronto of the West," with the exhibition slated to serve as the showcase for all of the Canadian West and not just the lower Fraser River Valley.[69]

6

Prosperity in Times of Trouble, 1930-1939

Despite such serious public controversies as the 1925 Joint Investigation, the debate over the Hastings Park lease, and the amalgamation question, the Vancouver Exhibition Association emerged from the 1920's in remarkably stable condition. Permanent arrangements were in place regarding the payment of federal and provincial grants, attendance appeared to be on the verge of surpassing 300,000, and some measure of credibility with the agricultural community had been gained, especially after the decisions to sponsor a Winter Fair and erect new livestock facilities. These gains, however, had been achieved in the booming twenties, a time of record economic expansion and unparalleled prosperity in the City of Vancouver. The following decade was to see a complete reversal in the city as the pall of the Great Depression descended over Canada.

By 1930, signs of financial distress were abundant throughout the country. The number of unemployed men continued to mount, and thousands who were unable to find work "rode the rails" to Vancouver, where the more salubrious climate lessened the impact of poverty somewhat. With relief rolls swelling at an alarming rate, reaching such an extent that the City of Vancouver faced financial ruin, the annual exhibition seemed out of place. Despite the widespread hardship and to a certain degree because of it, however, the fair continued throughout the decade, serving as a beacon reminding the people of past prosperity and future prospects.

The depression, with its attendant financial and personal dislocation, had rather surprising consequences for the annual exhibition. Attendance, expected to fall with the drop in the economy, actually went in the opposite direction, reaching a reported 377,000 in 1936 and remaining above the 300,000 mark for much of the decade. These figures cannot be taken entirely at face value, however, for they served a publicity function and the evidence suggests they were frequently bent to that purpose. In 1936, for example, admission ticket sales totalled only $62,445, with the standard charges being fifty cents for adults and twenty-five cents for children still in effect. In addition, fully $38,000 of the admission receipts came from the sale of advance tickets. Many of the holders of these tickets, interested more in the prizes offered than in the exhibition, would not have used their stubs to enter the grounds. The discrepancy between receipts and attendance again raised the question of whether the V.E.A. was allowing thousands of free passes, simply doctoring the figures for publicity purposes, or, most likely, doing both. Regardless, the procedure of "padding" attendance figures was frequent in exhibition circles and should not detract from the fact that the Vancouver Exhibition Association actually improved its attendance during very trying times. That the number of patrons would rise during a period of widespread economic distress indicates the escapist function of the fair. The carnival, with its wide variety of sights, sounds, and smells, was more attractive than ever. A similar phenomenon has been observed with movie theatres, as patrons by the thousand flocked to the extravagantly staged musicals which inundated the North American silver screen during the depression years. Like the exhibition, the movies provided a valued escape hatch, a means of abandoning, even if only momentarily, the dreary realities of life.

Befitting the apparent demand for extravagance and frivolity, the Exhibition Association moved in 1935 to add a parade to its yearly cycle of activities. Spurred on by Vancouver Mayor G. G. McGeer, who was looking for a suitable outlet for a demonstration of civic pride and determination, the V.E.A. agreed to stage a parade on the opening day of the fair. The project was not undertaken without considerable apprehension, especially since the decision to hold the event was not made until mid-July, barely a month before opening day. With civic backing, including a sizeable monetary grant, the exhibition association was able to pull it off, and on 20 August 1935, it staged an elaborate exhibition parade complete with marching bands, floats, and clowns through downtown Vancouver. This marked a distinct departure from the modest procession of dignitaries traditionally held on opening day.[1]

Perhaps more surprisingly, the exhibitions of the 1930's proved even more successful financially, returning an average annual profit of almost $35,000, up significantly from previous years. The profit increased steadily through the decade, rising from $15,740 in 1930 to over $61,000 in 1936, with only a minor decline thereafter. The returns from the fair were used to sustain ever-expanding year-round activities of the V.E.A. and to pay for minor improvements and maintenance at Hastings Park.

The widespread economic distress and the high unemployment had other important implications for the V.E.A.'s plans for the physical development of Hastings Park and the operation of the annual fair. The vast number of unemployed in the city made work at the annual fair a valued prize. In 1930, over one thousand people applied for two hundred available jobs, which meant the association could use selective hiring practices. Whenever possible, they hired from lists of returned soldiers provided by local veterans' organizations, with preference given as well to civic ratepayers and married men with families.[2]

Since it was a civic institution, the exhibition was eligible for relief grants and was allocated large gangs of relief labour to work on the grounds. The men were employed on a variety of projects, including the golf course, park extension and ground clearance, renovation of the race track oval, and sundry other chores. In return for their work, the association usually paid the men's streetcar fares and supplied the required tools and materials, while the city gave the unemployed workers meal tickets.[3] These relief operations were often substantial affairs, involving fifty or more men working on one project at a time. However, the erratic and unreliable character of this assistance sharply compromised its value.

In addition to improvements made possible through relief grants, the association was also eligible for special make-work grants from the civic and federal governments. Under the federal Unemployment Relief Act of 1930, substantial amounts of money were available to the City of Vancouver and, indirectly, to the Vancouver Exhibition Association. Much of the construction on the new exhibition buildings (Forum, Pure Foods, and Manufacturers) was undertaken by relief gangs as were a variety of maintenance projects on the grounds. The association also appealed on its own to the federal government for further financial assistance, arguing successfully that the construction of new livestock buildings at Hastings Park would not only assist the V.E.A.'s agricultural programme, but would also assist in alleviating unemployment in the city.[4] Indeed, in appealing for funds in 1935 to complete one of the livestock structures, President Walter Leek of the V.E.A. managed to link the two, writing that: "We again urge upon you the necessity for the completion of the building not only to relieve unemployment but to assist in the development of agriculture, through which agency further relief of unemployment will come."[5] Through the use of relief labour, special civic grants and federal assistance for construction projects, therefore, the Vancouver Exhibition Association was able not only to weather the financial storms of the 1930's, but also to continue with the development of the Hastings Park grounds and facilities.

In the other traditional area of financial support, the consequences of distressed times were more as one might anticipate. As the various levels of government moved towards financial restraint, the V.E.A. found the annual subsidy programmes worked out in the previous decade being altered significantly. The provincial government dropped its arrangement of providing the association with a set percentage of the parimutuel tax from the Hastings Park race track in 1930, opting instead for a straight grant of $5,000. That amount was reduced to $4,000 the following year, and to $2,000 in 1932. In the next year parimutuel taxes were again the basis for V.E.A. funding, and the association's percentage in 1933 brought $9,700, the most money yet received from the provincial government. The percentage of parimutuel offered by the province continued to serve as an important source of revenue throughout the remainder of the decade, returning as much as $28,000 in 1936. Civic financing was similarly erratic, although far less remunerative. The V.E.A. received a specific allotment each year for park maintenance, and the appropriation declined steadily. Each reduction elicited an immediate reaction from the association, with development plans being shelved, staff let go, or wages cut.[6] On the federal level, for two years the V.E.A. received the full $5,000 grant that went with its new Class "A" designation. The grant was slashed in half in 1932, although it was restored to its former level three years later. Disruptions in federal subsidies continued, however, and the allotment was again reduced in 1936, this time to $4,000, where it remained for the rest of the period. This apparent instability in government funding, with grants fluctuating widely according to the yearly condition of the economy, made it difficult for the Vancouver Exhibition Association to plan for future fairs. The fact that the various government subsidies constituted only a minor segment of the association's budget softened the impact somewhat, but certain areas such as agricultural prize lists and park maintenance were hit hard by the confusion.

The V.E.A.'s approach to the 1932 fair reveals in sharper focus the association's disjointed response to the country's economic disorder. Choosing "Back to Prosperity" as the theme for the year's activities, the association then proceeded to act as if prosperity was the most unlikely occurrence. Prize awards were decreased across the board, which led to a substantial decline in the number of exhibitors and competitors. As if to further emphasize the financial problems, the V.E.A. then cancelled the annual Winter Fair, ostensibly because the federal government refused to provide a $2,500 grant for operating expenses. To put the association's actions in perspective, the fiscal-year profit exceeded $14,900. The Winter Fair was reorganized in 1933 and was staged essentially as a cattle auction, with any pretentions that it was a major agricultural event largely removed.[7]

The prospect of increasing losses from the operation of the winter show and the possibility that the attendance of the annual fair would drop off substantially as the depression worsened, which seemed imminent in 1932, were enough to convince the fiscally conservative directors of the V.E.A. to cut losses wherever possible. Reducing the prizes and cancelling the 1932 Winter Fair were not financially necessary in the short term, but they suggest that the association had been infected with the prevailing depression mentality. At the same time, the V.E.A. continued to provide ringing public declarations that all was well with the exhibition and that every effort was being made to continue operations uninterrupted.

One group directly hurt by the V.E.A.'s actions during the 1930's was the association's own permanent employees. Despite consistent and comparatively high profits, wages for all staff were reduced by 8.75 per cent in 1931 and even more two years later. The manager, J. Matheson, saw his salary plummet from $6,000 in 1930 to $5,500 the next year, and even further to $4,800 in 1933. The decline was not permanent, however, and as early as 1934 the association was beginning to revise the salaries upwards, with the first general increase being 5 or 6 per cent. During this period as well, the exhibition's outside workers saw their pay fall below the salaries paid to civic employees in similar positions. The city was, for example, paying 53⅛ cents per hour for jobs where the V.E.A. paid only 42½ cents. In the 1923 lease, the V.E.A. had agreed to pay its employees according to the city's wage rates, a factor which apparently did not weigh heavily upon the minds of the V.E.A. directors. They were criticized by the Trades and Labour Council for refusing to adopt the pay scale, but with unemployment so high, few employees were willing to complain too vociferously. The employees did, however, keep their positions throughout the thirties, since the various projects undertaken by the Vancouver Exhibition Association were sufficient to justify retaining a small permanent staff.[8]

During the harsh depression years both organizations and individuals associated with the exhibition floundered in the economic chaos. The first casualty was the British Columbia Amusement Company which operated rides and concessions at Hastings Park and which had taken over the operations of "Happyland," keeping the amusement area open through much of the summer months. Indications that all was not well with the B.C.A.C. first appeared in 1930, when a series of contract violations were reported, including the non-payment of rent and the construction of new facilities without permission. The matter came to a head the following year as the company teetered on the edge of bankruptcy, throwing the management of carnival activities at the fair into considerable disarray. The V.E.A. approached the B.C.A.C. with an offer to pick up a two-year option to purchase the company with the price for the company's assets to be $250,000 if the option was acted upon. The B.C.A.C. turned down the offer, and the V.E.A. called for the immediate payment of all outstanding debts and threatened to seize the assets if suitable arrangements were not concluded forthwith. Fearful of their impending losses, the many creditors of the amusement company then approached the V.E.A. and appealed to the association to take over the B.C.A.C. The company continued to refuse the V.E.A.'s offers, however, and the creditors, aware that the association's tender would leave them out in the cold, took matters into their own hands. In April, 1932, an agreement was finally reached among the three groups. The creditors formed the Pacific Coast Amusement Company, assumed control of the assets of the B.C. Amusement Company, and signed a five-year lease with the exhibition to provide permanent amusement facilities at Hastings Park.[9]

The situation was hardly what the Pacific Coast Amusement Company would have chosen. Over the next four years, the company worked assiduously to wrangle better terms from the Vancouver Exhibition Association. Despite their complaints and generally declining revenues, the P.C.A.C. was able to post a profit in each of the first four years and moved steadily towards retiring the debts of the former owners. In 1936, a new lease was negotiated between the amusement company and the V.E.A.; the rental was based on a set percentage of gross receipts, and the association agreed to reduce the minimum rental from $3,000 to $2,000 a year. Appeals by the P.C.A.C. to have the rental reduced even further or to have the V.E.A. assist with maintenance were rejected, as the exhibition association continued to refuse to commit itself to any assistance for sub-lessors. The P.C.A.C. only reluctantly accepted the fact that it now enjoyed long-term tenancy at Hastings Park, and it required some time for the irate creditors to coalesce. By 1938, however, it was clear that the company had not only accepted its role with the exhibition, but was also profiting substantially from it. In that year, the V.E.A. received more than $9,000 from the company for fair-time and year-round rentals, far in excess of the $2,000 minimum. Like the B.C.A.C. before it the Pacific Coast Amusement Company did not have exclusive rights to provide amusements on the grounds, and during the annual fair the P.C.A.C. facilities were supplemented by other games, shows and attractions brought in for the occasion.[10]

While the B.C. Amusement Company's bankruptcy and reorganization were a decided inconvenience, the second financial problem of the decade was to prove far more serious. Suggestions that something was amiss with the finances of the Vancouver Exhibition Association were rumoured in 1935 when unsubstantiated accusations were made that the accounting practices of the association were not entirely above board and that there was a hint that someone in the association had been embezzling funds. Feeling that the association's credibility was at stake, the V.E.A. called for either a resolution of confidence from City Council or an investigation by a Supreme Court judge. The city decided to take the issue up itself and William Tucker of the Internal Audit Department was assigned to conduct an investigation in the summer of 1935. Work elsewhere, particularly in the corruption-riddled relief department, drew the auditors away from the exhibition grounds temporarily, but the required V.E.A. documents were sealed and locked inside the Directors' Room. To this point, the matter was entirely internal, involving only the city and the V.E.A., but it did not remain that way for long. Tucker, a loner and iconoclast, began addressing public meetings on the matter of V.E.A. finances. He alluded to certain shortfalls in the account books and suggested as well that someone associated with the organization had breached the trust of the Internal Audit Department by entering the sealed Directors' Room.[11]

On 3 December 1936, following stepped-up investigations by the city's auditors, L. H. White, an accountant with the Vancouver Exhibition Association, was arrested and charged with the embezzlement of more than $41,000 in civic funds between May 1932 and November 1936. The V.E.A. directors reacted swiftly to the revelations, asking City Council to continue their financial investigations and quickly proclaiming that "It was the general opinion of the Exhibition members that responsibility lay with the auditors," Price, Waterhouse and Company, who had failed to note anything extraordinary in their annual audit of the association's books.[12] White confessed to the defalcations and explained that the embezzlement had evolved out of the system used to pay civic wages for work done at Hastings Park. Under the arrangement, the V.E.A. paid not only its own employees, but also those civic workers engaged at the grounds. White, who handled the payroll, would issue cheques to both groups of men and then would invoice City Hall for repayment. By sending in altered invoices, the accountant was able to hold back substantial sums of money for himself.[13]

Outgoing Mayor G. G. McGeer led the subsequent charge against the Vancouver Exhibition Association. Indeed, the issue had quickly spread from the matter of White's embezzlement to the possibility of mismanagement by the association. Longtime antagonists of the association, somewhat surprisingly including Mayor McGeer who had co-operated effectively with the association the previous year in planning for the opening day parade, used the issue as a means of attacking the V.E.A., and the whole debacle quickly became far more serious. Accusations flew wildly; McGeer and other councillors suggested that the association had withheld access to its financial records and there were threats that the association's lease might be revoked.[14] The association was stunned by the disclosures and the council-led onslaught, and in an attempt to soothe mounting public criticism suggested that a proper inquiry be conducted. At the same time, however, the V.E.A. refused "to be investigated in any private manner such as we understand the City Council intend to do on their own behalf."[15] It was decided to approach council and have the civic auditing department investigate the association's affairs. In addition, a study group composed of three prominent directors was appointed to review the financial arrangements and suggest revisions in the association's business practices.[16]

City Auditor Wardhaugh conducted a personal audit of the V.E.A.'s finances, suggesting in his final report that a financial manager should be appointed, that a continuous audit of all business records be implemented, that an adequate accounting system be installed, and that trial balances, or monthly statements, be issued.[17] The V.E.A. moved quickly to adopt Wardhaugh's recommendations since it was imperative to retain public confidence. While White's embezzlement was the only crime uncovered within the Vancouver Exhibition Association, it was part of a larger discovery of corruption within the city government. Led primarily by the crusading W. A. Tucker, whose public disclosures of his discoveries and whose antagonism towards his employers led to serious personal difficulties with the civic administration, the Internal Audit Department cut a swath through the government, ferreting out corrupt individuals, particularly within the Relief Department.

As far as the V.E.A. was concerned, the matter did not end with White's arrest nor even after the recommendations of the internal auditor had been implemented. Apparently, they still wanted a scapegoat, someone who could be held responsible for what had happened within the association. Two men in particular, General Manager J. K. Matheson and Assistant Manager G. S. Hockley, were selected for attack. During the investigation by the internal auditor, Hockley was suspended without pay pending a review of his status. The assistant manager was not, however, willing to accept his suspension without a battle. He demanded, and received, the right to defend himself against the public charges, but he was not successful. Hockley was given the opportunity to resign, and he agreed to step down on 15 April 1937.[18] Initially, everyone was eager to place the blame solely on the shoulders of White and Hockley, and it was noted with more than a little satisfaction that the possible dismissal of both men had been discussed by the board of directors the previous October, with Hockley being criticized for his disloyalty and lack of a "spirit of co-operation."[19] Such remonstrances were primarily post-hoc attempts by the V.E.A. directors to absolve themselves of any responsibility for the embezzlement. It was soon clear, however, that the assistant general manager had had nothing to do with the thefts, but still, the V.E.A. wanted to "have nothing more to do with him"[20] and instead of being rehired Hockley was given a new dismissal notice and a month's pay.

Hockley was merely the first to be pulled overboard in the wake of the discovery of White's embezzlement. An in-house investigation in March 1937 concluded that General Manager Matheson "must accept a major part of the responsibility."[21] The situation was complicated by the fact that Matheson was seriously ill and was then convalescing at the association's expense.[22] An easy way out of this potentially embarrassing situation was found. Matheson's contract was up for renewal at the end of July, and the directors made it readily apparent that they had no intention of retaining his services. There was some remorse that the long-term manager was to be released, but as V.E.A. President Walter Leek explained in a letter to Matheson it was necessary.

> The intensive effort we all, including yourself, put into the operation of our Exhibition, the lamentable condition in which we discovered our internal affairs was nothing short of heartbreaking. As our General Manager, you must assume the responsibility of that position. I am afraid in view of the disclosures made, that it will take some time to recover confidence in our management.
>
> In view of the importance of the Exhibition to the Community, only a complete re-organization will satisfy the General Public, on the good will of whom depends so much of our success.[23]

Two important considerations, the desire of the directors to absolve themselves

and the need to restore public confidence in the association culminated in the firing
of Matheson. Through the "sacrifice" of Hockley and Matheson, the V.E.A.
hoped to divert attention from White's embezzlement, thus allowing the association to return to exhibition matters.

The first matter to be settled, though not without controversy, was the hiring
of a new manager to replace Matheson. After an extensive canvass which, given
the high unemployment of the depression, drew a large number of applicants, S.
C. McLennan was selected for the post. The new general manager, who had
previously served with the Department of Agriculture in Ottawa, was given a
salary of $350 per month and the use of an automobile, plus approved expenses.
Hiring an employed easterner elicited considerable public criticism, and several
individuals and groups questioned the judiciousness of the V.E.A.'s selection,
particularly as it was felt that any number of Vancouverites or British Columbians
could have filled the position.[24] But hiring McLennan was significant for another
reason as well. By selecting an applicant with an extensive background and
interest in agriculture, the V.E.A. was signalling its intention to increase its
emphasis on that aspect of its exhibition.

Despite the tumult attending the revelations of White's embezzlement and
other difficulties associated with the depression, the internal organization of the
Vancouver Exhibition Association remained stable. There were suggestions that
all the honourary directors, area or organizational representatives who served a
strictly ceremonial role, be eliminated, but no action was taken. Further, it was
argued that the directors were losing touch with the duties of the departments they
were responsible for and that the number of committees should therefore be
reduced from more than twenty to a more manageable ten, with the personnel of
the new committees being given "real responsibilities" instead of rubber-stamp
positions.[25] Once again, nothing was done, and the number of active committees
continued to grow. A new constitution was ratified in February 1939, but the
document contained only cosmetic changes to the structure of the organization.
This internal inertia of the V.E.A. was primarily caused by the severe manpower
shortage in the organization. The number of individuals and businesses holding
memberships, which had recovered during the 1920's from the depths experienced
during World War I, plummeted again in the 1930's. In 1938, at the bottom of the
slide, the V.E.A. had a paltry forty members, barely sufficient to fill the required
boards and committees. The association's limited numbers were later swelled by a
series of outside appointments from agricultural organizations, the Vancouver and
New Westminster Chambers of Commerce, the Vancouver City Council, and a
variety of other groups, but it was obvious that the permanent core of members had
dropped ominously low. Unable to draw on a broadly based membership, the
V.E.A. fell back on its small but enthusiastic management and directorate which
cemented together the shrinking Vancouver Exhibition Association and carried it
through the depression.[26]

Perhaps more remarkable than the V.E.A.'s ability to operate at a profit and maintain the organization throughout the 1930's was the flurry of construction at Hastings Park, which saw more building than had been seen since the opening years of the fair. The association's control of the property had been recognized again in 1933 when City Council, with very little debate, agreed to extend the V.E.A. lease until 1960, tagging fifteen years onto the existing agreement. This extension did not silence those proponents of an east-end park, Parks Board Commissioner C. W. Thompson, for one, suggested in 1933 that a major five-hundred-acre park, incorporating the exhibition grounds, be established in that area. Like other such proposals, this one was never seriously considered. Hastings Park belonged to the exhibition, and at this time few Vancouverites were prepared to challenge either the use of the property or the V.E.A.'s control. [27]

Within the boundaries of the park itself, the association continued to expand, peeling back the forests to provide more room for the development of additional exhibition facilities and the extension of the golf course, which was itself actually the vehicle for expansion. As President Leek reported to the membership in 1937:

> We looked upon the golf course as a good investment as we were clearing a future exhibition site. We have arrived at the time now that we must use the portion west of Windermere Street for Exhibition purposes; we have pleaded with City Council to procure all of the lands extending to Rupert Street so that they might be cleared for golf and provide sufficient space for the final development of the Exhibition. [28]

The golf course served as the exhibition's vanguard. The arrangement was quite judicious, since public opposition to the expropriation or purchase of land for a golf course was likely to be far less vociferous than if the areas were being taken over simply to add more land to the exhibition.

That such expansion was necessary only twenty years after the founding of the exhibition reflects not only the increasing size of the fair, but also lack of foresight on the part of the early management of the association. In their haste to erect suitable facilities in time for the first exhibition, the directors had built a series of wooden structures with a life expectancy of no more than twenty years. Not only had they accepted less than adequate engineering and construction practices in the first structures, they had also spread the financing for the buildings over forty years. [29] The Industrial Building and School Building, two of the earliest facilities, both came down during the 1930's, and the Forestry Building followed shortly thereafter. This put the association in the rather precarious position of still having to pay the mortgages for facilities no longer in use or greatly restricted in utility, while at the same time requiring major new developments to handle the demand for exhibit and display space.

The first spate of construction came in 1930-1931 after the passage of the $300,000 by-law. This civic loan enabled the association to build three new structures, the Forum, Pure Foods Building, and a Women's and Arts Building. Erected at a cost of $235,000, these structures marked a significant shift in the physical orientation of the exhibition.[30] Whereas the fair had previously focused on the Northwest entrance, these buildings were placed in the Southwest corner, an explicit acknowledgement that Hastings had replaced Powell Street as the principal east-west corridor out of the downtown core.

These three buildings were the major physical legacy of the 1930's, and it can readily be seen that both in gestation and implementation they were more a part of the expansive 1920's than of the depression years. The economic downturn, however, did not end the Vancouver Exhibition Association's plans for further developments, although it did seriously constrict the capital available for exhibition projects. The difficulty of financing additional construction is best illustrated by the association's endeavours to secure the money necessary to complete the livestock facilities for the summer and winter fairs. The first phase of the expansion was completed in the late 1920's, and plans and designs were in place to finish the project. The V.E.A. went to work on the Conservative government in Ottawa late in 1930, appealing for $150,000. The Conservative administration, no friend of the Liberal-dominated V.E.A., rejected the justifications presented in the association's applications. A Department of Agriculture memorandum circulated in February 1931 doubted the V.E.A.'s claim "that it is supreme, in comparison with other Class "A" fairs in Canada (the Canadian National Exhibition excepted)." Indeed, the author of the report made it clear that in the opinion of the Livestock Branch officers, New Westminster had always been a far better agricultural show and that, despite Vancouver's comparatively high expenditures on prize lists, the fair was doing little towards the advancement of agriculture.[31] A series of appeals to various dominion authorities fell upon deaf ears, and without federal assistance there was no money forthcoming from the provincial and civic governments.

A consequence of the fiscal restraint exercised by the Conservative government in power from 1930-1935, the strong Liberal orientation of the V.E.A., and the fact that the association's application was not particularly strong, the second phase livestock building went unbuilt. When Mackenzie King led his Liberal Party back into office in 1935, however, the complexion of the issue changed markedly. The directorate quickly fired off a letter to Prime Minister King requesting support for their plans and suggesting that continued assistance for Toronto's exhibition without similar aid for Vancouver's fair "savours of favouritism."[32] Discussion over a variety of proposals for financing followed. The matter was finally resolved in 1939, when the dominion authorities agreed to pay $100,000 over a ten-year period, with the city to add $47,300 over the decade. The province also expanded its grant, giving the exhibition 50 per cent of all parimutuel earnings from the

Hastings Park racetrack, provided $5,000 went into the building fund. With further negotiation the Vancouver Exhibition Association was able to get funding for the Garden Auditorium added to the arrangement and to have the tripartite agreement extended to cover both the auditorium and the new livestock building. In October 1939, the association secured a $257,000 loan from the Bank of Montreal and quickly proceeded with construction. This debate over the livestock building indicated a feature of exhibition financing that was becoming increasingly apparent and unavoidable. As much if not more than need, politics was to be the determining factor. The V.E.A. management was particularly adept at playing the shifting winds of federal and provincial politics to its own advantage and was able to use this expertise to ensure the continued expansion of the Vancouver fair.[33]

The new second phase of the Livestock Building, a facility which originated more in political patronage than demonstrated need represents the true legacy of the decade. The bigger and more glamorous additions, the Forum, Pure Foods, and Women's and Arts buildings, actually belonged to the twenties in terms of impetus and financing. Few plans generated during the 1930's ever came to fruition. A 40,000-seat stadium was proposed, ostensibly as a relief project, but failure to secure financing killed the grandiose plans. A second project, the proposed Empire Building, proceeded much further. Slated to serve as a display house for the manufactures of the British Empire, the building was initially intended to be financed by contributions from a variety of British industrial and commercial interests. Rough plans were developed, but when the British funding failed to materialize, the plans were reluctantly set aside. Although the depression effectively killed new construction proposals, ironically, the 1930's saw more construction at Hastings Park than any other time. Those projects were clearly remnants of the previous decade and not an adequate reflection of cautious approach to physical expansion endemic in the 1930's.[34]

One further event affected the physical plant in this period. On 27 January 1935, in the midst of one of Vancouver's heaviest snowfalls, the expensive lamella roof of the Forum Building gave way. No one was hurt in the collapse, and the City Council quickly made $70,000 available to reconstruct the roof. In the aftermath of the calamity, recriminations flew, with Architect H. H. Simmonds, the Lamella Roof Company, and the City Building Department alternately being singled out for criticism, usually by each other. More significant than the scramble to assess blame for the incident was the resulting acrimonious debate between council and the V.E.A. over the financial responsibility for the reconstruction. This conflict took on more importance because of the concurrent controversy concerning V.E.A. finances and auditing procedures. Although the city granted a loan in order to renovate the building immediately, it then attempted to attach a provision that the city's internal auditors be allowed to investigate the association's financial records.[35] The V.E.A. rejected both sides of council's "offer," recording that "this

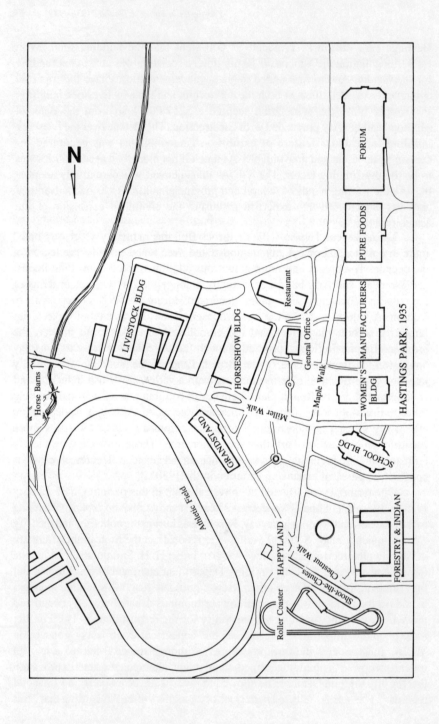

N

Horse Barns

Athletic Field

LIVESTOCK BLDG

HORSESHOW BLDG

Restaurant

General Office

GRANDSTAND

Maple Walk

Miller Walk

HAPPYLAND

Roller Coaster

Shoot-the-Chutes

Chestnut Walk

WOMEN'S BLDG

MANUFACTURERS

PURE FOODS

FORUM

SCHOOL BLDG

FORESTRY & INDIAN

HASTINGS PARK, 1935

Board [of Control] respectfully but firmly denies any responsibility either for the collapse of the building or for the payment of reconstruction costs."[36] The matter continued unresolved until December 1937, when the V.E.A. agreed, in the interests of maintaining cordial relations, to pay a total of $9,446 over seven years towards the interest charges of the $70,000 cost.[37] Technically, all of the Hastings Park facilities were owned by the city and were included in the annual $1 rental paid by the association. It was the V.E.A.'s contention that the Forum was therefore the responsibility of the city, although the association normally paid for construction. While the resolution of the forum roof controversy was satisfactory in the short term, it did nothing to lay to rest the question of who really owned, and was therefore responsible for, the exhibition facilities.

Notwithstanding this conflict, the Forum was a significant addition to the V.E.A.'s facilities. The erection of the Forum and particularly the fact that it included an ice sheet, greatly increased the year-round use of Hastings Park. Hockey, both amateur and professional, public skating, tennis exhibitions, and sundry other sporting and entertainment events were scheduled in the Forum, Pacific Coast League soccer was played in the race track oval, and the tennis and badminton courts were rented out to local clubs, thus utilizing otherwise idle facilities.[38] With the multi-purpose Forum leading the way, the V.E.A. was gradually expanding its year-round operations. Increasingly, the area was being used not as a free public park, as had been the case since 1908, but as a location for the activities of private citizens and organizations.

By renting the buildings during the year, the V.E.A. provided themselves with yet another cushion against the uncertainty of the exhibition's profit. In the 1930's there was a decrease in the reliance on the fair as a source of revenue, though it provided an average of 67.6 per cent of the yearly revenue in the decade, down from 77 per cent in the 1920's and 87 per cent between 1910 and 1919. At the same time, the proportion of expenditures on non-exhibition activities increased, reaching an average of 50 per cent during the depression years, up substantially from 33 per cent the previous decade, and 18 per cent in the first ten years of the Hastings Park fair. The Vancouver Exhibition Association was undergoing a major transformation, from the sponsorship of an annual exhibition to the management of an integrated, year-round sports and entertainment facility. The change was gradual and not really acknowledged by the association. To the directors and members, the annual fair was the "raison d'être" of the V.E.A., and the additional rentals were merely an insurance policy against poor weather or low returns from the fair.

Another non-fair activity which took on increasing importance was horse-racing. S. W. Randall's Ascot Racing Association, lessees of the Hastings Park racetrack, applied for an extension of its contract in 1933, requesting that a new agreement run until 1960. In return for the extension, Randall promised to pay $7,000 for a one-week meet in July and $7,000 for the exhibition-week races.

Additionally, Randall agreed to effect a major improvement of the racing facilities, including new barns, stables, and fences, with the costs to be borne entirely by the Ascot Racing Association and the ownership of the structures falling to the city. Before the V.E.A. could grant Randall the lease he requested, the association needed to have its own lease extended, a matter attended to with few difficulties that same year. Realizing the tremendous profits to be made from racing, the association had actually applied for a racing charter of its own in 1932, but the federal government's reluctance to grant such a privilege resulted in the long-term agreement with Randall. Racing proved to be consistently remunerative, especially since the association was not required to pay any expenses. In 1931, for example, the V.E.A. received the $14,000 rental from Randall, plus over $12,000 as its percentage of the provincial parimutuel taxes — a total of over $26,000 from a branch of operations which cost the association next to nothing. A mark of the association's valuation of the racing facility was the decision in 1935 to fill in the ravine, long a "beauty spot" in the park, to make way for racetrack and exhibition expansion.[39]

While internal matters remained fairly stable throughout the 1930's external relations with other exhibitions and with fair associations underwent some dramatic changes. In the previous decade the Vancouver Exhibition Association spurned local associations in favour of west coast and international fair associations, but now the trend was reversed. A series of programmes were implemented to improve relations with other British Columbian fairs, including the donation of challenge shields to Class "B" fairs in Chilliwack, Kamloops, and Armstrong, with the awards intended for the best regional exhibit at each fair. The arrangement, it was believed, "would be a very friendly gesture which would find response in the hearts of the people operating the B fairs and among the country people generally."[40] Other concessions made to local fairs and exhibitions included subsidies to certain regional displays intended for the Vancouver show and helping small regional fairs to secure suitable entertainment.[41]

At the same time, the V.E.A. was contracting its activities in larger associations. For example, while membership in the Pacific Coast Fairs Association was retained, participation in both the Western Canada Fairs Association and the International Association of Fairs and Exhibitions ceased. The Vancouver Exhibition Association did not end its involvement with all west coast and international organizations, continuing to send representatives to the Pacific International Show to arrange dates and attractions and participating in the attempt to revive the dormant North Pacific Fairs Association. The regional focus of the association was, however, increasing markedly as the V.E.A. became convinced of the need to establish cordial relations with exhibitions and the agricultural community throughout British Columbia if Vancouver's presentation was ever to deserve full status as the major provincial fair.[42]

The 1930's had been an unusual decade for the Vancouver Exhibition

Association. In this time of general economic distress, the association had prospered. As the pall of war replaced the gloom of depression in 1939, the association remained strong, vibrant and expansive.

7

The V.E.A. and World War II, 1939-1946

Canada's preoccupation with the severe economic problems of the depression ended with dramatic suddenness on 1 September 1939, when the armies of Nazi Germany were unleashed on Poland. By the tenth, Canada had declared war. The 1939 fair was in progress at the time war broke out in Europe, but it ended before Canada entered the conflict. The Vancouver Exhibition Association was once again faced with the decision whether it should continue to hold annual exhibitions, as it had done during World War I, or cancel the fair for the duration of the fighting. As before, it was hastily decided to proceed.

For a number of reasons, the fair did not continue throughout the six-year war, though it was staged in 1940 and 1941. The dominion government supported the decision of many exhibition associations to proceed with their annual shows, once again noting that it was important for public morale that life continue on as before as much as possible. However, the government did not back up its declaration of support with continued assistance for the agricultural fairs. Except for several long-term building grants, all funding was cancelled in 1940, and it was not reinstituted during the war. With some pleasure, the Minister of Agriculture, James G. Gardiner, was later to note that the suspension of financing did not seriously affect the various fairs and that instead the exhibitions enjoyed consistent success both at the gate and in the cash box. The V.E.A. reacted to the loss of federal assistance by reducing prizes for agricultural competitions by 25 per cent. Faced with considerable opposition over the reduction, especially as it occurred during an exhibition which returned a profit of $64,900, the V.E.A. raised the allotment for prizes by 12.5 per cent the following season. The association clothed itself in patriotism, claiming that the increase did not result from pressure from the agricultural community but because of the great importance of agriculture to Canada.[1]

The two wartime exhibitions were highly profitable, with the 1941 surplus of $59,000 almost equalling the excellent return of the previous year. Attendance rose to an all-time high of 386,000 in 1941, indicating widespread support for the association's decision to proceed with wartime fairs. There was some opposition to isolated aspects of the show, including a minor protest by some prominent businessmen, who opposed the continuation of an exhibition parade and favoured instead a display of Canadian military might. Major-General R. A. Alexander, Officer Commanding, Pacific Command, quickly allayed such concerns by offering his "100% support" to the V.E.A.'s plans, stating that the military was not prepared to provide such a parade.[2] Resistance to the skid-road gambling continued as well, but it was dismissed by the V.E.A. with the usual promises to clean up the operation. Most important, and in striking contrast to the controversy generated in 1914, holding an exhibition during war never became a public issue.

The onset of war had an immediate effect upon the fair. Introduction of special taxes and regulations by the Federal government hit the amusement sector hardest. Early in 1941, the federal government changed the recently imposed blanket tax for carnivals, which required American carnivals to pay $500 per month for the right to perform in Canada. The new tax called for licences of $100 for each riding device, $50 for each side show, and $25 for each concession for every calendar month the carnival company was in Canada. The company capable of supplying all the amusement needs of the V.E.A., the Amusement Corporation of Canada, faced added costs of $5,000 as a result of the new taxes. To secure the A.C.A., the Vancouver Exhibition Association was forced to pay one-half of the taxes. The company did come to Vancouver for the 1941 exhibition, but attempts to secure a contract for the following season fell short as the new taxes and regulations simply proved too onerous.[3]

Additional controls threatened the exhibition, but appeals to the government proved successful. A special amusement tax was created in 1941 which would have placed a surcharge on all admission and grandstand fees. The commissioner of excise tax quickly granted an exemption to fairs for the debatable reason that "many persons entering the grounds are not interested in amusement but rather in education or recreation."[4] Similarly, when "dim-out" regulations required the City of Vancouver to restrict the number of lights visible in the evening, the V.E.A. again requested special consideration.[5] The 1942 exhibition was cancelled shortly thereafter, and the issue was not resolved. It is doubtful that the government would have succumbed to the V.E.A.'s last suggestion.

The most outstanding feature of the 1940 and 1941 exhibitions was the opening of the two newest facilities. In the previous decade, plans had begun for the second unit of the Livestock Building and the Garden Auditorium. The V.E.A. had secured the necessary funding after arduous negotiations with the dominion, provincial, and civic authorities. Finally, construction began: the three-thousand-seat auditorium, costing over $110,000, and the three-acre Livestock Building, which cost $157,000, were completed in time for the 1941 exhibition.[6] Thus fair activities were expanded although exhibitions remained similar to those of the pre-war era. The most noticeable change was the military flair present in the parades and many of the exhibits.

One casualty of the war years was the Winter Fair, which had been staged annually since 1925 (except for 1932). It was cancelled in late September 1939. This show had evolved over the years into a simple business operation, providing the livestock producers of British Columbia with access to the lucrative Vancouver market. As President Dunsmuir noted: "our Directors were of the opinion that the outbreak of war has made it unnecessary for us to assist producers to either market or obtain better prices inasmuch as there is already a better market at better prices, which most people seem to believe will continue along these lines."[7] Stating that it was the association's intention to re-establish the Winter Fair after the war, Dunsmuir pointed out that the V.E.A. was concerned that the military might require the buildings even though several of the old wooden structures usually used for the winter show were being demolished to make way for the new Livestock Building. However, the Department of Agriculture accepted the Vancouver Exhibition Association's decision, even offering the organization 50 per cent of the standard fair grant to defray any expenses already incurred.[8] The Winter Fair was gone for the duration of the war, and although it was not apparent at this time, the show was never again to form a part of the V.E.A.'s activities.

In August 1942, for the first time since 1910, the Vancouver Exhibition did not stage its annual fair. Its uninterrupted history marked it as something of an anomaly among Western Canadian fairs, and its closure came as a surprise. That the Vancouver exhibition was not held was a result of two factors: the military's demand for the use of the grounds and facilities and, less directly, the Japanese attack on Pearl Harbor. Arrangements for the military occupation of Hastings Park had been made immediately after the outbreak of war. The Department of National Defence agreed to pay twenty cents per square foot per annum for the buildings used and agreed to the V.E.A.'s request that the Forum, golf course, and Happy-land not be included. However, complete possession of the exhibition facilities did not occur until late in 1941, although the military was making use of parts of the grounds and several buildings at various times. In August 1941, the Air Force declared its intention of using the Industrial and Women's Buildings and of building additional structures immediately after that year's exhibition.[9] Recognizing that the establishment of Hastings Park as a military base was almost inevitable, the Vancouver Exhibition Association continued to impress upon the government "the necessity that the buildings, if occupied, must be vacated for the operation of the exhibition."[10] Once again, the V.E.A. was prepared to fulfil its patriotic duty, provided that those obligations did not interfere with the normal functioning of the annual fair. Events soon conspired to ensure that the V.E.A.'s immediate concerns would be altered.

On 7 December 1941, Japanese forces launched a surprise attack on Pearl Harbor, changing the entire complexion of the war, and in the resulting turmoil Hastings Park was completely taken over by Canadian military authorities. Though not clear to the public at the time, the federal government's decision to assume control of the V.E.A.'s facilities actually had little to do with the threat of possible Japanese attack on British Columbia.

Racial tensions were brought to the surface exposing the embitterment in British Columbia's social and political environment.[11] The most virulent wave of racial hatred ever to infect the province swept across B.C. as a result of the attack on Pearl Harbor. The hostility was directed towards the Japanese, or more correctly, Japanese Canadians living in the militarily vulnerable coastal areas. Whites throughout the province called immediately for federal government action to handle the "Jap" menace. General Alexander noted that: "The situation with regard to the Japanese resident in British Columbia is assuming a serious aspect. Public feeling is becoming very insistent, especially in Vancouver, that local Japanese should be either interned or removed from the coast."[12] Public pressure for the removal of the Japanese grew rapidly, and a wide range of Vancouver groups, individuals, and politicians added strength to the outcry. Faced with the possibility of racially inspired violence, the federal government reluctantly agreed to order the evacuation of all Japanese within certain "protected zones" along the Pacific Coast for, as it was euphemistically put, "their own good."[13]

To effect the removal of the Japanese population, estimated to be in excess of twenty thousand people, the federal government established the British Columbia Security Commission on 4 March 1942. Chaired by Austin C. Taylor and managed by a twenty-member advisory board, the commission was charged with the removal of all Japanese from "certain strategic areas of British Columbia" and with their relocation to the interior of the province. Although the B.C. Security Commission was responsible for the development and administration of the Japanese camps, usually located in deserted mining communities inland, the organization's first priority was peaceful evacuation from the Vancouver area into the isolated regions of the interior.[14]

Only at this point did the potential use of Hastings Park as a support to the B.C.S.C. become a serious possibility. Indeed, late in January 1942, the real estate branch of the Department of National Defence had informed the Vancouver Exhibition Association that it would not require the exhibition facilities for the forthcoming year. With the decision to remove the Japanese, however, Hastings Park once again became the subject for negotiation. The association was extremely reluctant to surrender the grounds, for it was apparent that the occupation would include most if not all of the facilities and that the takeover would force the cancellation of the 1942 exhibition. After extended and often acrimonious negotiations between the Department of Labour, the B.C. Security Commission, and the V.E.A., an agreement was made to rent the Livestock Building and the Women's

Building for $2,000 a month. A further agreement allowed the Royal Canadian Mounted Police to lease the racetrack and grandstand as storage space for the cars and other belongings being seized from the Japanese.[15] Eventually, the V.E.A. agreed to relinquish control of the Forum for an additional $2,000 a month. The strength of their reluctance can be measured by the remarks of the government agent handling the negotiations who noted that "The Exhibition authorities at first were not very cooperative . . . but when they found out that the Government meant business, they came to these terms."[16]

It soon became evident, however, that the facilities surrendered by the Vancouver Exhibition Association would not be sufficient to handle the needs of the B.C. Security Commission. After surveying the grounds, federal agent Colonel Gibson recommended that all grounds and buildings except the golf course and race track be taken over. He ensured that the government would pay all carrying charges. Aware that such extensive possession meant not only the demise of the 1942 exhibition but also the end to all association activities on the grounds, the V.E.A. protested the government's decision vigorously and refused to accept the federal offer. During the early war years the control of the exhibition facilities was not immediately essential, but in 1942 the federal government was completely unwilling to broach any resistance. When threats of expropriation failed to sway the V.E.A., the government acted. Citing the association's reluctance to conclude reasonable arrangements for the leasing of the property, Ottawa assumed control of the grounds and buildings by Order-in-Council on 14 April 1942.[17]

Rudely jolted by the awesome plenitude of federal power, the Vancouver Exhibition Association gave in, now aiming to regain only a modicum of control over the facilities and to secure some revenue from the take-over. By early June 1942 an agreement was signed with the V.E.A. which effectively dictated rental terms for the facilities of $50,000 in 1942 and $54,000 per annum each year thereafter. Individual buildings would be returned to the association if they were no longer required, and the government was given the right to use the grandstand and first nine holes of the golf course at no extra charge if they were required.[18] The legalities straightened out, Hastings Park was then turned over to the B.C. Securities Commission for use as a transshipment point for the Japanese.

Reviewing the task at hand, the B.C.S.C. decided to develop the property into an assembly site, a place where Japanese slated for deportation could be brought and detained for an indefinite period until their locations inland were prepared. Workmen descended upon the grounds, quickly turning the former livestock building into a temporary dormitory. Muriel Kitigawa, who visited the structure in the midst of the evacuation process, provided a vivid description of the environment in a letter to her brother.

The whole place is impregnated with the smell of ancient manure and maggots. Every other day it is swept with dichlorine of lime, or something, but you can't disguise horse smell, cow smell, sheep, pigs, rabbits and goats. And it is dusty! The toilets are just a sheet metal trough, and up until now they did not have partitions or seats. The women kicked so they put up partitions and a terribly makeshift seat. Twelve–year–old boys stay with the women too, you know . . . as for the bunks, they were the most tragic things there. Steel and wooden frames with a thin lumpy straw tick, a bolster, and three army blankets . . . no sheets unless you bring your own. These are the "homes" of the women I saw . . . these bunks were hung with sheets and blankets and clothes of every hue and variety — a regular gypsy tent of colours, age and cleanliness — all hung in a pathetic attempt at privacy . . . an old, old lady was crying, saying she would rather have died than have to come to such a place . . . there are ten showers for 1,500 women.[19]

It was no doubt a heart-rending experience for all the Japanese and Japanese-Canadians involved, as they were torn from their homes, dispossessed of most of their belongings, often separated from family and friends, and forced to move to unknown communities.

It quickly became evident that the temporary holding site first envisaged would not suffice and that more substantial arrangements were required. The Pure Foods, Manufacturing, and Forum Buildings were brought into service, cooking facilities were expanded, a small store was opened, and additional sleeping arrangements were provided. Even with the expansion and improvements, the centre was still hardly hospitable. The evacuees were separated by sex and age, with men, women and children being placed in different sleeping quarters, removing the last vestige of normality remaining in the lives of many families. The dormitories themselves allowed for virtually no privacy as bunks were jammed close together, although in some buildings blankets hung from ceilings served as rudimentary partitions. Few incidents marred the evacuation procedure, although the "residents" occasionally took umbrage with the quality of the food being offered and refused to eat.[20] For the most part, as the B.C. Security Commission noted, the "Japanese co-operated and resigned themselves to their new environment."[21]

Ken Adachi, a journalist who went through the evacuation procedure as a child, was less sympathetic to the government's handling of what were largely Canadian citizens, and later wrote bitterly: "the great majority were a psychologically bruised, badly puzzled and frequently apathetic group of people . . . They bore little resemblance to the image of the sly, ruthless, Empire worshipping fanatics which the white public persisted in creating as the prototype of the evacuees."[22]

The evacuees had few people willing to fight for their interests, and in fact there was considerable opposition in Vancouver to the "good" treatment being meted out to the Japanese [23] The only official agent acting for the Japanese in

Canada was the consul-general of Spain. The Spanish authorities did request and receive an investigation of the medical facilities at Hastings Park. In replying to the request, H. A. Waring, undersecretary for external affairs, noted that "the medical arrangements which existed at Hastings Park, prior to its closing, were adequate to any reasonable demand upon them and considerably superior to those enjoyed by a great majority of the occupants of the Park, prior to their taking up residence there."[24] Shorn of their right to protest, the internees fell into an uneasy apathy, unable to work effectively for the betterment of their conditions and apprehensive about what lay ahead.

Although it appeared for a time as though the government had decided to use the Hastings Park holding centre as a permanent depot for the internees, a possibility which elicited widespread complaints from the citizens and politicians of Vancouver,[25] the B.C. Security Commission decided to continue the evacuation as initially planned in order to prevent outbreaks of violence. Ghost towns, referred to as "relocation centres," such as Greenwood, Kaslo, New Denver, Slocan City, and Sandon, all long-abandoned mining towns, were reopened. Beginning in July 1942, the resettlement process began. The commencement of the removal inland did not mean that Hastings Park was quickly emptied. Quite the contrary; the facilities became even more active after that date, as Japanese were brought in greater numbers to the park as a preparatory step to relocation.

In all, some eight thousand Japanese and Japanese Canadians passed through Hastings Park, with the number of people on the site reaching as high as 3,866 in early September. Reflecting the bureaucratic mind which had handled the entire operation, the B.C.S.C. noted, not without some pride, that 1,542,371 meals had been served with a "raw food cost" of $0.0933 per meal.[26] The entire process had been handled in a businesslike manner, and the "processing" of the Japanese had proceeded with few difficulties. The evacuation was fully completed by 30 September 1942, at which time the Hastings Park Assembly Centre was finally shut down, ending a brief but tragic episode in the history of Vancouver's exhibition. For many who passed through the park in the tumultuous months of 1942, the legacy of Hastings Park would live on as the indignity of being huddled in cattle barns, jammed into cramped quarters, forced to eat cheap and often alien food, and the trauma of the evacuation itself became an indelible part of the collective memory of the Japanese Canadian community. For Vancouverites, however, the Japanese "menace" was finally constrained by late September 1942, when the last internees were sent to the interior. The deportation complete, the grounds and buildings of the Vancouver Exhibition Association now stood empty. However, they were not to be freed for exhibition purposes for quite some time.

Even though the occupation of Hastings Park had been initially undertaken for the Japanese evacuation, the military did not surrender control of the property following the departure of the last internee. Instead they maintained a strong presence at Hastings Park until after the end of the war. The golf course was used for army manoeuvres, several buildings were kept in service as dormitories, and other structures were used as storage depots. Unlike World War I when Hastings Park had served as the major military installation in the city, the property was used in a more ancillary role between 1942 and 1945. Although the site of considerable activity, it was not the focus of Department of National Defence activities in Vancouver.

Following the end of the internment process, the D.N.D. formally took control of the property from the B.C. Security Commission, leaving only a few small buildings and the second nine holes of the golf course for the V.E.A.'s use. A new lease was drawn up between the association and the federal government with the accord extending to 1952, although a provision in the contract allowed for the D.N.D. to cancel the lease in any year provided notice was given by 1 April. As the war ground on and the D.N.D. expanded its interests elsewhere, sections of the park were gradually returned to the association, such as the Forum in October 1943 and the first nine holes of the golf course the following year. When they accepted back leased buildings and grounds, the V.E.A. insisted that the government restore the properties to their pre-war condition, particularly the golf course which had been used for military manoeuvres.[27]

One of the most interesting developments of the occupation occurred in 1944, when Major-General George R. Pearkes attempted to involve the Vancouver Exhibition Association in a departmental squabble. Pearkes approached the V.E.A., asking for a letter declaring the association's desire to regain possession of their property. Apparently he hoped that such a request would assist his own efforts to secure additional permanent military facilities in the Vancouver area. The V.E.A. wisely chose to stay out of the internal dispute, sending Pearkes a non-committal reply which stated simply that the association would be pleased to have the buildings returned as soon as they were no longer required for the war effort.[28]

The war dragged on into 1945, and even when the conflict ended in that year it was clear that the site would not be returned in time for a 1946 exhibition, meaning that the fifth consecutive fair had to be cancelled. As the end of the occupation approached in 1946, the V.E.A. appointed Architects McCarter and Nairne to survey the grounds in order to ascertain the amount of compensation to be sought from the federal government for damage done during the occupation. Control of the grounds ultimately was returned to the Vancouver Exhibition Association on 12 July 1946, but a final settlement of the compensation issue had to wait for several months. McCarter and Nairne completed an eighty-page report on the cost of reconstructing the various buildings to an appropriate state and on the basis of that report and further negotiations with the government, an agreement was reached in November 1946. Although the V.E.A. had pressed for total compensation of $424,000, they agreed to accept $375,000. The settlement ended more than four years of possession by the various branches of the federal government and finally freed the Vancouver Exhibition Association to stage a fair again.[29]

Unable to hold an annual fair, the V.E.A. might have slid into inactivity for the duration of the war, but in fact the association was extremely active throughout the period, using the hiatus in public programming to put its house in better order. Indeed, the V.E.A. even managed to keep one small aspect of its exhibition, the Junior Farmers Show, operating. An arrangement was worked out with the Chilliwack Exhibition whereby the Vancouver organization would provide the necessary funds to present an agricultural competition for children from the Lower Mainland. The young visitors were provided with dormitories, food, and chaperones. The effort was not major nor expensive, costing the V.E.A. approximately $2,000 to $4,000 a year.[30] However, the arrangement did allow the association to continue what many members saw as the most important agricultural and educational aspect of the fair.

Although actual construction on the grounds ceased during the war years, plans for additions continued unabated. A new gate was proposed for the corner of Hastings and Renfrew, plans were drawn up and estimates were made.[31] Other suggestions for physical expansion included a proposal that a major building be erected to house displays of British Columbian manufacturers and industries. Those facilities which remained in, or were returned to, the hands of the V.E.A. were fully utilized throughout the war, especially the golf course and the Forum Building, the latter being a particularly popular spot for sporting events.[32]

Another attraction kept open through the war years was the Edward and Mary Lipsett Indian Museum. The Lipsetts were lifelong collectors of artifacts from among native groups of North and South America and members of the V.E.A., and early in 1941 they approached the board of directors with an offer to deposit their collection at Hastings Park permanently. The association leapt at the opportunity and agreed to renovate the Aquarium Building to house the materials. In making their gift, the Lipsetts declared that it was their wish that the collection always be free to the public and that it become the permanent property of the exhibition. While the collection itself was a major one the Lipsett Museum represented only a slight increase in wartime activities at Hastings Park. The opening of the museum provides, however, further indication of the V.E.A.'s determination to maintain as many events and attractions on the grounds as their limited resources would allow.[33]

Perhaps the most remarkable aspect of the association's wartime activities was the expansion of land holdings near the exhibition grounds. Even though the eighteen-hole golf course provided ample space for extension in the near future, the V.E.A. continued to look far down the road towards the time when the annual fair would outgrow the bounds of the original 160-acre Hastings Park grant. The first addition to the V.E.A.'s holdings came not as a result of the association's activities, but rather as a gift. By agreeing to cancel a $6,000 property tax debt, the city acquired Con Jones Park from Mrs. Ada Stevenson, niece of the original owner, John Callister. Located just west of the exhibition grounds along Renfrew Street, the property had been developed as an important sports facility complete with playing field and grandstand. It was then turned over to the V.E.A. for an annual rental of $1.00 with a provision that the association would pay back taxes out of money earned from the operation of the park. Renamed Callister Exhibition Park in honour of its pioneer owner, the land was a significant addition and allowed a resumption of several sporting activities which had been cancelled following the military occupation of Hastings Park.[34]

The more important land acquisitions began in 1943 when the V.E.A. moved to purchase additional lands to the east of the golf course. Ostensibly, only the course was to be expanded, but in fact this manoeuvre served once again as a convenient vehicle for the extension of the grounds. By 1944, a $100,000 programme of land purchases, transfers from the city, building removal, and golf course construction was underway in the area between Rupert, Hastings, Eaton, and Cassiar Streets, although the eastern boundary was irregular and did not adhere strictly to the latter throughfare. City Council agreed to pay 50 per cent of the costs of the twenty-seven-acre extension, with the expected $50,000 contribution to be spread over ten years.[35] The project proceeded through the remainder of the war, with an agent of the V.E.A. purchasing lots in the area as they became available and arranging for the removal of the houses to lands east of Cassiar Street. The V.E.A. did not assume a high profile in the negotiations, largely in an effort to keep costs down. "As a general policy," it was explained to the V.E.A. directors, "he [Mr. Stibbards, the real estate agent] has contacted residents on a personal basis and the name of the Vancouver Exhibition Association has not appeared in the negotiations."[36] There were nontheless a few problems encountered in the expansion process, particularly since wartime rent controls and regulations made it difficult to force a tenant to leave a rented home without six months' notice. Occasionally owners proved reluctant to sell, in which case the city and the V.E.A. resorted to expropriation.[37] By the time the V.E.A. regained full control of their facilities, the extension of the grounds was complete, with the exception of land held by a few recalcitrant residents.

Another aspect of the Vancouver Exhibition Association's activities to undergo major transformation during the war years was the horse-racing at the exhibition grounds race track. Racing at Hastings Park did not proceed uninterrupted throughout the war and was rescheduled on several occasions to allow for military activities. Early in 1942, it was decided to concentrate all lower mainland racing at Hastings Park, and the Vancouver Thoroughbred Association, West Coast Jockey Club, Ascot Jockey Club, and the Brighouse Park group joined together and held six weeks of racing together instead of the traditional two weeks staged by the Ascot Racing Club. This arrangement continued throughout the war with occasional modifications and proved to be highly remunerative for the association. The consortium of racing interests paid, for example, $9,000 per week for five weeks of racing in 1945, plus a fixed percentage of gross receipts from betting. In this period as well, S. W. Randall, owner of the Ascot Jockey Club and manager of the racing facilities, began formulating plans for the redevelopment of the track, grandstand, and stables. One section of the grandstand was renovated in 1942–1943, but by the end of the war Randall had far more grandiose dreams. A new five-furlong track was to be laid and complete new areas for both horses and spectators were to be provided, all to be paid for by the Randall interests. In return for the privately financed redevelopment scheme, Randall requested an extension of his lease arguing that such construction was not feasible without the stability of a long-term commitment. Randall's plans were not implemented by war's end, but they reflected the direction that the future development of horse racing at Hastings Park would take.[38]

It should be clear that the V.E.A. pursued a very active course during the war years, carrying on activities as much as possible and even expanding certain aspects of its operation. Another area which the association considered carefully during this period was the internal structure of the organization. The directors and membership took advantage of the hiatus to re-evaluate the inner workings of the Vancouver Exhibition Association. Several changes were made to adjust the activities of the association to the wartime realities. Financial constraints and the military occupation of Hastings Park in March 1942 led to severe cutbacks in exhibition staff, and all employees except seven managerial staff were terminated the next month. Without a fair, committees seemed superfluous and the number of active groups was slashed in half. Those remaining committees could proceed at a more leisurely pace owing to the reduced work load. It was also decided to limit the number of meetings and to hold them only when required instead of on a regular basis.[39] S. C. McLennan, general manager of the exhibition, left the association for a year and a half to assist with the administration of the Hastings Park Assembly Centre, and then joined the army as a major. At the exhibition he was replaced by Ida Rae, long-time secretary of the V.E.A., who was named "Acting Secretary in Charge."[40] McLennan returned as manager in April 1944, but his re-entry to exhibition life was to be short and stormy. Resigning over a "difference in policy" McLennan left the V.E.A. in May 1945 and was quickly hired by the Brandon Exhibition.[41] Since there was no exhibition scheduled for 1945 and one was not likely in the following year, the association took time in selecting a new manager, finally settling on V. Ben Williams for the post in May 1946.[42]

More substantive changes also took place. Led by Alderman J. Price in 1944, a group of citizens began to press for major restructuring of the association management. They called primarily for the public election of directors, along the lines adopted by the Parks and School Boards. City Council refused to back Price's suggestions, but it did empower the alderman to discuss the matter with the association. President Walter Leek argued that the existing system was the only way good citizens could be interested enough in the organization to get them to serve as directors. Oddly, while the V.E.A. vigorously rejected Price's proposal, it was seriously considering other ways to instill "new blood." While privately admitting the need for new directors with fresh ideas, the association was extremely reluctant to open up the board of directors to non-members and openly rejected the idea of public elections. In the end, a plan to ensure more dynamic leadership led to revisions in the constitution which were intended to interest younger men in the V.E.A. Directors over the age of sixty-five were automatically elevated to the new status of advisory director, providing they had served for at least fifteen years. The number of advisory directors was limited to nine, and they were required to resign after an additional ten years. A further attempt to open opportunities within the association was made by the passage of a regulation restricting the presidency to three consecutive one-year terms, after which election to that post was no longer possible. These changes were seen as a means of ensuring mobility within the Vancouver Exhibition Association, of attracting new people into the organization, and of preventing the directorate from ossifying into a closed clique.[43]

Further evidence that the V.E.A. was not viewing the cancellation of the exhibition as an occasion for stagnation and inactivity came with the establishment of a Post-War Planning Committee early in 1943. It was to investigate all aspects of Vancouver's fair and make recommendations on future physical and organizational development. A central co-ordinating committee was formed, with sub-committees delegated to study each of the branches of the V.E.A.'s activities, including Agriculture, Boys' and Girls' Competitions, B.C. Products, Construction Industry, Education, Electrical and Engineering Industry, Fishing, Mining and Forest Products. The Post-War Planning Committee considered a wide range of alternatives. Several were eventually adopted, such as a new B.C. Building and a new site for the amusement area. Others disappeared after only short deliberation, most notably a dormitory designed to house Boys' and Girls' Department competitors. As President John Dunsmuir noted, "our first post-war exhibition should present to the public our present facilities renovated, improved and modernized."[44] That goal was not realized by the 1947 fair, but the committee did provide a base for the future development of Exhibition Park and brought to the fore several innovative ideas for reforming the fair.[45]

More than anything, the establishment of the planning programme shows the increasing professionalism of the Vancouver Exhibition Association. A technical advisor was hired, a special operations committee was formed to lay the plans for the first post-war fair, the press was invited to all meetings in an effort to generate publicity for the association, and representations were made to federal and provincial authorities in an attempt to secure future funding.[46] A new exhibition association was emerging out of the turmoil of the war, one that retained the self-confidence of the pre-war V.E.A. but which also contained an expanded business expertise and orientation.

The culmination of this "professionalization" was the production in 1948 of the first integrated development plan for Hastings Park. It was drawn up by J. A. Walker and R. Riley of Harland Bartholomew and Associates, an internationally known firm of urban planners from St. Louis, Missouri, whose association with Vancouver was highlighted in 1929 by their presentation of a comprehensive development plan for the city. The plan called for a new set of playing fields inside the racetrack oval, a coliseum and swimming pool, and an array of new exhibit buildings. The main thrust of the report was that the V.E.A. should endeavour to keep as much open green space as possible and that the buildings should adhere to a consistent design. While the plan was never implemented, it does reveal that the association was planning for the future.[47]

The Vancouver Exhibition Association had changed in other important ways as well. One crucial alteration was signalled in 1943 when President Leek noted in his annual report: "While agriculture in all its phases has been, and will continue to be, of major importance, it has for some time past been the opinion of the Board of Control that insufficient attention has been given to other phases of our provincial industrial activities and that henceforth lumbering, mining, fishing, manufacturing, merchandising and tourist travel must be vigorously and aggressively sponsored and featured."[48] Agriculture would have to share the limelight with other activities. The association, however cautiously, was moving to modernize its presentation, attempting to keep the fair in step with the development of British Columbia. The post-war exhibitions would not only be more professionally managed, but they would reflect the new mood with which the nation had emerged at war's end. The traditional agricultural fair was becoming an anachronism, and although the V.E.A. was not yet prepared to abandon that aspect of its show, it was moving to diversify the fair to account for the ever-widening range of industrial and commercial activity throughout British Columbia.

It was, therefore, a "new-look" exhibition association which followed from the Second World War. Different in approach and different in style from its predecessor, the "new" association dropped its old name in 1946, choosing instead to be known as the "Pacific National Exhibition." At the same time, Hastings Park was renamed Exhibition Park, a change first suggested in 1939 but shelved until after the war in face of public opposition.[49] "Pacific National Exhibition" was an appropriate designation for the redesigned fair; it symbolized an amalgamation of the association's provincial ambitions and new international aspirations. Vancouver's fair had matured, but in turning from local connections in favour of the greater potential of a fair of national and international standing, it still displayed the booster mentality that marked its origins.

The Pacific National Exhibition: The "New" Fair and the British Empire Games, 1946-1954

Dressed with a new name, a new approach and, for the first time, the rudimentary beginnings of a development plan, the Pacific National Exhibition approached the post-war era with renewed vigour and confidence. The financial problems of the depression seemed far removed and the public opposition to the exhibition which had reached an appex in the 1920's appeared to have dissipated. With five years of planning behind it, the P.N.E. was anxious to test public reaction to a "new" exhibition programme that it anticipated would commence a new era in the association's history.

As planning for the first post-war exhibition in 1947 progressed, it became clear that the war-time preparations had been valuable. Continuous discussions and planning with representatives of the livestock and agricultural associations, a series of meetings with past and potential exhibitors, and the many improvements to the fairgrounds laid a solid foundation. The various committees of the P.N.E. had had more than enough time to prepare for the fair, arranging for participants, exhibit space, prizes, judges, and other requirements. The planners and organizers were working in virtually optimum circumstances. Ample lead time had been provided, public support appeared on the upswing, prosperity appeared to be widespread with the country showing few signs of falling into a depression similar to that which had followed on the heels of the First World War. Optimism was undoubtedly at a high point as the exhibition approached.

The 1947 exhibition exceeded even the Pacific National Exhibition's inflated expectations. Over 580,000 patrons were reported to have passed through the turnstiles during the week-long fair, and the exhibition itself returned a profit of in excess of $113,000, both all-time highs. Vancouverites had been most enthusiastic in their response to the return of the exhibition and the results augured well for future developments. With such a firm indication of public backing, the P.N.E. was able to approach future plans with increased energy, confident that the city was likely to look upon its efforts with approval.

In many ways, the fair was little different from its last predecessor five years removed. Happyland was still operated by the Pacific Amusement Company, and although one of the most important landmarks at Exhibition Park, the Big Dipper, had been demolished for safety reasons, the bulk of the presentation had changed little. To supplement the permanent devices, the Pacific National Exhibition also returned to a traditional ally, hiring the Amusement Company of America yet again. Attempts to secure additional shows or to contract with an alternative amusement company were unsuccessful, still reflecting Vancouver's isolation from the major exhibition centres in North America. Grandstand shows, long a standard feature of the fair, were once more scheduled, and the P.N.E. paid more than $20,000 for a series of performances. The presentations were held in front of the race track grandstand following the end of each day's racing card, with an awning atop the stage serving as protection against poor weather.[1]

Given that the association had had five years to plan for the 1947 exhibition, it is perhaps surprising that so few changes had actually occurred in the structure and content of the fair. In the P.N.E.'s actions, there was a certain hesitancy to innovate, a reluctance that was probably based on the directors' doubts about the manner in which Vancouverites would receive the exhibition after a five-year hiatus. The directors decided therefore to stay with tried content and structure, to test public response, and then restructure the fair more substantially in the following years. Although the 1947 exhibition was strikingly similar to past fairs, there were nonetheless some indications that the presentation was changing. One major addition was made to the industrial displays, a B.C. Products show devoted entirely to the exhibition of the province's newly expanded manufacturing output. Plans were soon to be formulated for the construction of separate B.C. Products Building, but in 1947 the presentation was housed in a section of the former Women's Building.[2]

A second minor change in 1947 suggested that a significant reorganization of the agricultural components of the fair was in the offing. The dairy show, traditionally only a small segment of the exhibition, underwent a major alteration. Representatives of the dairy industry of British Columbia had decided to forego competitions in butter and cheese categories in favour of an educational exhibit. The provincial dairy commissioner stated the industry's belief that it would "now be of more benefit to the Dairy Industry as a whole to feature a display of an educational nature, depicting with the aid of show cases, graphic exhibits and films, some of the steps involved in the production of pure, wholesome milk and milk products."[3] The change was hardly dramatic and most of the exhibition's patrons barely noted the new format. Symbolically, however, the alteration was crucial. Up to this point, the agricultural show had been oriented primarily towards the farming community, with the encouragement of excellence through competition being the principle aim. With the new dairy show, at least one branch of the agricultural display was abandoning the traditional goal in favour of public education. Long proud of its rural roots and orientations, Vancouver's exhibition was showing the first signs of developing an awareness of the contradiction inherent in staging an agricultural fair in an urban environment. From this point on, the emphasis was increasingly on integrating farm and city. Agriculturalists were encouraged to use the exhibition as a showpiece for their products, while the urban manufacturers displayed their wares for the farmers.

While the new direction of the dairy show was significant in the long term, for the most part the fair provided few indications of the changes to come. In the next seven years, however, a "new look" exhibition unfolded, the fair that had been envisaged by the wartime planners. Starting in 1948, the Pacific National Exhibition began introducing changes in its format and in the type of entertainment being offered. By themselves they were mainly minor, but the cumulative result was a significant transformation of the fair.

The most important single change was the addition of internationally renowned shows staged indoors which were intended to be one of the most effective drawing cards of the fair. Plans to hire a "star" were first implemented for the 1948 fair, when Jimmy Durante was brought in to headline a show slated for the Forum. Similar attempts the following year to arrange for the appearance of Doris Day or Kenny Baker, popular American singers, were unsuccessful, but the association eventually was able to come to terms with Edgar Bergen. Hiring the big-name performers did not prove financially remunerative, and the directors decided to try a slightly different tack the following season. Replacing the big-budget American acts for the 1950 exhibition was a "Western Music Round-up." Offering prize money in a variety of musical classes, the P.N.E. succeeded in attracting a large number of country music performers, especially from Western Canada. Successful from an organizational standpoint, the Round-up failed miserably as a public attraction. Revenues were more than $20,000 less than expected. Having lost heavily on both name stars and amateur shows, the P.N.E. continued to look for an inexpensive entertainment which would attract crowds. Ironically, the solution was found in a presentation that had been a nemesis of the exhibition for over forty years.[4]

The association's dilemma was solved by the circus, a show that visited Vancouver regularly. The travelling circus had been in competition for the entertainment dollar since the fair's inauguration in 1910. The association had tried repeatedly to convince City Council to withhold a permit from any circus wishing to perform in the city within two months of the annual fair. No formal agreement was ever reached on the issue, but the exhibition association and council did reach an "understanding" that the circus would not be allowed to interfere with the fair.

The problem emerged again in the post-war period when the Polack Brothers Circus allied with a local charitable organization, the Gizeh Shrine Temple, declared their intention to stage a circus two weeks before the exhibition.[5]

Faced with such competition, the P.N.E. directors decided to explore the possibility of hosting the circus on the exhibition grounds during the annual fair. While plans for 1947 were too far advanced to include the circus, negotiations were launched to arrange for a showing the following year. The Forum was the only P.N.E. structure capable of providing space for both performers and spectators. Other displays, particularly the Horticultural Show, would be without proper facilities as a result, but since the circus was expected to generate $40,000 to $50,000 annually it had top priority. There was an outcry at the displacement of the Horticultural Show but entertainment had clearly replaced agricultural content at the P.N.E.[6]

With a building set aside for the performance, the P.N.E. could conclude negotiations with the Shrine and Polack Bros. In the agreement reached early in 1948, the association agreed to pay $18,500 for the performance and tentatively accepted a 50/50 profit split with the Shrine, the sponsors of the show. The circus proved to be a consistently popular attraction, selling out virtually every show and returning sizeable profits to the Pacific National Exhibition and the Gizeh Shrine Temple. The circus gained steadily in popularity, and in 1951 the P.N.E. temporarily abandoned its search for "big-name" entertainers and decided instead to enter into a long-term contract with the Shrine and Polack Bros. Circus.[7]

The immediate post-war years saw the addition of yet another new feature, the Miss P.N.E. pageant, held for the first time in 1948. Communities throughout British Columbia were granted "franchises" in the competition which allowed the selection of a girl from their town to represent them in the contest. The pageant followed the lines of the classic American beauty contest, with poise and appearance being the main criteria for success. The geographic arrangement of the contest added a lively regional rivalry to the competition. Margie Brain of Prince Rupert, who was the first winner, helped inaugurate an event that enjoyed wide popularity. By adding yet another entertainment feature, the exhibition continued to move away from its farming and manufacturing base.

The conflict and, in many ways, contradiction between the carnival atmosphere generated by rides, games, stage acts, and horse racing and the stated educational and promotional aims of the exhibition were inherent in the structure of the fair itself and had been present since the Vancouver Exhibition Association was formed. A large urban audience was not to be gained by a fair whose principal focus was livestock competitions and regional displays of fruits and vegetables. Such attractions were important to some Vancouverites, but in order to be truly viable the association had to add a variety of amusement and entertainment features. These would draw fairgoers who would also view the various agricultural and industrial displays and competitions which allowed the association to fulfil its primary function. To provide such a balance, it was necessary to ensure that entertainment did not overwhelm the central basis of the exhibition. Until the Second World War, the balance had been maintained, although on several occasions the Vancouver Exhibition Association flirted with allowing the amusements to supersede the educational and competitive displays. In the immediate post-war era, the pendulum was clearly swinging in the entertainment direction. The new character of the Pacific National Exhibition was increasingly remote from the fair's agricultural and industrial roots, but the new P.N.E. was popular with Vancouverites and British Columbians.

Despite opposition from livestock exhibitors, the fair was expanded from a seven to an eleven-day show in 1948.[8] Even with the additional five days, attendance that year was disappointing, with only 57,000 more fairgoers than the previous year. Annual attendance levelled off at approximately 640,000 until 1952, when the number of patrons was reported at over 750,000. By 1954, a year in which attendance was swollen by the fortuitous proximity of the British Empire and Commonwealth Games held two weeks earlier, over 870,000 people entered the grounds during the exhibition. That total was more than twice as high as any pre-war figure and provided the P.N.E. with all the evidence needed to justify the revisions made to the exhibition programme. Financially, the exhibitions held between 1947 and 1954 proved just as rewarding, returning an average annual profit of $155,000 with a high of $240,000 in 1953.

Buoyed by such returns and eager to continue the expansion of the fair, the P.N.E. directors undertook to redevelop Exhibition Park to suit the new and changing demands of the exhibition which in turn reflected the changing lifestyle of urban British Columbia. Although proposals for additions or deletions from the physical plant came from many directions, the P.N.E. attempted to ensure that some continuity remained in the planning. A series of new projects, most minor, were initiated in this period ranging from new sheep barns to a five-furlong race track. Both of these were opened in time for the 1948 exhibition. Other changes made shortly after the war included a $24,000 driving range with a pro shop and coffee bar facilities erected in 1950 and a new nine–hole golf course, built on recently acquired lands, replacing sections of the links swallowed up by the expansion of the fair grounds. The following year, 1952, saw the construction of three new structures, the Dog, Cat, and Mink Show Building, Poultry and Pet Stock Building, and Works Area Building, at a total cost in excess of $154,000. The Outdoor Bowl was also built in the centre of the grounds to serve as an exercise ring for livestock and as the venue for horse-team driving competitions.[9]

The single most important project undertaken by the Pacific National Exhibition was the long-planned B.C. Products Building, a structure intended to house government and industry displays representative of the diversity of economic activity in the province. By 1952, the association had prepared a full set of plans, expanded to encompass both a central B.C. Building and two flanking commercial exhibit buildings. To finance that project, the P.N.E. resorted to its traditional source of major funding, the civic ratepayers. Although there were fears that the by-law would be lost owing to public attention on Empire Games financing, the request for $1,000,000 passed handily. Commonwealth Construction Company was awarded the contract for the $1.25 million facility, and work began early in February 1953. Initial plans called for the completion of the building in time for that year's exhibition, and the P.N.E. proceeded to rent out exhibit space. Manufacturing and commercial exhibitors readily signed up to reserve areas in what was intended to be the fair's major showcase, and even the provincial ministry of trade and commerce agreed to lease a large exhibit spot. Construction did not proceed quickly, however, and as late as 12 August the facility was not yet available for exhibitors' preparations. Though the still incomplete building was pressed into service, problems continued to haunt the building that first year, as poor planning and building delays severely hampered the flow of spectators past the various displays. Exhibitors were understandably upset with the conditions and convinced the P.N.E. to reduce the rental rates. Although the association attributed these problems to construction difficulties, later experience was to show that the design of the building itself was not well suited for exhibition purposes.[10]

One positive aspect of the new facility was that it provided a new home for the Challenger Relief Map. Owned by Challenger Cartographers Limited, the 80 x 76 foot map was a remarkable large-scale relief model of British Columbia. It had been housed in the Poultry Building, which was slated for demolition in 1951. Since the map was expected to cost between $50,000 and $60,000, the P.N.E. was somewhat hesitant to purchase it, and, indeed, the first vote on the motion to buy it was defeated. An agreement was finally arranged when the association offered to pay the owner $47,000 over a ten-year period. It was quickly decided that the best location for the relief map was in the B.C. Building, and in order to provide better viewing facilities, the P.N.E. even agreed to install a $9,000 platform that tracked above the map surface, to allow spectators to observe all sections of the province.[11] The new B.C. Building housed as well a four hundred-seat educational theatre and the Lipsett Indian Collection.

Not all projects proceeded with as much dispatch. Suggestions which fell by the wayside included a drive-in theatre in the southeast corner of the park and a large community swimming pool. One major proposal, for an arena/auditorium, not only did not get off the ground in this period but also stirred a significant civic controversy. The association had been contemplating building a ten thousand-seat arena two decades earlier, but nothing had come of the plans. When the idea came up again in 1949, there were two conflicting proposals. The P.N.E. felt that the arena should be located at Exhibition Park. Others in the city, however, argued that it should be erected in the downtown area. For a short time in 1952 it seemed that the decision to locate the British Empire and Commonwealth Games in Vancouver might provide the necessary impetus to build the facility, but that hope faded quickly. The Pacific National Exhibiton had not given up and proceeded with a request to City Council in 1953 asking that a coliseum for Exhibition Park be included in the city's Five-Year Plan, a new funding arrangement whereby annual by-laws were replaced with a complete half-decade package for capital expenditures. To the P.N.E.'s disappointment, council did not accept the suggestion.[12]

When proponents of a downtown arena then came forward with a comprehensive plan for a convention hall-arena, the directors of the P.N.E. were quick to challenge them, pointing out that they would be in direct competition with the P.N.E. and that the exhibition was in dire need of such a building. In addition, they noted that the association had access to government funding through its status as an agricultural fair, monies unavailable to the competing group. The P.N.E. faced considerable opposition, with the Vancouver Board of Trade among other civic groups coming out strongly in favour of the downtown site. The battle intensified early in 1954, as supporters rallied around the two sides polarizing civic opinion.[13]

City Council provided the forum for what appeared to be the final battle over the issue. Overruling the reports of the Technical Planning Board, council invited the P.N.E. to present its plans for a ten thousand-seat coliseum. At this time, the rebuke of the city planners was seen as a major victory for the exhibition association. The matter appeared finally settled on 19 May 1954 when council voted to reject the convention centre/arena proposal and asked the P.N.E. to proceed to draw up plans. The issue was far from dead, however, and the supporters of the downtown coliseum declared their intention to fight on. The Pacific National Exhibition had only won the first skirmish. Only a year earlier, the citizens had enthusiastically endorsed the decision to build the Empire Games stadium on the exhibition grounds, but a vocal minority was now questioning the location of all of Vancouver's major sports facilities on the P.N.E.'s property. Considerable intra-city boosterism is apparent in this conflict as well. The downtown business community came out strongly in favour of a proposal which would enhance property values in the downtown area, increase their accessibility to sports and other entertainment features, and help attract convention business to the city. Round one of what was going to be a long, and at times embittered, contest went to the P.N.E.[14]

It was a development which had little to do with the annual fair that was to stimulate the most important physical expansion in the immediate post-war era. An international sports event, the British Empire and Commonwealth Games, was staged in Vancouver in August 1954, providing exciting sports action throughout the city and leaving behind an impressive physical legacy. As plans and developments progressed towards the Games, however, the role of the Pacific National Exhibition was never clearly spelled out, and it evolved instead out of a curious series of public negotiations, policy reversals, and inconsistent planning.

When it was first learned that the Games would be coming to Vancouver, the P.N.E. immediately indicated its interest in participating. The first proposal was for a ten thousand-seat indoor coliseum, an idea the P.N.E. had been unsuccessfully promoting since 1949. Though this plan soon collapsed, the association was nonetheless still willing to participate, providing that construction would not interfere with the exhibition and that the P.N.E. would not become involved financially with any structure not well-adapted for fair-time activities. The urgent need for a site for a thirty-five thousand-seat outdoor track and field facility, however, soon offered the P.N.E. a new avenue to pursue.[15]

Initial plans for the games called for the construction of a $600,000, forty-two thousand-seat stadium at the University of British Columbia, at first slated to be the primary competition site. University President Norman MacKenzie took exception to the grandiose plans and suggested that unless the stadium was scaled down to an eight thousand-seat facility it would not be allowed on the U.B.C. campus. There was no shortage of alternate sites — Capilano Stadium, Central Park in Burnaby, Lansdowne Park in Richmond, and a gravel pit in West Vancouver were all offered as possibilities. The P.N.E. proposed Callister Exhibition Park as a prospective location, although they later indicated that the park was not really a satisfactory option. As late as September 1952, however, the British Empire Games Society was declaring their intention to stick with U.B.C., proposing that a small permanent stadium be built and that temporary seating be used to bring the facility up to the required capacity.[16]

As time wound on, however, public opposition to the U.B.C. site grew. Point Grey residents were concerned about potential traffic problems while others in the Lower Mainland complained about its comparatively isolated location. Stepping in, the Pacific National Exhibition indicated a willingness to make additional lands in the southeast corner of their property available. Led by Mayor Hume and sports columnist Eric Whitehead, the opponents of the Point Grey stadium convinced the B.E.G. Society to choose the P.N.E. site. Sports groups throughout the city enthusiastically endorsed the proposed twenty-five thousand-seat "Citizen's Stadium."[17]

While citizens and sports groups grew increasingly excited at the prospect of a stadium at Exhibition Park, the directors of the P.N.E. began to have second thoughts. From the plans, it was clear that the stadium would destroy the driving range. At a special meeting with City Council, the P.N.E. directors noted that going ahead would mean the loss of the $30,000 invested in the range and would as well probably force the closure of the public golf course. Much more important, it could threaten the association's financial viability. On the positive side was the prospect of profit from the management of the stadium and the fact that the P.N.E. had an obligation to assist with such an important civic event. Feigning greater reluctance than they actually felt, the Board of Control passed a motion declaring that "the Pacific National Exhibition agree to the request of the British Empire

Games Society to provide our Driving Range area for the erection of a Stadium for the Games and agree to assume the responsibility for Stadium operation and management after the Games, provided the Stadium will be a properly finished building, attractively landscaped with all necessary services and free of all encumbrances." In addition, the P.N.E. requested that additional lands south of Hastings Street be provided for parking and that City Council agree to back the association's by-law then being presented to the ratepayers.[18]

With the necessary agreements finally in place, design and construction could begin on a facility that was now expected to cost $1.25 million. The stadium was to be funded jointly by the British Empire Games Society and the City of Vancouver, with the former providing $500,000 and the latter approaching the ratepayers for permission to borrow the remainder. The Pacific National Exhibition was not totally satisfied with the arrangement, particularly since they were afraid that they might lose the by-law request for $1 million for the B.C. Building as a result. A strenuous publicity campaign directed towards conquering the "danger on election day . . . of over-confidence and apathy" was launched in support of the P.N.E. by-law.[19] These efforts were successful, and the by-law for Exhibition Park received a solid 73 per cent favourable vote, while the request for stadium financing similarly received more than two-thirds of the ballots cast.[20]

With financing for both buildings secured, attention could now be focused on the construction of the structures. Late in November, the Board of Control received the unexpected news that the stadium would require far more land than initially thought, forcing the P.N.E. to surrender a considerable portion of the golf course. Original plans were hastily revised and a new series of proposals were brought forward, ranging in cost from $1.25 million to $1.4 million. Attempts to keep costs down led to a number of other changes in the original design, including alterations in the size of the roof, elimination of dressing rooms, and, most important to the crowds which later filled the stadium, a major reduction in the capacity of the lavatory facilities.[21]

Construction finally began and on 25 June 1953, barely one year before the games were scheduled to begin, Percy Williams, the two-time Olympic champion sprinter, turned the first sod. Although it was completed on time, there were more than the expected number of delays. The "natural site" for the stadium, a depression in the southeast corner of the park, proved to be a poor selection. The generally unstable land caused frequent difficulties both before and after completion, but never more so than in March 1954, when it was noted that the nearly completed south side of the stadium appeared to be sinking.[22] It was the portent of things to come, in the long run hasty planning and last-minute financially motivated revisions in design were serious errors. It meant that maintenance and renovation costs would continually mount.

One final matter had to be settled — the name of the new stadium. The P.N.E.'s Board of Directors planned to use "Empire Stadium" during the games, and then change it to "Exhibition Bowl."[23] The action spurred considerable controversy and the *Vancouver Daily Province* even held a competition to select a more appropriate name. Dismissing such suggestions as Totem or Evergreen Bowl, the association decided to retain Empire Stadium.[24] Attention was now placed where it properly belonged, on the games themselves.

Officially opened on Friday, 30 July 1954 at a gala celebration in Empire Stadium, the games ran through to 7 August at various locations in the city. The P.N.E. hosted the opening and closing ceremonies and the track and field events at Empire Stadium, and other facilities on the grounds were in operation during the games. The Exhibition Forum, with a seating capacity of 6,650, was the site for the boxing matches, while weightlifting competitions were held a short distance away in the Garden Auditorium. The highlight of the games, and one of the most memorable moments in sports history, occurred in Empire Stadium in the finals of the one-mile race. The first man to break the four-minute mile, Roger Bannister was challenged by Australian Frank Landy. The contest was a classic confrontation, with Bannister pulling ahead in the stretch and with both competitors breaking the four-minute barrier. In all, the British Empire Games were a major success for Vancouver and, more directly, for the Pacific National Exhibition.

The new facilities and the increasingly business-first attitude of the P.N.E. led to a substantial expansion of year-round activities. Since the first days of the exhibition, various sports, cultural groups, and commercial interests had rented the facilities when they were not in use. Sports had been a feature at Hastings Park since the 1890's and the opening of Vancouver's first race track, but they had seldom served as major attractions. In the 1950's, however, Vancouver, and particularly the P.N.E., began to expand as a professional sports centre.

Professional hockey had been hosted off and on at Exhibition Park from the opening of the Forum Building in 1930. Since it held only 3,500 spectators, the facility could not attract a major league team. Repeatedly shunned by the National Hockey League, Vancouver did obtain a franchise in the Pacific Coast Hockey League, a forerunner of the Western Hockey League. Named the Vancouver Canucks, the hockey team proved to be a valuable source of income and the P.N.E. held the right to first refusal should the owners of the team decide to sell. The arrangement with the Canucks indicates something of the emerging business character of the association. In 1951, for example, it was decided not to sponsor amateur hockey in the Forum for the debatable reason that "amateur hockey might harm the attendance at the professional hockey and might not be worthwhile." The bottom line for the P.N.E. seemed to be profit maximization and not community service.[25]

In 1954, owner Coleman Hall made public his intention to sell a half-interest in the team, and the P.N.E. agreed to purchase a share of the franchise. To conduct the transfer, a complex and confusing arrangement was worked out. First, Vancouver Ventures Limited was formed, with the exhibition association and Coleman Hall as the only partners. The new company purchased the franchise from Hall who, in a surprising and never adequately explained move, was then given a contract to manage the Forum.[26] The agreement, which brought considerable profit to Hall, was reached with a larger purpose in mind. By controlling the only professional hockey franchise in Vancouver, the Pacific National Exhibition believed it could see that the city was awarded a National Hockey League franchise. And having intimate ties with the Canucks made the association confident that it had secured the upper hand in the ongoing negotiations for a civic coliseum. The hockey team was the P.N.E.'s trump card; it could claim that any arena built anywhere but at Exhibition Park would have to function without professional hockey.

For a long time, hockey was the only professional sport of any magnitude in the city, but Canadian football also came to Vancouver in this period. Previous attempts to have Vancouver included in the Western Interprovincial Football League had been unsuccessful. But with Empire Stadium Vancouver was to have one of the finest facilities in Canada. Early in 1953, Vancouver's request for entry into the league was accepted, although the team was not scheduled to begin operations until the 1954 season. In August 1954 a contract was reached between the P.N.E. and the city's entry, the B.C. Lions Football Club.[27] The arrangement with the Lions, an arms-length contract which saw the P.N.E. take no financial interest in the operation of the team, stood in marked contrast to the agreement with the Canucks. Since there was a suitable stadium already in place at Exhibition Park, the P.N.E. saw no direct benefit from involving itself in its tenants' financial affairs. Another notable prospect opened up by the arrival of Canadian football in Vancouver was the possibility that the Grey Cup Game, the annual final in Canadian football, and up to this time firmly entrenched in Central Canada, could be held on the west coast.

The years from 1947 to 1954 saw the Pacific National Exhibition not only continue its traditional non-fair activities, such as horse racing,[28] commercial shows and amateur sports, but also expand into new areas. The association was still set upon broadening its revenue base and lessening its financial dependence upon the annual fair. However, as the P.N.E. adopted a business-like stance and attempted to operate at optimum fiscal efficiency, such concerns as public access and community service were set aside in favour of fiscal gain.

While these major changes in activities at Exhibition Park were taking place, the exhibition association was not prepared to discard its status as an agricultural show piece. When the provincial government imposed a 17.5 per cent amusement tax on the exhibition in 1952, the P.N.E. claimed that it was really an agricultural fair and went to Victoria to request a special dispensation. The tax was subsequently reduced to 5 per cent, even though the minister of finance had not been overly impressed with the P.N.E.'s position. Similarly, when the B.C. deputy attorney general gave notice that the province would no longer allow the advance sale of tickets for the exhibition, the P.N.E.'s main "insurance policy," representatives of the association scurried off to Victoria and later to Ottawa in an attempt to secure an exemption. On both these occasions and during the debate over the location of the civic coliseum the Pacific National Exhibition repeatedly reverted to its claim for special status as an agricultural fair. In this period, however, governments were taking a firmer look at their fairs' policy, and, at least in the case of the provincial administration, they were not overly sympathetic to the P.N.E.'s[29] pleas for special consideration.

Other important North American exhibitions were also becoming more professional, and fair management was becoming increasingly complex. The "seat of the pants" operations conducted by the pre-World War II directors were no longer appropriate to the magnitude of operations in the 1950's. Recognition of the growing importance of fair management came in 1946, when the Western Fair Association, an international west coast organization, established an Annual College of Fairs in California. The P.N.E. manager and several directors attended the five-day course, which was designed to introduce the participants to the mechanics of the exhibition and to keep them abreast of changes in amusements, displays, techniques of exhibiting, crowd control, management of facilities, and long-term planning.[30]

The P.N.E. also maintained its membership in regional fair associations, such as the Western Canada Association of Exhibitors, Western Fairs Association, and the B.C. Fairs Association, continuing to use them primarily as a vehicle for arranging exhibition circuits and contracting amusement companies and entertainment operators.[31] Aware of its steadily improving status as one of North America's largest fairs, the P.N.E. noted: "the Pacific National Exhibition, or the other major exhibitions, should set their dates and the smaller fairs in the province should then group their dates around our Exhibition."[32] Eager for international recognition, the P.N.E. would hardly allow small regional fairs to influence the selection of dates. The crucial West Coast circuit was another matter, however, and in 1950 the association agreed to permanently entrench its exhibition in the eleven days surrounding the September 1st weekend.[33] The P.N.E. clearly aspired to match the size, scope, and status of the Los Angeles, Dallas, and Toronto exhibitions.

Less noticeable perhaps than the physical changes, the changes to the management and content of the annual fair were no less important. Professionalism changed the focus of the annual exhibition, and the fair was no longer the sole "raison d'être" of the P.N.E. With most of the major sporting teams playing out of Exhibition Park, and with various cultural and business organizations renting space at other than fair-time, the P.N.E. appeared to many to be the entertainment centre of Vancouver and British Columbia.

The citizens welcomed the expanded role of the P.N.E.; attendance rose at the fair, and ratepayers seconded the expansion plans of the association through their resounding support for the 1952 by-law request for $1 million. When the

P.N.E. agreed to accept the British Empire Games stadium at Exhibition Park, their stock in the community rose even higher. At a time when the image of Vancouver was clearly at stake, many thought it fitting that the major showcase of the event be built in conjunction with one of the city's most progressive organizations.

In the seven years between the first post-war fair and 1954, the exhibition had emerged with an established direction and a commitment to the future. Public response was consistently favourable, except for the controversy over the location of the civic auditorium complex. Even then, however, it appeared by the spring of 1954 as though the issue had been resolved in favour of the P.N.E. These had clearly been banner years for the Pacific National Exhibition, and the organization faced the post-Empire Games era confident that it enjoyed substantial civic backing for its plans for the continued re-orientation of the annual fair and the redevelopment of Exhibition Park. The next six years were to prove how quickly that support could dissipate.

9

Fall From Favour, 1954-1960

With the completion of the British Empire Games and an overwhelmingly successful 1954 exhibition when a record 870,000 fairgoers visited Exhibition Park, the Pacific National Exhibition had put behind it the difficulties associated with re-establishing the fair after the Second World War. A "new look" P.N.E., stressing entertainment and amusements and laying claim to being Canada's great showcase on the Pacific rim had been brought forth to replace the more narrowly focused exhibition of the inter-war period. Buoyed by the enthusiastic public response to its new endeavours, the P.N.E. assumed a new confidence in its dealings with the city and various levels of government that, at times, seemed to border on arrogance. The altered presentation and the evolving attitude did not generate antipathy in Vancouver. Nevertheless, while the public generally lauded the P.N.E.'s continuing attempts to restructure the exhibition programme and continued to support the fair after 1954, new problems could be identified on the horizon.

As the P.N.E. expanded its year-round activities and pursued a vigorous expansion programme, an important transition in the public perception of the P.N.E. was underway. In the public mind, the exhibition association was becoming disassociated from the annual fair. Until this time, largely as a result of the activities and orientation of the Vancouver Exhibition Association, the yearly exhibition and the management of Exhibition Park had been inseparable; it was impossible to attack one without criticizing the other. But as the P.N.E. became synonymous not only with the fair, but also with professional hockey and football, horse-racing, and a wide variety of year-round operations, it became easier to differentiate between the two. It was this distinction which allowed the annual exhibition to enjoy continued public support at the entrance gates, with attendance rising as high as 963,000 by 1960, at a time when the association itself was coming increasingly under attack.

Developments at the fair up to 1961 followed essentially along the lines adopted since 1947 — an increase in attractions and entertainment, with a series of additions designed to stimulate even greater public interest in the fair. The circus remained the headline act, although the attraction was usually supplemented with other performers, including a "Water Follies" presentation in the Forum in 1959. Several other features were also added; in 1959, for example "Old MacDonald's Farm," a petting zoo for small children, was opened under the sponsorship of Super Valu Stores, as was a trackless train providing transportation around the exhibition grounds. In 1960, the P.N.E. staged a Timber Carnival, consisting of competitions between a number of local lumberjacks exhibiting the skills of the forest. The carnival was one of the "outstanding successes" of that year's fair and, although it had been conceived as a once only event, the Timber Carnival was soon to reappear as one of the free feature attractions.[1]

New attractions were not always greeted so positively, and several of the events staged at Exhibition Park reflected poorly on the P.N.E. During the 1954 fair, a local jeweller sought permission to stage a complete wedding ceremony on the grounds. The suggestion elicited considerable criticism, and moved one director to argue that the "whole plan is undignified and makes a mock of the marriage ceremony."[2] The original plan called for the bride to wear $1 million in jewels, for the event to take place in the jeweller's exhibit booth, and for the newlyweds to then go to the Outdoor Stage to display their accoutrements. The P.N.E. eventually buckled under public pressure and refused to allow the cere-mony to take place. They did, however, agree to rent the Outdoor Stage to the jeweller and, after the couple had been married outside the grounds, they were allowed to proceed to the stage where they exhibited their finery before a large and enthusiastic audience.[3]

A second public faux pas occurred under the glare of the national spotlight. In 1959, Prime Minister John Diefenbaker agreed to open the exhibition officially. The whole programme was reminiscent of Laurier's appearance at the 1910 exhibition, when the prime minister was booed by spectators viewing a horse race and the whole event degenerated into a near riot. The P.N.E.'s elaborate plans for Diefenbaker began to come unstuck when it was discovered that the reins for the horse-drawn carriage in which he was to ride to the grandstand had been stolen and substitutes had to be hastily secured. Next, as Diefenbaker was ushered forward to make his grand entrance, the organizer found to his dismay, that a motorcycle aerial act was still in progress, and the crowd's attentions were clearly focused on that performance. Any hope of restoring order finally disappeared when the crowd rose to sing the national anthem at the request of the public address announcer, and it was discovered that the band had already left. In good humour, Diefenbaker was not overly distressed by the mismanagement and successfully carried off the opening ceremonies. These temporary embarrassments, however, detracted little from the generally favourable response to the fair.[4]

There were no significant changes in either the agricultural or industrial segments of the programme in this period. Among the structures, the B.C. Building and attached exhibit wings were proving less than satisfactory. The complex had not been designed to maximize pedestrian circulation, and exhibitors became increasingly critical of the poor traffic flow. Attempts were made to improve attendance, including the offering of special prizes for fairgoers who ventured into the buildings, but the structures continued to be a major disappointment and concern to the management of the fair.[5]

If the content of agricultural and industrial exhibits changed little, there was at least one important change in display technique. Displays such as the Pacific Food Carnival, which featured commercial producers distributing small samples of their merchandise, were prominent attractions at the fair. Two similar displays, B.C. Products Group and "Show Window" give out samples of new items, including ceramic lamps and such innovations as soft drinks in cans.[6] While in themselves only minor additions to the fair, these sample booths signalled a major shift in the orientation of the displays. It was becoming increasingly popular to provide samples of products, particularly in the agricultural departments. These exhibits were run by large-scale processors, but they did set an example for the various farming organizations also active at the exhibition. Within a decade, the sample booth would become the order of the day for the marketing associations, serving not only to indicate the quality of produce, but also to educate the public in the possible use of the commodities.

Although the livestock exhibits retained their traditional competitive format, they also underwent minor revisions in this period. As the fair expanded, first to eleven days and then, in 1958, to fourteen, it became increasingly difficult to convince livestock exhibitors to keep their animals at the P.N.E. for the duration of the show. Stockbreeders who wanted to display the animals in more than one exhibition or who were concerned about the high cost of feed for the two-week period, resorted to removing the cattle from the grounds contrary to the competition regulations. Recognizing the exhibitors' difficulties, the Pacific National Exhibition reconciled the problem by splitting the show, with the competitions for individual breeds and in particular classes running for only a portion of the exhibition. Only two sections of the livestock show, heavy horses and dairy classes, were present for the entire fair, and they were the highest profile breeds, the animals that drew the greatest attention. This device once more underlines the priorities of fair organizers and suggests the true status of agriculture at the new fair. By keeping the two classes most demanded by the fairgoers, they could maintain the façade of a true agricultural fair. Otherwise, agricultural competitions retained their now traditional secondary role in the exhibition.[7]

In addition to these changes, the P.N.E. also made modifications to coincide with local or provincial celebrations. In 1958, for example, several special attractions were added to the programme as the exhibition association's way of participating in British Columbia's Centennial. The focus of the P.N.E.'s efforts on this occasion was a mysterious "Project X."[8] The proposal was kept secret until the eve of the fair, when it was revealed that the attraction was a display of modern rocketry. The highlight of the show was a large standing rocket, complete with simulated blast off. Other displays included a Space Science club run by the Canadian Legion, a fifty-foot high American army missile, and earth satellites. A presentation by the Canadian army rounded out the attraction. Centennial activities were not restricted to "Project X" and included a ski-jump display in Empire Stadium as well as various minor attractions. The Centennial Committee, operators of the ski-jump, had to build a large tressel-like structure to hold the ramp, but they expected to recoup their expenses through the sale of admission tickets. However, the ski-jump and, to a lesser extent, Project X were major disappointments, attracting small paying crowds which hardly justified the expenses incurred. While these new shows were unsuccessful, the centennial year was an overall success, drawing a record 924,000 patrons to the expanded fourteen-day exhibition.[9]

To continue this 1950's format, it was necessary to come up continually with new feature attractions. Meeting this challenge created an important new departure in the structure and direction of the annual fair. It was agreed that while the core of the exhibition would remain unaltered from year to year, the adoption of an annual theme would allow for a regular change in special attractions and permit the "Chairmen of Committees to build around a central theme that will be in keeping with the tone of the whole fair while still allowing the committee members free rein for their imagination and also aid in giving a new appeal and new look to the Exhibition."[10] Rigorous guidelines were suggested for the selection of a suitable focus; the theme would have to be adaptable to the Exhibition Park facilities, help commercial departments by encouraging industrial exhibitors, lend itself well to new and different free attractions, and allow for suitable decorations. With the new approach, the P.N.E. could assume a "new face and new dress" each year, ensuring greater publicity and raising the stature of the exhibition.[11]

The P.N.E. was not alone in making this move. Marketing the exhibition did become more and more important, but the exhibition association's involvement with other North American fair organizations no doubt also influenced the decision to move to a central theme. Like several other innovations designed to market and "modernize" the fair, it followed closely on the heels of the P.N.E.'s participation in the College of Fairs.

A "Salute to the Pacific" was chosen for the first year, 1959, and the Pacific National Exhibition attempted to interest Pacific Rim countries in hosting displays. In concept, the plan was wide-ranging, encompassing not only trade and industrial exhibits, but also displays and attractions depicting the social and cultural life of the various nations. The first attempt at organizing the exhibition around a single theme nearly proved disastrous. Representations were made to a number of countries, including India, Thailand, Cambodia, Japan, Hong Kong, Korea, and South Vietnam, and initial indications were that most would attend. As the fair approached, however, many countries backed out, leaving the P.N.E. with a thematic fair but few relevant exhibits. In the last ten weeks before the exhibition, however, several nations recanted and agreed to provide attractions, as did a number of ethnic groups within the City of Vancouver. Although the first attempt had generated more than its share of headaches, the use of a single annual theme promised a wide range of organizational advantages, and from 1959 on the association selected a central focus for its fair.[12]

Not all efforts to revise or expand the exhibition proved so successful. One spectacular rejection of a P.N.E. move to expand the fair occurred in 1960–61 and centred on the association's attempt to temporarily take over control of New Brighton Park. This 10.6-acre park, located just north of the exhibition grounds on the shores of Burrard Inlet, seemed ideally suited for the association's 1961 fair. The theme for that year was "Maritime Festival," and the P.N.E. planned to hold boat races and stage a historical pageant in the waters off New Brighton Park beach. The Parks Board agreed to the use of the park,[13] and the association proceeded with further planning for the event but they had miscalculated local reaction. East end residents, led by the Cassiar Ratepayer's Association, moved to prevent the use of the property, arguing that: "The Pacific National Exhibition is continually encroaching on this district and commercializing it. They have developed it with complete disregard for the residential area."[14] A special committee of the P.N.E. tried to placate area residents by assuring them they would have complete and unimpeded access to the park during the fair.[15] Despite this conciliatory attitude, the P.N.E. condemned what they saw as narrow-minded criticism. In a public statement, General Manager Morrow asked: "Why is it when anyone comes forward with an idea which means progress they are immediately assailed by small-minded individuals who love to vilify anything constructive?"[16] In the end area residents won, leading the P.N.E. to decide that the project was not worth the problems incurred. Plans for the Maritime Festival were scaled down from a grandiose regatta on Burrard Inlet to a relatively minor boat show staged in Exhibition Park on a lake formed by flooding the Livestock Bowl.[17] More important than the loss of the festival was what this controversy signalled about the relationship between the P.N.E. and the east end of Vancouver. For the first time since the inception of the fair fifty years earlier, the residents and the association had become embroiled in a bitter conflict. Even though the matter was settled in favour of local interests, the citizens of the east side were becoming increasingly suspicious of the designs of the Pacific National Exhibition. What the association saw as progress was viewed as rampant commercialism by many residents and the groups appeared headed on a collision course. All previous controversies involving the P.N.E. had been city-wide. In the New Brighton Park conflict the association found its most severe critics right at its doorstep for the first time, and the debate foreshadowed more serious problems in the future.

One further development in the annual fair programme of the 1950's is worthy of note. Late in 1954, the federal government moved to restrict the use of advance ticket sales at fairs across Canada. Used traditionally as rain insurance, these sales provided the P.N.E. with approximately $200,000 annually. It was not the tickets themselves but the prizes attached to them that were declared illegal. The P.N.E. decided to proceed with the sale in 1955 without the lottery, and the number of tickets purchased dropped from 218,000 to only 90,000. To compensate for the loss, the P.N.E. countered by adding a list of prizes to the programme sold to guide fairgoers through the exhibition. Attempts to secure a re-interpretation of the law banning the advance sale were unsuccessful, but as the souvenir programme sale became equally remunerative, the association did not carry its protest on long. The programme concession was allocated to the Vancouver Ventures Limited, a P.N.E. subsidiary, until the company was dissolved in 1959. At that time, the management of the programme concession revolved to the exhibition association itself, and a committee was established to oversee marketing and promotion.[18]

While the period from 1955 to 1961 saw considerabe change in the content of Vancouver's annual fair, the organization in charge of the programme was also being modified. Although the alterations were not dramatic, they mark an important stage in the evolution of the association. The Pacific National Exhibition and its predecessor the Vancouver Exhibition Association had worked under essentially the same constitution since the 1908 incorporation of the V.E.A. As President Moffitt said in 1955, "The charter of 1908 under which we are operating is like an old suit of clothes — we need new ones for 1955. We propose the same type of charter held by the Canadian National Exhibition and other non-profit exhibitions." He went on to state, "No radical departures are proposed, it is just a face lifting of the old constitution."[19] Actually, the proposals were more sweeping than Moffitt intimated and Alderman T. R. Orr and City Solicitor R. K. Baker, in a report on the P.N.E.'s plans, claimed that the alterations would allow the association to borrow money, acquire property, mortgage assets, and lease facilities, all without council's approval.[20]

There was as well some rather vigorous opposition from another quarter to the P.N.E.'s proposed constitutional reform. Ben Morley of the Building Service Employees Union commented strongly on the changes, calling the association's action "a pretty piece of skullduggery" and claiming that the union "should oppose strongly a private company taking it [Hastings Park] over. It is commercialized to the point where it is no longer a Park."[21] Public clamour increased as the Trades and Labour Council joined in voicing its concern over what it saw as the "privatization" of the exhibition association and the perceived loss of public control over Exhibition Park. The growing fear was that the P.N.E.'s proposals were too extensive and that the association was attempting to garner too much power and control for itself.[22]

Meetings between the P.N.E. and City Council led to some modifications in the two positions. As finally enacted, the new constitution included a few revisions in the organization of the P.N.E. and some minor changes in the powers of the association. The Board of Control was renamed the Board of Directors, with the group formerly bearing that title becoming the Board of Governors. The Board of Directors, which served as the management of the P.N.E., was composed of eighteen elected directors selected from among the membership, advisory directors who counted among their number all city councillors and anyone who had served more than fifteen years as a director, as well as an undetermined number of appointed directors. This latter group was intended to ensure appropriate occupational representation on the board, with the constitution declaring that: "the Board shall, as far as the same is practicable, select such additional directors to be representative of the agricultural and other industries not already represented by the elective directors."[23] The Board of Governors served strictly an advisory capacity and included among its members the premier and government ministers, all the mayors and reeves in the province, and other individuals as desired by the P.N.E. Membership on this board was strictly honorary with few powers or privileges.

City Council retained the right of final approval over all P.N.E. borrowing and land acquisitions. In all, the 1955 constitution did not significantly alter the duties and powers of the Pacific National Exhibition's members and directors, and those organizational changes which did occur were largely cosmetic. Even the stated objectives of the association retained their traditional form: "to encourage and promote the welfare of the agricultural and other industries of the country, and matters having to do with civic improvement generally and other matters or things having a civic, national, patriotic, scientific, agricultural, artistic, educational, social, recreational, or sporting character, or any other object, except profit useful or beneficial to the people generally, and to provide facilities for the same."[24] With such an omnibus declaration, almost any legal activity could come under the P.N.E.'s umbrella, thus assuring the association wide latitude in the management of the Exhibition Park grounds and facilities.

The 1955 constitution placed considerable emphasis on agriculture, but it was extremely careful not to limit the association to that single aspect. Although the P.N.E. could confidently declare in 1958 that "We are an agricultural fair and will always remain so. We are a member of the great family of fairs throughout the Province, across the dominion and across the border."[25] it was clear that the P.N.E. could legally become what it wished, retaining or eliminating agriculture, expanding or contracting commercial aspects, highlighting or downplaying amusements.

Though the arrangements had obvious advantages for the management, it made it very difficult for the public, and at times for the directors, to know exactly what the focus of the exhibition was to be.

A major concern in the aftermath of the debate over the new constitution was the question of membership. Some felt that public involvement remained distressingly low, and it was suggested that the fees be lowered "to broaden the opportunity for membership and get more people interested in PNE."[26] Finding support in the example of Toronto's Canadian National Exhibition, the majority of the directors decided on the opposite tack, restricting the entrance of people into the organization to prevent the membership from becoming "more unwieldy than the one we have at the present time." A further examination of the membership practice of exhibition associations in Regina, Edmonton, Calgary, Texas, and California found that they were also restrictive. Even those individuals who troubled to penetrate the association found their powers circumscribed. Under the constitution, for example, the eighteen elective directors were far outnumbered by the advisory and appointed directors, with the result that effective control of the fair lay in the hands of non-elected officers.[27]

P.N.E. subsidiaries such as Vancouver Ventures Limited also expanded. The company was given not only the contract to manage the Canucks and the Forum Building, but also exclusive rights to handle the lucrative sale of prize programmes during the fair. Two years after its formation, Coleman Hull sold his equity, an interest that had cost him three dollars, to the P.N.E. for $75,000. The company continued to operate until December 1959, but its establishment, its rather unusual functions, and particularly the dubious relationship with Hull was to become the focus for considerable debate in 1961, when the P.N.E. became embroiled in a major conflict with City Council. A second subsidiary, Tyroe Estates, established in 1959, was to act simply as an agent for the P.N.E. in negotiations for the purchase of property on the west side of Cassiar Street. The association feared that if its role in the transactions became widely known the asking price for the properties would skyrocket. And, indeed, when the ownership of Tyroe Estates was made public in April 1961, the firm lost its effectiveness and it was quickly dissolved.[28]

To provide a firmer financial base, the P.N.E. directors moved repeatedly to expand year-round activities. Major entertainment events continued to be staged on the grounds, the highlight undoubtedly being the 1957 performance by Elvis Presley in Empire Stadium. The show attracted 22,000 adoring fans and degenerated into a near riot as Elvis "rocked the kids into such a frenzy of joy that they nearly kicked each other to death." In the aftermath of the concert, it was generally agreed that Elvis and his "wriggling songs" would never be allowed back to Exhibition Park.[29] Other one-time events staged in P.N.E. facilities included a "warehouse sale" held by Wosk's Department Stores in the Showmart Building in 1958, one of the first retail shows held on the grounds.[30]

In addition to the growing number of single occasion events, the P.N.E. also began a search to encourage more permanent users. The Vancouver School Board became a valued tenant, renting a series of buildings for use as a welding school, an aeronautical school, and for other vocational education purposes. Even apparently non-productive areas such as the Swine Building were occupied; this particular facility was leased by B.C. Packers for storage. The Vancouver Police Academy also became a temporary tenant at the P.N.E., renting space in the new Administration Building for a training school. The P.N.E. seemed particularly well suited as the site for a permanent police school, especially since plans were being formulated for the establishment of a metropolitan police force, and negotiations were begun to arrange for permanent quarters for the academy. The plan for permanent facilities, like those for an area-wide police force, fell by the wayside, but for a time the Police Academy was a valued tenant in what otherwise would have been an underused building.[31]

The most important single tenant secured by the P.N.E. in this period was the B.C. International Trade Fair. Established and financed by the B.C. Department of Trade and Industry to co-incide with the 1958 centennial, the fair was intended to "emphasize the importance of import and export trade in the development of British Columbia by providing central facilities for foreign exhibitors to exhibit their products."[32] The 1958 show returned a satisfactory $29,000 to the P.N.E.[33] Suffering from a lack of preparation time and being perhaps overly ambitious in conception, the fair was not as satisfactory to the government. Businessmen, however, approved of the venture, noting that it served as "a challenge to our B.C. Manufacturers," and would "provide opportunity for local manufacturers now to meet foreign buyers as well as to observe the quality of competition they face in the markets of the world."[34] Spurred on more by the potential than by the success of the first International Trade Fair, the Department of Industrial Development, Trade and Commerce decided in 1959 to hold yet another show, this one scheduled for April to May 1961.[35]

By far the greatest non-fair activities held at Exhibition Park were the professional sports events, particularly hockey, football, and horse-racing. From 1956, the Pacific National Exhibition was the sole owner of the Vancouver Canucks, although the association retained former partner Coleman Hall as general manager until 1961. When Hall's term expired, the P.N.E. established a special committee to handle the club.[36] The P.N.E.'s ownership of the hockey franchise did not pass without controversy; a number of prominent civic politicians, most notably Alderman Frank Fredrickson, saw the relationship simply "as a trump card in the decision as to where the city should build an all-purpose coliseum."[37] The fact that the association continued to operate the team, despite increasing deficits, poor on-ice performances, and declining attendance, suggests that Fredrickson was not far off the mark.

The B.C. Lions Football club was more profitable for the P.N.E. The Lions, in fact, were eager to improve and expand Empire Stadium, lending money to the P.N.E. at one per cent interest to allow for the construction of end-zone bleachers and an extension of the west side roof. Having the Lions on site brought additional events to the P.N.E., the most important being the 1955 and 1958 Grey Cup matches. Empire Stadium was one of the largest facilities of its type in Canada, but to secure the 1958 Grey Cup game the P.N.E. was still forced to reduce its "final" offer substantially to defeat a competitive bid entered for Toronto's Varsity Stadium. The most contentious issue concerning the Lions and the exhibition association centred on the football club's demand for exclusive rights to the stadium. In 1960, a group of local businessmen led by Peter Graham attempted to secure an American Football League franchise for Vancouver and had designs on the P.N.E.'s largest facility. The P.N.E. therefore attempted, although they did not press the matter with much vigour, to convince the Lions to sign a contract with no guarantee of exlusive rights. The club not surprisingly rejected the suggestion, and a number of city aldermen questioned the propriety of the P.N.E.'s action. The A.F.L. issue then died quickly.[38]

Horse-racing continued at Exhibition Park, and the Jockey Club's unusual relationship with the Pacific National Exhibition was unchanged. They paid a yearly rental and a percentage of the parimutuel take for the use of the property, and constructed and maintained all racing and stabling facilities. Although the P.N.E. and the city were the nominal owners of the structures, both were completely excluded from the management of the track. Late in 1960, the Ascot Jockey Club merged with the B.C. Jockey Club, which had operated an annual slate of races out of Lansdowne Park in Richmond. The Lansdowne track was relegated to a training facility, and all lower mainland thoroughbred racing was concentrated on the P.N.E. grounds. Under the agreement, the number of racing days was expanded from 40 to between 74 and 80.[39] While the P.N.E. was not directly involved in the merger, it was of obvious benefit to the association since it ensured increased revenue from parking, parimutuel percentages, and lease arrangements.

The P.N.E. greeted this pattern of expansion and diversification with enthusiasm.[40] While the revenue base was shifting away from the fair, however, the association remained firm, at least publicly, about what it saw as its essential purpose. The exhibition remained paramount, the major focus for the association's endeavours, and all other activities were justified solely as a way of providing the revenue required to sustain the show. At the same time, however, the public no longer saw the P.N.E. as solely or even primarily an exhibition, let alone an agricultural fair. It was now an exhibition, a sports centre, and an entertainment site. While the P.N.E. could argue that it was remaining consistent with its principles, the association was becoming more of a facilities management organization, concerned primarily with filling existing structures with paying tenants and adding additional buildings.

Given the increased emphasis on renting the exhibition facilities throughout the year, the association decided to make the Garden Auditorium Committee responsible for locating suitable tenants. Similarly, the Executive Committee agreed to allow the general manager to hire a salesman exclusively to rent space in the Showmart Building.[41] All of these efforts manifest a recognition of the tenuous nature of annual fairs and are consistent with the "management" approach to fair operations that grew out of the immediate post-World War II period. In order to provide operating capital, to set aside money for future developments, and to keep the employee infrastructure needed for the exhibition, the buildings had to be used on a more regular basis. It would no longer serve to leave facilities empty if a profitable use could be found for them.

In the second half of the 1950's, there was also further construction. An early addition was a new Administration Building, opened in 1956 at a cost of approximately $270,000.[42] More important developments were, however, in the offing.

Happyland, the permanent amusement area long entrenched in the northwest corner of the grounds, was the first part of the grounds to undergo renovation. The move to reconstruct the carnival area was another of the P.N.E.'s recurring attempts to provide an amusement area that was at once profitable to the association and acceptable to the general public. In 1955, dissatisfied with the performance of the Pacific Amusement Company, the P.N.E. began to investigate the possibility of assuming the management of Happyland.[43] Two years later, in the midst of what was inappropriately called a "comprehensive development plan," the association decided to force the removal of the P.A.C. and relocate the amusement area. Two sites were considered: the northwest and the northeast sections of the park.[44] Initially, the P.N.E. decided on the northeast, planning to build the centre just north of Empire Stadium. After approving the application of a new firm, Burrard Amusements, to develop the area, the P.N.E. then opted for yet another site, this time between the stadium and the B.C. Building. Construction of Playland began in December 1957, and it was completed in time for the 1958 exhibition.[45] In the typically booster fashion characteristic of P.N.E. officials, President Ferguson noted that the new amusement park would be "one of the best" in North America.[46] Area residents were less enthusiastic, claiming that Playland would serve to attract the "hoodlum element" to the region.[47] The old Happyland suffered an ignominious end; it was completely razed by October 1957 and replaced by a parking lot. The rather haphazard manner in which a site was selected for Playland indicates how "comprehensive" the P.N.E.'s development plan really was. Construction on the grounds continued on an ad-hoc basis, with facilities erected whenever need was demonstrated and financing was available.

The development of Playland was, however, greatly overshadowed by the proposal to build a coliseum for Exhibition Park. The question had already generated considerable controversy in the city, though it had apparently been settled in the P.N.E.'s favour. After receiving council's support, the association turned its attention to the problem of financing the proposed $3 million structure. A committee led by directors Ferguson and Dunsmuir launched confidential negotiations with the federal and provincial governments. In initial meetings with Minister of Agriculture James Gardiner, they could only secure a promise of $200,000, although it was implied that if the P.N.E. could gain civic and provincial support, the federal authorities would doubtless raise their offer.[48] Next they went to City Council with a request for a $1 million by-law submission for December 1956.

The resulting campaign was bitter. The P.N.E. launched a massive blitz in support of the Exhibition Park proposal. Publicist Dorwin Baird orchestrated radio addresses, advertising in local papers, television spots, billboard signs, press conferences, and public meetings. As he stated a week before the vote was to be held, "The utmost has been done."[49] The P.N.E.'s opponents, led by the Downtown Business Association, who were pushing their own coliseum proposal, did not back away and presented an opposing campaign. The Technical Planning Board, a civic body charged with defining development priorities for Vancouver, joined the opposition to the P.N.E. and, on the eve of the vote, released a special report which was highly critical of the exhibition association's plans. Despite the board's protestations to the contrary, the P.N.E. was convinced that it was "part of an organized plan to upset the Coliseum by-law."[50] The electors demonstrated on voting day that they had not been swayed by the P.N.E.'s efforts, and the by-law secured only 42 per cent of the total vote. Adding insult to injury, the P.N.E. was then attacked for having expended public funds in an attempt to convince the citizens to spend their own money.[51]

The issue, however, was far from settled. The P.N.E. still emphatically declared that the exhibition needed a new building. The Downtown Business Association also gave notice that it was proceeding with plans for an arena in the city centre when they approached council with a request that a by-law for $3 million be submitted to the ratepayers in December 1957.[52] Within the P.N.E. there were suggestions that a different tactic might be adopted. Recognizing that both the federal and provincial governments had based their proposed grants at least publicly on the assumption that the building was to be used for agricultural exhibits, Dr. J. C. Berry, a director of the association, suggested that:

we should consider commencing for the erection of a coliseum type of building for the use of agriculture because . . . if by this means we could indicate our faith in what we are attempting to do and show the citizens evidence of our good will and intentions; having done this it should not be difficult to get the balance of the money particularly once the general public are made aware of our intentions and what we are proposing to do.[53]

The proposal was very simple: forget the plans to develop a major coliseum and focus instead on the immediate needs of the exhibition, namely a new livestock arena.

Meetings between the P.N.E. and the Vancouver Board of Trade resulted in an agreement to build two structures, a coliseum and a livestock arena, the latter to be placed at Exhibition Park. This arrangement hardly pleased the association, but they decided nonetheless to "proceed on the basis of doing currently what is possible within the money which we have in sight and expand if and when funds become available."[54] City Council also supported the new proposition, although they made it clear that their support was conditional upon the P.N.E. not turning the livestock arena into a multi-purpose facility.[55]

The P.N.E. quickly brought forward a proposal for an eight thousand-seat facility capable of housing between 150 and 200 horses and of being converted into an ice rink. With $1 million already offered by civic and federal governments and confident that additional funds would be forthcoming, the P.N.E. felt it could go ahead with the $1.5 million structure. Choosing the location seemed to be the only outstanding issue, but subsequent events were to prove that the directors' confidence had been misplaced.[56]

Although they acknowledged that including an ice rink turned the livestock arena into a multipurpose facility, the P.N.E. defended their decision to ignore council's restrictions, arguing that the city was capable of supporting two ice rinks.[57] Opponents reacted at once, claiming that the association was using the livestock building as a "subterfuge for a new sports arena"[58] and referring to the proposed building as a "monumental tomb for the frustrated wishes of the voting citizens."[59] City Council dissolved in acrimonious debate over the issue, but not before agreeing to withhold any financial support for the building until a specially appointed Citizen's Committee had had time to study the matter.[60]

The Pacific National Exhibition quickly retreated. The building reverted to a livestock arena; it was scaled down to 3,000 to 4,000 seats, and the ice rink was dropped. Having had to accept a building it did not really want, the P.N.E. decided not to commit any of its own money to the project, financing the structure on government grants alone. Chastened by the turn of events, the association even agreed to work with the supporters of a downtown arena and promised to move the Vancouver Canucks to the new building wherever it was located.[61]

In effect, the P.N.E. had been trapped by the contradictions inherent in their organization. Though they professed to be an agricultural fair and stated repeatedly that the arena was needed primarily as an exhibition showcase, the P.N.E. really wanted a home for their hockey team. They were being deliberately deceptive, and, too clever by half, the P.N.E. in the end got what they were publicly arguing for. It was a lesson they would not forget.

With the final designs calling for a 3,500-seat arena with a 230 by 100 foot ring, covered by a 50-foot high domed roof, to be built abutting the old livestock barns, the new building was much diminished from the proposals first brought forward in 1954. The $3 million budget, which included substantial P.N.E. fiscal involvement, was slashed to $1 million, with the association all but withdrawing from financial participation.[62]

More important than the forced reduction in the size of the arena was the negative effect the coliseum-arena controversy had on relations between the City Council and the Pacific National Exhibition. After the Empire Games, council and the association enjoyed a cordial and mutually supportive relationship, best evidenced by the aldermen's decision to back the P.N.E.'s coliseum proposal in 1954. During the next seven years the link was greatly eroded. The P.N.E. began to appear more and more autonomous, acting without the backing of City Council and sometimes undertaking projects and plans in direct opposition to the civic government. Soon a new dispute broke out which was to envelope all of the P.N.E.'s operations.

The question of the distribution of powers between council and the P.N.E. boiled to the surface. Trying to re-establish some control over what was ostensibly a civic body, council demanded the right to audit the association's books and to approve the yearly budget for capital expenditures. The P.N.E. directors agreed to allow the city auditors to serve as external auditors for the association, but refused the second request, offering to submit the budget for information, but not for approval. The conflict escalated from there, with council expanding its demands and the P.N.E. remaining adamant in defence of its autonomy. To strengthen their position, the aldermen made the $280,000 grant for the Livestock Arena conditional upon the P.N.E. agreeing to a list of special conditions, including a renegotiation of the Exhibition Park lease, that would allow council to approve the capital budget and have the city's auditors examine the association's financial records.[63]

Before the issue was finally settled, the various participants engaged in several rounds of name-calling and sabre-rattling. Thomas Campbell, a mayoralty candidate, questioned the connection between the P.N.E. and the Non-Partisan Association, a local political organization. Pointing in particular to the active roles played by P.N.E. directors John Dunsmuir, Mort Ferguson, and J. S. C. Moffitt in the N.P.A., Campbell claimed "that the interests of the taxpayers are being ignored and a private kingdom is built to satisfy the ego of the select few."[64] Other critics took broader swipes, questioning not only the political allegiances of the directors, but also the judiciousness, if not the legality, of such P.N.E. practices as not publishing tenders for certain projects and granting other contracts without calling for public bids[65] as well as the whole matter of the ownership and management of the Vancouver Canucks.

The debate continued into November, hitting a high point when the arena grant was withheld. A new P.N.E. president, Thomas Fyfe, was elected that month, and he began his tenure by declaring that "That Pacific National Exhibition should be a place for fun, not for politics.''[66] Fyfe quickly agreed to accede to council's requests. Budgets were to be submitted to the aldermen, and the lease was to be opened for renegotiation. Eager to be as conciliatory as possible, he stated that "Council is the senior body. It should have control over expenditures of public money. We want to have a harmonious relationship with Council from now on.''[67] The conflict seemed settled in November 1961. Still, it would be several years before the differences were finally reconciled and the ill-feeling generated by the controversy was tempered. The Pacific National Exhibition accepted the defeat somewhat philosophically. It was, after all, a civic body, and council did have legal control over the facilities and grounds. If anything, the conflict demonstrated the tenuous and unusual situation of the P.N.E., owning none of the buildings it managed yet existing as a semi-independent organization with only weak contractual links with the civic government.

This seven-year period, 1954 to 1961, which started on the positive euphoria surrounding the British Empire Games and a level of public acceptance unrivalled in its history, obviously ended much differently. The major legacy of the period, the livestock arena, was, perhaps an appropriate reminder, a building that the P.N.E. did not want in the form it finally assumed. Equally important was the power play with City Council. The exhibition association had lost, and the wounds would never entirely heal.

10

Politics of Change, 1960-1973

The bitter debate over the Pacific National Exhibition's new livestock arena had once again drawn the association into a significant civic controversy. As before, the P.N.E. emerged bruised but intact. More important, the apprehensions and antagonisms aroused were not readily soothed. Although the P.N.E. publicly adopted a conciliatory manner towards City Council, the contradictory division of powers and responsibilities between the association and the civic government ensured future flare-ups.

The decade from 1962 to 1972 was one of remarkable change for the Pacific National Exhibition, with major additions to the physical plant, expansion of year-round activities, significant alterations in the structure and content of the fair, and important shifts in public and government opinion concerning the association. Old trends, such as the increasing emphasis on entertainment, were confirmed and expanded, and new departures, including alterations in the agricultural component of the show, took place. As the fair was adapted to suit a changing urban environment, many former events and attractions were unceremoniously dropped, indicating the association's willingness to allow the exhibition to develop and change with the times.

Grandstand shows continued to draw publicity as the highlight of the annual exhibitions. However, the Shrine P.N.E. circus, part of the fair since the late 1940's, was dropped from the programme in 1967. Citing declining attendance, competition from the Stadium Show, and the need to renovate the seating arrangements in the Forum, the P.N.E. eliminated the circus in favour of an Oriental bazaar and revue. This new attraction, encompassing a stage show and a series of booths featuring Oriental craftsmen, food outlets, and manufacturers' displays, was not successful, and it was soon replaced with other features. The Shrine

Circus, on the other hand, was not forgotten and re-emerged as a significant non-fair-time event at Exhibition Park.[1]

Like the circus, the Empire Stadium Show fell on hard times as the 1960's progressed and in the winter of 1967-1968 the Attractions Committee even recommended scrapping the feature. The Board of Directors rejected the suggestion on this occasion, but the fact remained that the show was too expensive, and owing in large part to the stadium's out-of-the-way location, the expected audiences were simply not materializing. The completion of the new Pacific Coliseum in 1968 offered a way to solve the problem, and in 1969 it was decided to move segments of the Stadium Show to the new facility. With a more attractive setting, the P.N.E. could turn from its accustomed practice of offering free entertainment, as it had often done in Empire Stadium, to charging admission. The entertainment packages put together for the Coliseum shows, designated the "Star Spectacular," were far from being a sidelight to the exhibition, as its predecessor had occasionally been. The 1971 presentation, for instance, featured such international performers as Tom Jones, Ray Charles, the New Seekers, and Jimmie Rodgers, and Canadian attractions Anne Murray, the Irish Rovers and the R.C.M.P. Musical Ride. The annual show became a highly publicized media event designed to attract people to the exhibition and to provide the P.N.E. with additional revenue.[2]

The Pacific National Exhibition added a number of features in addition to the grandstand shows and the Star Spectacular designed to draw teenagers to the fairgrounds. For example, a teen dance was held in the Garden Auditorium in 1963. The dance represented a revival of an old programme, for the dance hall had been a prominent exhibition-time feature from the first years of the fair to the late 1940's. Two years after the dance was inaugurated, a separate "Teen-Fair" was opened in conjunction with the exhibition. Held in a cordoned-off area and run by a private interest, the attraction included disc jockeys, record sales, hair stylists, and other booths and displays of interest to teens. Teen-Age Fair Inc., the producers of the show, had staged similar events at other exhibitions, and the P.N.E. directors hoped the new feature would attract an increased number of teenagers to the fair. After two reasonably successful years, the directors decided that they no longer required the expertise of Teen-Age Fair Inc. Refusing to renew the company's lease in 1967, the P.N.E. went ahead with its own version of the teen fair, while the firm that had brought the concept to Vancouver was forced to set up shop in the Seaforth Armouries and run its show in direct competition with the exhibition. However, the P.N.E.'s Teen Fair proved somewhat less successful than its predecessor and the concept was soon dropped from the programme.[3]

One feature which remained popular throughout the period was the P.N.E.'s annual "lottery." Fair programmes containing tickets on a major draw were sold on the grounds, with the top prize usually being a "dream" home. The prize programme, instituted in the 1950's to replace the outlawed advance ticket sale, drew considerable annual attention, but never more so than in 1968. In that year, it was decided to offer a new prize, a $50,000 gold brick, in place of a home. For the winner, the prize was anything but a dream come true as she soon found herself embroiled in an acrimonious dispute with her husband, who claimed that the winning ticket was supposed to have been put in his name. In the end, the courts ruled that the lady was to split her winnings 50-50 with her estranged husband and the matter was finally laid to rest. The P.N.E., upset at the negative publicity, dropped the idea of a gold bullion prize and returned to offering the now traditional dream home.[4]

The theme format begun in the previous decade was applied with special vigour for Canada's centennial year fair. The P.N.E. actually began planning for the 1967 fair a full four years in advance. A committee was established in 1963 to select a theme and decide upon a project that would allow the participation of the exhibition association in concert with the federal, provincial and civic governments. Various proposals were brought forward, including a military tattoo, and a National Beard Growing Contest. A two-year plan was finally adopted, including a 1966 fair focusing on the province of British Columbia, to be followed the next year with a Centennial Exhibition highlighting the regions of Canada. A suitable focus offering a regional and national dimension was soon found. Recalling the exceedingly favourable public response to the Timber Carnival in 1960-1961, the P.N.E. decided to resurrect that theme and stage a B.C.-wide forestry contest in 1966 followed by a nation-wide "Festival of Forestry" in the Centennial year. The forestry theme was supplemented during 1967 with a Centennial Tattoo, a B.C. International Trade Fair, a Centennial Square Dancing Jamboree, and a Birthday Party staged in Empire Stadium on July 1. The 1967 exhibition which followed these presentations was an extravaganza of national pride, and the forestry theme proved so popular that it became a permanent part of the annual fair.[5]

Ironically, within a year of having hosted a centennial fair which celebrated national unity and harmony, the P.N.E. once again became embroiled in a public dispute. Perhaps it is not surprising that the often heated protest politics of the 1960's would affect the Pacific National Exhibition. Indeed, the 1965 parade had been interrupted by demonstrators attempting to confront Prime Minister Lester Pearson. But that incident paled in contrast to a 1968 controversy. The conflict centered around Regulation 25 in the P.N.E.'s manual of exhibition rules and regulations, a broadly worded passage which banned partisan political displays on the grounds. Under this provision, a series of groups including the B.C. Peace Council, Canadian Campaign for Nuclear Disarmament, Communist Party of Canada, and the Peoples' Cooperative Bookstore Association, were refused permission to exhibit in 1968. Representatives of the banned groups met with the P.N.E. directors and argued that the association was violating the United Nations Charter and preventing the implementation of programmes dedicated to world peace. The directors voted to retain the ban and declared that they would not back down. The protesters were not ready to give in and threatened to picket the fair. On the eve of the exhibition the P.N.E. capitulated, retaining its ban only on bona fide political parties. Embarrassed by the situation, and prodded by the B.C. Civil Liberties Association, the P.N.E. directors quickly agreed to drop the contentious Regulation 25 from the association's books.[6]

On its own volition or, as in the case of Regulation 25, pulled by outside forces, the Pacific National Exhibition was moving with the times and with the changing character of Vancouver and British Columbia. One major departure from past practice was the 1968 decision to open the exhibition on Sundays. As early as 1963, the P.N.E. had looked for ways of securing special dispensation to open for the entire week. When the Canadian National Exhibition in Toronto opened on Sunday for the first time in 1968, the P.N.E. was quick to approach City Council for the appropriate revisions in the by-law covering Sunday openings. Council acted swiftly on the request and on 11 December 1968 the required approval was granted. A few decades earlier, such a move would have touched off a charged public debate. In 1968, the issue passed with barely a murmur of public opposition.[7]

While the Pacific National Exhibition was willing to alter the exhibition to suit the changing needs and demands of the community, its ultimate concern for attendance had resulted in a remarkable conservatism when it came to the question of admission charges. Indeed as late as 1965, the standard adult entrance fee stood at 50 cents, the same as it had been in 1910. Confronted with a $14,000 deficit in 1965, it was finally decided to double the adult admission the following year. In an attempt to prevent a drop in attendance, the P.N.E. staged a series of free attractions on the grounds. The result was disappointing, with total attendance falling approximately 6,000 despite the added entertainment. Admission charges were again revised upwards only five years later, with the adult ticket increasing to $1.50 in 1971. Again, increased costs and declining revenues were cited as the reason for the change. The drop in attendance was more substantial on this occasion, but fell well short of the decline of 30,000 budgeted by the P.N.E. management. Both moves, in 1966 and 1971, significantly increased gate receipts without seriously harming attendance.[8]

Such changes in the annual fair did not represent substantive alterations in the focus or direction. In one area, however, there was substantial and important change. Legally and constitutionally, if not in the public's eye, the Pacific National Exhibition was an agricultural fair and most of its government assistance was derived from that fact. As the association's annual report noted in 1967, "Agriculture today plays an ever increasing role in the modern world and the Pacific National Exhibition is proud to present a showcase for agriculture on the Pacific Coast."[9] That showcase was not, however, a static object and it underwent a series of important revisions in this period.

A major alteration came in 1968 when the B.C. Federation of Agriculture opted for a different format in agricultural display. Named "Acres of Food," the exhibit included booths from a variety of agricultural producers' associations. Fairgoers were offered samples of the various products and were provided with special recipes. The first show, held in the Pacific Coliseum, did not draw as expected and the following year the whole display was moved to the Forum. The B.C.F.A. was pleased with the success of the venture at the new location and noted that all the groups participating, including the Milk, Broiler, Egg, Turkey, Mushroom, Oyster, Sheep, Vegetable, and Flower industries, were enthusiastic about the project. The sample booths proved to be particularly popular and it was recorded with a mixture of pleasure and astonishment that the mushroom booth alone had handed out over 1900 pounds of mushrooms.[32]

The intent of the agricultural show — to establish and expand markets for the agricultural products of British Columbian producers — had not changed, but the form of presentation had been altered. Sample booths and dispensing recipes to consumers represented a more sophisticated approach. The competitive displays of earlier years had similarly been designed to enhance consumer awareness of farm produce, but the agricultural associations were realizing that the old system was no longer adequate. Rather than focusing on competition, which placed an inappropriate emphasis on the individual producer, the various groups decided upon a collective marketing approach. The intention was still to encourage consumption of local products, but with the establishment of the "Acres of Food" concept the producers were displaying a willingness and ability to adopt modern and more relevant publicity techniques.

The federal government, long a backer of the competitive format, supported and even encouraged the shift in emphasis. The government urged that the new format respond to the fact that "the primary responsibility . . . is to the customer paying at the gate while the secondary responsibility is to the exhibitor." Anxious to encourage the development of "displays which will inform and impress the city and urban population of their dependence upon agriculture," the federal government allowed all exhibitions to use up to 20 per cent of their allotted prize moneys for agricultural displays and educational exhibits.[11]

On the surface the transformation was simple and, to some, insignificant. The move did, however, reconcile one of the outstanding contradictions of the urban agricultural fair: to many, the exhibition was in fact two shows, a carnival directed at the city dwellers and an agricultural competition aimed at rural farmers and producers who travelled to the city to compete in the "big money" city fair. The new emphasis on educational rather than competitive displays was actually an obvious means of achieving what had long been the P.N.E.'s stated goal. The fair was there, in theory, to educate urbanites in the ways and means of agriculture, to familiarize the city dweller with the use of farm produce, and to emphasize the continuing interdependence of city and country. The P.N.E. was not now, and indeed had never been, an agricultural fair in the traditional sense. Vancouver's exhibition did, however, have an agricultural fair as an important component of its programme, and it was repeatedly declared that the Pacific National Exhibition would remain as the meeting place for the urban residents and the farmers and livestock breeders of British Columbia.

Just as the structure and content of the annual fair underwent significant revisions between 1960 and 1973, so too did the Exhibition Park physical plant. This decade saw the completion of the contentious livestock arena, the construction of a sports coliseum, as well as a series of smaller projects. The P.N.E. directors continued to look to the future, albeit in a rather haphazard manner, as they brought forward a long list of development proposals for consideration.

The livestock arena, the first project undertaken in this decade, really started in the previous period. Discussion and debate leading up to the actual construction had begun early in the 1950's and had been largely responsible for the 1961 conflict between the P.N.E. and Vancouver City Council. With that controversy behind them, and city, province and federal governments committed to funding, the association went ahead with the $1,050,000 structure. Ready in time for the 1963 fair, the building was no sooner finished then it was discovered that interior acoustics were, to say the least, abominable. Indeed, reverberations within the dome-style building, or Agrodome as it had been christened, were so poor that City Council quickly agreed to provide $23,000 to improve the sound quality. Like most of the P.N.E. structures, the Agrodome had not been the result of extended planning and analysis. The hasty design was partly the product of public criticism faced by the association during the debate over the location of the civic sports arena. The building that emerged was functionally a one-use structure and had few non-fair time uses, especially as a P.N.E. plan to install an ice-sheet was vetoed by City Council. Having few uses, the building sat empty much of the year, a mute reminder of the P.N.E.'s surrender to political expediency in 1960-1961 and of the stubbornness of the association.[12]

Soon after construction of the new building was completed, the issue of the location of a civic sports coliseum resurfaced. The P.N.E. directors, arguing that "Inasmuch as a large segment of taxpayers, tenants, columnists and other ardent supporters of the Pacific National Exhibition, both within the City boundaries and in suburban areas, look to the Pacific National Exhibition to offer a plan for a sports arena . . .," formed a special sub-committee to review the matter.[13] The action immediately reopened the heated debate of four years before, although the response on this occasion was generally more favourable to the P.N.E. proposals. The association went out of its way to generate support, eliciting approval from groups favouring the Exhibition Park site, and holding meetings with the Vancouver Board of Trade, City Council, Downtown Business Association, and other civic groups to explain their plans. Council agreed to allow the P.N.E. to proceed, although they set some rather stringent conditions. The building had to be up to National Hockey League standards, able to accommodate 16,000 spectators, and be readily adaptable for exhibition and trade fair purposes. More importantly, the P.N.E. was given only three months, until 31 October 1965, to finalize all financial arrangements. If the association failed to meet that deadline, the P.N.E. was required to "agree to support the Vancouver City Council in any programme they may adopt to erect a similar structure at any other location within the boundaries of the City of Vancouver."[14]

Buoyed by council's somewhat tenuous support, the Pacific National Exhibition moved quickly to assemble financial commitments. The most troublesome problem was securing the estimated $6 million required to build the facility. With substantial lobbying by P.N.E. directors and Vancouver-area Members of Parliament, and backed by the efforts of Erwin Swangard, Managing Editor of the Vancouver *Sun* and a supporter of the P.N.E. plans, who made timely use of his contacts with Prime Minister Lester B. Pearson, a promise was elicited from Ottawa that one-third of the cost would come from federal coffers. The decision to provide funding represented a rather abrupt about-face, for only three months earlier the federal government had turned down the P.N.E.'s request for assistance, arguing that the proposed structure was not really an agricultural or exhibition facility. The B.C. government had earlier committed itself to matching any federal largesse and accordingly came up with $2 million. The City of Vancouver promised $1 million, leaving the P.N.E. to raise the final $1 million on its own. With the required capital secured before the 31 October deadline, the P.N.E. was free to continue with the design and construction stages. Initial plans had called for an architects' contest to select a design for the new facility, but it was decided that such a competition would not allow for completion by the target date of early 1967. The P.N.E. proceeded directly to engage Phillips, Barratt and Partners as engineers and architects for the new Exhibition Park showpiece.[15]

While the decision to fund the coliseum was generally welcomed by the citizens of Vancouver, the financial arrangements did raise some questions about the propriety of the government grants. As usual, the P.N.E. applied for government assistance on the basis of its status as an agricultural exhibition, and all buildings thus financed were to be suited for exhibition purposes. While the federal government's assistance programme had, by the 1960's, been expanded to include "community" facilities, the exhibition component was still, in theory, a requirement. The provenance of the federal government's funding for the coliseum, coming more from the timely intervention of prominent Vancouverites than as the result of the validity of the P.N.E.'s appeal, suggests that political considerations were a key factor in the dispersal of large government grants. The development was hardly new or startling, for the P.N.E. had on several earlier occasions benefitted greatly from the association's strong connections with the federal Liberal Party.

In the now typical pattern of P.N.E.-City Council relations, the arena matter did not proceed smoothly. Mayor Bill Rathie criticized P.N.E. President Captain

N↑

CASSIAR ST.

EMPIRE STADIUM

Roller Coaster

Timber Show

PLAYLAND

Outdoor Stage

GRANDSTAND

LIVESTOCK BLDG

AGRODOME

B.C. BLDG

PACIFIC COLISEUM

ROLLERLAND

SHOWMART

FOOD BLDG

Administration Bldg

GARDEN AUDITORIUM

FORUM

RENFREW ST.

HASTINGS ST.

EXHIBITION PARK 1982

Harry Terry in April 1966, claiming that the association was not co-operating with the city in planning the facility. Terry, for his part, rejected the city's proposed parking requirements and argued that the city planner and Board of Administration were still waging a campaign to build the arena downtown. City Council eventually agreed to allow construction to proceed, although some concern was expressed that the association would have difficulty raising its $1 million share of the final cost. Alderman Bob Williams, a resident of the east end of the city, continued to oppose the project, declaring that he was "sick and tired of the long song and dance from that little empire on the east side." To Williams' dismay, council in the end actually increased its commitment, offering to provide an additional $750,000 on the condition that the P.N.E. assume responsibility for any costs in excess of $5,750,000. Work finally began in the spring of 1966 on the 15,000 seat Exhibition and Sports Building, and on 8 January 1968 the newly named "Pacific Coliseum" was officially opened.[16]

While the Agrodome and Pacific Coliseum attracted most of the attention in this decade, the P.N.E. also undertook a series of smaller developments to update and expand its physical assets. The old P.N.E. restaurant, torn down to make way for the Agrodome had to be replaced and in 1962-1963 a new facility, the Dogwood Room, was opened in the basement of the B.C. Building. The Forum, built in 1930, was in serious need of renovation and although the General Manager argued for the demolition of the structure, the P.N.E. felt compelled to go along with council's demand that a skating rink be maintained in the city's East End and therefore agreed to allocate more than $900,000 for repairs to the building.[17]

These alterations represented short-term and poorly planned additions. At least partially conscious of the problems inherent in ad hoc planning, the association attempted to implement a park-wide "Space-Age Look" development plan in 1965. The proposal called for a $1.6-million Women's Building, a "vertical feature" similar to Seattle's Space Needle, a sky-ride, a covered Olympic-sized swimming pool, tennis courts, landscaping, and a variety of smaller projects. The most noticeable additions derived from this "plan" were a 1450-foot long sky-ride that could take fairgoers from Playland to the exhibition buildings on the west end of the grounds and a 330-foot space tower. Other aspects of the so-called plan met with less success. In essence, the 1965 development plan was a "plan" only in a very narrow sense, designed to add new facilities rather than a comprehensive proposal to restructure the grounds.[18]

A more sophisticated redevelopment plan was brought forward in 1971 calling for a new multi-purpose structure in the centre of the grounds. The low-slung building was to incorporate parking, agricultural and exhibit space in three underground levels. The P.N.E. greeted the design with considerable enthusiasm and actually approached the federal government for funding. The concept would have had significant implications for the shape and direction of the exhibition, but like many of the association's proposals the suggested development never advanced beyond the planning stage.[19] This put the P.N.E. back in its usual position without an adequate management plan. Instead, the practice was to respond to short-term exigencies and needs. The result was that the P.N.E. facilities were inefficient for the purposes intended and the association was saddled with a set of buildings that were often ill suited for the exhibition.

But if the buildings were not the best, they were all the P.N.E. had. Far from complaining about the poor facilities or restricting the use of inefficient structures, the P.N.E. continued to expand its year-round operations. While the expansion led to increasing attendance figures and revenues, it also led to a growing suspicion in the community that the P.N.E. was as much concerned with the profitable management of Exhibition Park as with the staging of the annual fair. The contradictions between the aims of the yearly exhibition and the fact that the P.N.E. now controlled the best set of sporting, entertainment, and exhibit facilities in Vancouver was never satisfactorily resolved, nor for that matter was the association's position on the issue ever publicly clarified. To some directors, the P.N.E. managed the facilities simply to ensure that the association had the required buildings, staff and liquid capital to operate the fair. At the same time, however, these endeavours began to assume a life of their own, seemingly separate from the exhibition. The fair appeared to be simply one more event, albeit the most important, in the constant whirl of activity at Exhibition Park.

Not every facet of the Pacific National Exhibition's year-round activities was profit oriented and at least two prominent features, the B.C. Sports Hall of Fame and the Lipsett Museum, were designed as free educational features. The Hall of Fame was established under curator Eric Whitehead in 1966 with the aid of a $25,000 provincial grant. Featuring photos of inductees, souvenirs and historical artifacts, the display was given a prominent position in the B.C. Building. Although reluctant to provide funding, especially when a major redevelopment of the display was undertaken in 1971, the P.N.E. nonetheless found considerable satisfaction in the fact that the Hall of Fame filled an otherwise poorly used section of the B.C. Building. As well, the new attraction fit in nicely with the P.N.E.'s increasing sports orientation.[20]

Containing a remarkable display of Indian artifacts from throughout the Americas, the Lipsett Collection had been a feature at Exhibition Park since 1941 and had been installed in the B.C. Building soon after that structure was opened. When the new Centennial Museum was opened in Vancouver's Vanier Park in 1968, however, the civic government began to cast covetous eyes on the justifiably renowned collection and requested that the P.N.E. turn the materials over to the city. Recalling that the Lipsetts, when donating the collection, had emphatically declared that the display was to remain with the exhibition, the directors refused to comply, touching off another confrontation with City Council. Under their constitution and city lease, all P.N.E. capital properties were held in the city's name and, in theory at least, the government could reclaim such properties at will. After some debate, the matter was shelved for two years. In 1970, the Centennial Museum again approached the association, this time asking for only 31 specific items from the collection. The P.N.E. committee in charge of the museum was prepared to accept the offer and the issue appeared headed towards a resolution. City Council, however, refused to allow the collection to be dismembered and, re-affirming its claim to the materials, strongly suggested that the P.N.E. move as quickly as possible to turn the artifacts over to the Greater Vancouver Civic Museum and Planetarium Board. Meetings were held over the next year to resolve the dispute, and on 6 September 1971 the P.N.E. directors finally voted by a bare majority to pass the collection on intact to the Centennial Museum.[21]

This comparatively minor problem provides a useful insight into the changing character of the Pacific National Exhibition. While the majority of the directors saw little benefit in continuing the fight with City Hall over the museum, several of the older members of the association vigourously protested what they viewed as the alienation of essential P.N.E. property. Past President and long-time member John Dunsmuir expressed his perspective with the interesting observation that: "the entire Fair was becoming too much of a carnival and little by little we are losing valuable exhibits of an educational nature."[22] Those directors favouring the more business-like management of the fair were unwilling to protest the take-over of the Lipsett Museum. But members who could recall when educational displays enjoyed a more prominent position in the exhibition saw the loss of the collection as further evidence of the movement of the P.N.E. away from its stated goals. There were few issues in this decade which divided the directors into two camps, but it does seem clear that to at least a few members, the increasing professionalism and commercialism of the P.N.E. was becoming more difficult to accept.

Those in favour of the transfer were not simply trying to get rid of a costly and increasingly unattractive component of the Pacific National Exhibition. They successfully argued that the association lacked the expertise to care for the materials correctly and that the Lipsett collection would gain far greater attention as part of the new Centennial Museum. This view, incidently backed up by the Lipsett's daughter, did not sway the minds of those who believed that it was activities such as the museum which gave the P.N.E. its unique educational and public service function.[23]

While educational displays such as the Sports Hall of Fame and, while it remained, the Lipsett Museum, attracted a certain number of people to the grounds year round, the major focus of the non-fair activities at Exhibition Park was still professional sports. Horse racing in particular continued to prove to be a popular attraction. By the early 1960's, however, facilities had deteriorated to the point where major renovations were required. The B.C. Jockey Club, managers of the racing concession, renegotiated their lease in 1964, securing a 19-year agreement in return for a commitment to spend $1.3 million on new grandstand facilities and other minor alterations. The B.C. Lions, principal tenants of Empire Stadium, continued their operations, boldly suggesting in 1964 that owing to their greater expertise in stadium management they should be given full control of the football facility. The issue of greatest contention between the P.N.E. and the Lions was, not surprisingly, the question of rental rates. Faced with the problem of lower revenues and higher costs, the Lions petitioned the association in 1969 for a downward revision of the rental charge. The Board of Directors acceded to the request, an action which touched off a serious internal dispute. The P.N.E. Negotiating Committee, upset at being overruled, tendered their resignations. This conflict, one of the first internal squabbles to be aired publicly, was only resolved when the matter was referred back to the negotiating committee for further discussion. On this occasion the Lions' tenancy proved reasonably remunerative. While the tentative 1969 agreement called for a rental of $131,000, the 1971 accord required the football club to pay 15 per cent of gross receipts.[24]

In this period, the Pacific National Exhibition controlled not one but two playing fields: Empire Stadium and Callister Park. The P.N.E.'s control of the latter facility, managed by the association since the 1940's, was thrown into doubt in 1968. City Council, considering an alternative site for a civic soccer field suggested that Callister Park be turned into a children's playground. Anxious to ensure that the association retained control of the grounds, Captain Terry of the P.N.E. Negotiating Committee argued that the area could be blacktopped and used for much needed parking. The proposal was quite out of touch with popular sentiment and was quickly dropped. Badly in need of renovation, Callister Park was becoming a financial burden and although some directors felt that the grounds provided room for future expansion of the exhibition, most were pleased when council offered them an easy way out of the dilemma. Council suggested that the P.N.E. surrender the remaining five years on the Callister Park lease and in return the city would pay for the installation of synthetic turf in Empire Stadium. Aware that council could expropriate the property at will and anxious to shed the worrisome burden, the P.N.E. quickly accepted the offer, trading their soccer pitch for a field of rubber grass.[25]

Horse racing and football remained popular attractions at Exhibition Park but they were overshadowed at least temporarily by the arrival of the P.N.E.'s newest tenant — the National Hockey League Vancouver Canucks. Their predecessors, the Vancouver Canucks of the Western Hockey League had been sold to the New York Rangers by the P.N.E. in 1962 in the wake of public opposition to the exhibition's continued ownership. The Canucks role as a Rangers' farm team was short-lived, for as soon as the P.N.E. confirmed final plans to built a sports coliseum, attempts were launched to secure an N.H.L. franchise for the city. Vancouver's appeals to the league for entry had long been ignored because of the city's lack of a suitable hockey arena. With the construction of the Pacific Coliseum, it seemed as though the final impediment to entry into the league had been removed and sports enthusiasts looked forward to the granting of a franchise.

Although passed over in the N.H.L.'s first major expansion in 1967, a decision greeted with considerable bitterness in the city, a franchise was finally granted in 1969. The right to operate the Vancouver team was awarded to Medical Investments Ltd. (Medicor) of Minnesota. Negotiations between Medicor owners Thomas Scallen and Lyman Walters and the P.N.E. were protracted, with both groups attempting to secure control of such lucrative sidelights as television revenue, concessions, programmes, and souvenirs. The final agreement, which provided for a payment of 15 per cent of gross receipts and 15 per cent of television revenue, appeared to favour the Pacific National Exhibition. Importantly, the P.N.E. was able to fend off Medicor's attempt to secure an exclusive rights contract, leaving open the possibility of a hockey team from another league also leasing the building. These rather mundane concerns were pushed aside in the fall of 1970 when the Vancouver entry in the N.H.L. skated onto the ice of the Pacific Coliseum to begin its first season in the league.[27]

The various events discussed above constituted the primary non-fair activities at Exhibition Park. At the same time, however, they represented only a fraction of the many attractions staged on the grounds throughout the year. Rock concerts, including the triumphant Beatles' performance in 1964 and a riot-ravaged Rolling Stones show in 1972, provided a significant source of revenue. Trade shows, including the B.C. International Trade Fair, auto, boat and home shows began to appear as annual attractions. For the latter events, the P.N.E. merely rented the required buildings to businessmen and did not take an active role in the management of the shows. Similarly, the P.N.E. also granted a special lease to a businessman to operate a roller-rink in the building that was aptly renamed Rollerland.

Faced with a changing exhibition and rapidly shifting year-round activities, the association undertook a series of minor internal revisions in an attempt to keep abreast of the times. Reflecting changing social attitudes, the association made the increasingly obligatory declarations of intent to interest women in the directorate. Ways to make better use of the Board of Governors and endeavours to inject "new blood" into the organization were also subjects of consideration. All were "motherhood" issues and none of the suggestions brought forth seem to have spawned substantive change. While the P.N.E. perhaps lacked the desire to revise the composition of the Board of Directors, they did find it possible to respond more effectively to pragmatic operational requirements and significantly revamped management operations. The change in the organization of the P.N.E., which centred on a revised operations system, was a simple, and necessary, attempt to develop a more sophisticated internal structure to handle the demands of a more and more complex operation.[28]

The Pacific National Exhibition's relations with outside authorities also underwent significant alteration in the 1960's. The federal government remained an active partner in the agricultural fair, providing funding for the livestock competition prize lists and also giving generous grants for such building projects as the Agrodome and Pacific Coliseum.[29] Of more direct importance on a day-to-day basis was the civic administration. The decade had begun with a major controversy between council and the association over the livestock arena, a matter that seemed resolved by the end of 1961. The following year, however, the entire controversy resurfaced, leading to a series of charges and counter-accusations between the two groups. The P.N.E. directors only capitulated to council's request for greater control of exhibition budgets when the aldermen threatened to withhold civic grants for Exhibition Park construction projects. With the association accepting council's demands the matter was finally settled and a new lease incorporating the agreed upon revisions was signed in August 1963. The following year, a further agreement was reached, extending the lease from 1975 to 1994, with a provision for renegotiation of all terms of the lease every five years beginning in 1975. The P.N.E.'s decision to accede to council's requests was based on a simple but compelling premise — self-preservation. The conflict originating in the debate over the livestock arena clearly threatened the future of the association, a fact that the directors only reluctantly came to admit. City Council was becoming increasingly assertive of its rights to control the Pacific National Exhibition and there seemed a very real possibility that management of the fair and the fair grounds might be assumed by the civic government.[30]

In deciding to challenge the power and prestige of the P.N.E., City Council sensed broad popular support for such action. The feeling of estrangement is captured in a comment by a P.N.E. director who lamented at a board meeting that: "the Pacific National Exhibition seemed to be wearing the curious, if somewhat sombre crown of a mother-in-law of many years standing in a family indifferent to her many fine points but at the same time quite jealously possessive of her material assets."[31] To the directors, it seemed ironic that communities in the B.C. Interior applauded the P.N.E.'s success while Vancouver seemed oblivious to the accomplishments of the annual exhibition. While clearly concerned about declining local support, the directors seemed unable to appreciate the seriousness of the developing breach. Signs appeared with increasing frequency throughout the decade that residents of Vancouver's east side, for decades the staunchest supporters of the fair, were turning on the association and were beginning to resent the intrusion of P.N.E. activities into their lives. While the P.N.E. did not ignore the residents' protestations and met with them on several occasions in an attempt to find a solution, the problem was not easily solved.[32]

The growing breach between the P.N.E. and the area residents did not leave the association isolated, for as the organization was pulling away from the City of Vancouver it was drawing closer to the province of British Columbia. The citizens of East Vancouver called for greater responsiveness to local needs, and the P.N.E. directors argued that the association had to place province-wide concerns over local matters. Conflict was all but inevitable. The controversy finally broke over the unlikely issue of minor hockey in the Forum and eventually concluded with the termination of the sixty-year-old volunteer structure of the Pacific National Exhibition.

Controversy flared when representatives of the P.N.E. Minor Hockey League Association approached City Council with a request for assistance. The exhibition association, having leased the Forum to the annual boat show, had informed the hockey league in September 1972 that the ice rink would not be available to them for a week. In February of the following year, two weeks before the boat show was scheduled, the hockey association met with City Council in an attempt to force the P.N.E. to allow uninterrupted ice time. The P.N.E. directors remained adamant that the contract with boat show promoter Harmon O'Laughlin could not be broken and they refused to consider the league's appeal.[33] What was on the surface a seemingly minor affair was actually a manifestation of a more serious issue — the question of the responsibility of the P.N.E. to local residents and City Council.

The conflict, which picked up in tempo through February 1973, soon took on more serious tones as both the council and the provincial government began to cast covetous eyes on the P.N.E. The association was provincially incorporated, but that did not stop council from agreeing in principle that the exhibition should be brought fully under civic control.[34] The civic attack was led by Alderman Harry Rankin, who saw the P.N.E. as an unresponsive and unrepresentative institution. Early in February, Rankin wrote, "Today this publicly owned facility is operated by a small, self-perpetuating society of businessmen solely for the profit of private promoters, hockey, football, racing, etc. Any benefits to the people are incidental."[35] At the same time, in a move that would appear to have been planned earlier and timed to take full advantage of the public furore over the local controversy, the New Democratic Party government in Victoria also moved against the Pacific National Exhibition. Resources Minister Bob Williams, an M.L.A. from Vancouver's East End, had long opposed what he saw to be a self-serving organization. In Williams' view, the P.N.E. was controlled by "a middle-management elite that in many ways is almost self-appointed."[36] The image was shared by the N.D.P. caucus.

On 22 February 1973, Bob Williams stood in the B.C. Legislative Assembly to announce a bill designed to restructure the Pacific National Exhibition and make it publicly accountable and more responsive to local concerns. Williams' long-standing hostility to the exhibition was evident as he introduced the bill:

Too often the PNE is simply a burden on the people of the east side of town. They have to live with the traffic problem almost daily as a result of that development. They have to deal daily with the mammoth invasion or intrusion into their neighbourhoods. I know that that can't be washed away, but it would be easier for the people of that area to take if the PNE were more responsive to their own needs right in the community.[37]

As to the future of Exhibition Park, Williams pulled no punches, responding to opposition queries on the topic by stating, "You bet your sweet bippy we want to change it into a giant community centre."[38]

Central to Williams' plan was a revamping of the Board of Directors, replacing the unwieldly sixty-member board with a sixteen-person body. As well, the board was to conform to rather rigid requirements and was to include five members of City Council, one member from the Parks Board, representatives from the agricultural, industrial, business, artistic, sports, cultural and ethnic communities, the trade union movement, plus three directors who were to live within one mile of Exhibition Park.[39] With the exception of the official civic representatives, all the directors were to be appointed by the provincial government.

This latest debate regarding control of the P.N.E. was clothed in controversy throughout, and it is hardly surprising that the government's plans were not greeted with universal equanimity. The P.N.E. directors, as would be expected, saw the takeover as "politically inspired,"[40] and a Vancouver *Sun* editorial referred to the N.D.P. action as "a scandalous abuse of power."[41] A vehement attack on the proposed P.N.E. bill was launched in the legislature by Social Credit M.L.A. Bob McClelland, who claimed that the provincial government was: "just getting their sticky fingers into everything they possibly can. Most of all they must get at community-oriented organizations which are now served by volunteer people, and have been served well for years and years and years."[42]

After doing their utmost to rally public opinion behind their cause and furious at the government's precipitous action, the P.N.E. Board of Directors voted to resign en masse and attempted to turn over all assets to the city in a last ditch attempt to prevent the provincial take-over. The considerable bitterness within the association to the government's decision was apparent in vice-president Nairn Knott's assertion that: "It would be awfully naive to believe that this Bill was engineered by amateur hockey problems. It was an engineered political ploy." P.N.E. President W. M. Anderson in announcing the Board of Directors resignations agreed with Knott, noting "It's ironic, and tragic, that a parochial and presumptuous Bill such as that proposed by a B.C. government cabinet minister . . . a man who is supposed to represent all British Columbia has forced us to turn over the P.N.E. to the City of Vancouver. It was the only way we could ensure that the P.N.E. will remain an institution for everyone."[43]

The N.D.P. majority in the legislature passed the Pacific National Exhibition Incorporation Act on 18 April 1973. The legislation did not alter the aims and purposes of the organization, but it did make substantial alterations to the directorate. In addition, a special Agricultural Advisory Committee was established, with representatives from the various types of agriculture and the different regions of the province. This special group was empowered simply to advise the Board of Directors on agricultural matters and was given no real power to determine policy. Even though the assets remained nominally with the city, and City Council had substantial representation on the Board of Directors, the P.N.E. was now a provincial institution.[44]

The Pacific National Exhibition, as it had existed for over sixty years, was gone, although few would really notice its passing. On the surface, the P.N.E. remained as before. The annual fair was not directly affected, professional and amateur sports continued, and the many and varied year-round activities went on without interruption. The change was clearly more of style than of substance. The P.N.E. had evolved from a local to a provincial fair. This evolution had begun as early as the 1920's, when the P.N.E. showed the first signs of being more concerned about its provincial status than its standing in the local community. The resolution of the 1973 conflict, ostensibly designed to re-orient the association towards Vancouver actually had the opposite effect in the long term, drawing the P.N.E. further away from the local scene and towards the province as a whole. In 1910, Vancouver's exhibition was a local institution, supported strongly by the city government and the citizens. Sixty-three years later the Pacific National Exhibition emerged as a provincial institution, both in law and in practice. The fair had been Vancouver's. It now belonged to British Columbia.

11

Vancouver's Fair in Retrospect

Vancouver was the last major city in Western Canada to stage an exhibition, yet sixty years after the 1910 fair the city's annual presentation was the largest in the four western provinces and second nationally only to Toronto's Canadian National Exhibition. The development and evolution of the Pacific National Exhibition has been far from tranquil, and at many times the fair was rocked by conflict, scandal and controversy. But the exhibition association weathered these storms. They continued to expand the physical plant, develop new attractions and activities, and assert the P.N.E.'s role as first Vancouver's and later British Columbia's "playground."

For a variety of reasons, the P.N.E. has always had its critics. In the early years, gambling and horse racing raised the ire of church groups and temperance organizations who levelled a concerted attack on the association in an attempt to have the exhibition programme altered. At almost the same time, a small group agitated against the extension of the association's Hastings Park lease, hoping to convince the civic government to leave the site as a natural park. The voices of dissent, however, were soon lost in the resounding echoes of support for the exhibition. The decision to hold an exhibition during World War I, management problems in the 1920's, the New Westminster-Vancouver amalgamation issue, revelations of internal corruption in the 1930's, the downtown stadium controversy of the 1950's and 1960's, and the continuing debate over local access to the P.N.E. facilities are but the most visible conflicts which have engulfed Vancouver's fair. The P.N.E. has never been without its share of opponents. For the most part, however, the majority of Vancouverites and British Columbians have supported the exhibition. Attendance has increased steadily since 1910, more than keeping pace with the increase in population of both the city and the province. By their continued attendance the citizens were acknowledging that the P.N.E. had something to offer and in so doing made the fair an integral part of the Vancouver scene.

The fair which Vancouverites flocked to see has changed with the community in which, at times, it has been uneasily situated. Visually the exhibition grounds have constantly altered. That this physical development has been haphazard and often poorly planned is evidenced by the still present B.C. Building and Agrodome. Indeed, as the provenance of the various facilities is traced, one is at once astonished by the diversity and impressed by the frequent lack of foresight. Empire Stadium came as a result of the British Empire Games of 1954, the livestock buildings represent a fortuitous piece of political patronage, the Agrodome was a last-minute substitution for a major sports arena, and the building of the Pacific Coliseum was closely tied with the attempt to secure a National Hockey League franchise for Vancouver. The directors had often approached physical expansion on a yearly and building by building basis, erecting what was possible at the time and taking advantage of whatever funding was available, often with little reflection on the long-term consequences.

As the physical plant at Exhibiton Park changed dramatically, so too did the organization operating the facilities. Initially, the exhibition association had been concerned almost exclusively with the production of the fair. Although they were willing to sublet their buildings to suitable tenants, they did not actively pursue that potential source of revenue. Beginning with the construction of the Forum and particularly after World War II, the P.N.E. began to recognize the need to increase use of the facilities. Inherent in the development of improved fairtime activities was the need to use the buildings for non-fair events. In order to justify the capital expenditures and to defray maintenance costs, the association was forced to expand usage. While defensible on financial grounds, this development threatened to weaken the profile of the annual fair. With few reservations, however, the directors allowed a tremendous expansion of operations, with retail and home shows, a B.C. International Trade Fair, and a plethora of other activities filling the P.N.E. buildings. Sports became a predominant feature. The Vancouver Canucks played first in the Forum and later in the Pacific Coliseum. The B.C. Lions and the Vancouver Whitecaps both operated out of Empire Stadium, and the B.C. Jockey Club staged a full season of horse-racing out of the Exhibition Park racetrack. This move towards year-round utilization of the fairgrounds reflects in part the growing management orientation of the association. As the physical plant grew and as the operation of both facilities and exhibition became increasingly complex, the P.N.E. altered its direction substantially. In recognition of the fact that Exhibition Park was not just the site of an annual fair but also the sports and entertainment centre of British Columbia, the P.N.E. began to function more as a business than a fair organization.

As the P.N.E. administration changed focus, its relationship with the citizens of Vancouver also changed. Initially, the association drew its greatest support from those living closest to the fairgrounds. Year after year, east end residents provided the strongest support for exhibition by-laws and, through their regional, ratepayers' and business organizations, repeatedly backed P.N.E. expansion plans. This community of interests could not last, however, and as the size of the exhibition and the area's population continued to grow it was soon apparent that a major clash was unavoidable. The fair which had, in the early years, provided a community focus for the east end residents, in the end became a threat to the identity of the community and the eventual take over of the P.N.E. by the provincial government was primarily the result of the ever-expanding conflict between area residents and the association.

While the shift in the relationship between the east side of the city and the Pacific National Exhibition is a complex matter, it is important to note that as local support declined, and perhaps because of it, the P.N.E. began to move away from its Vancouver roots in favour of a province-wide and even national orientation. The fair had from its first days pretentions of becoming B.C.'s major exhibition, but by the late 1940's, the change in orientation had become more noticeable and was symbolically indicated in the change of name from Vancouver Exhibition Association to Pacific National Exhibition. The transformation from city to provincial fair was completed in 1973 when the B.C. government took over control of the P.N.E. and made it a provincial institution. An act ostensibly designed to give more local control, the takeover nonetheless allowed the fair to complete its shift from a local to a provincial event. The fair had been Vancouver's, but thanks to the government's action it now belonged to British Columbia.

The development of the P.N.E. has always been closely linked to the growth of Vancouver. Changes in the exhibition structure, content and emphasis, reflect the dynamic character of the community which it serves. The alterations in the fair over time, therefore, tell legions about the development of Vancouver. The balance between the three main components of the fair — agriculture, entertainment and boosterism — shifted as the city itself grew and changed.

In 1910, Vancouver was a curious amalgam of a frontier settlement and a progressive urban setting, rough around the edges but with great aspirations for future expansion. The "Industrial Exhibition" of that year, combining resource and manufacturing displays with gambling and horse racing, was an accurate reflection of the boisterous boosterism which infected the community. Only in the aftermath of the collapse of the New Westminster exhibition in 1930 did the fair's agricultural component come close to assuming the primary status that rhetoric had always ascribed. This artificial prominence did not accord with the reality of Vancouver's economic function and the exhibition soon reverted to its former and more appropriate emphasis. The city that was the focus of the more professional presentations of the 1950's and 1960's was vastly different. On display was the "new" Vancouver. Gone were the insecurities and wild development plans of the past, replaced by a noticeable maturity and stability. The fair was just as booster-oriented as it had been in 1910, but the emphasis was now on the pride of accomplishment and guaranteed prosperity. The demand increasingly was for entertainment, particularly of an international stature, and for major league professional sports. Vancouver's search now was clearly for status. The city demanded to be put on the map as an internationally renowned centre and the P.N.E. responded by bringing in big-name American entertainers, welcoming professional football and working assiduously towards securing an N.H.L. franchise. The annual fair, therefore, was more than just a passing amusement. Not just in Vancouver, the exhibition was of Vancouver, and the development of the fair, its trials and successes, provides evidence not only of the internal evolution of the exhibition, but also of the city of which it had been an integral part. The fair is in essence an image of its setting, providing a glimpse of how people view themselves and their region, what they feel they have accomplished and what they see as still to be done.

Epilogue: 1973-1982

Plus ça change, plus c'est la même chose.
Alphonse Karr (Les Goêpes, Jan. 1849)

The years since the restructuring of the P.N.E. organization in 1973 have not been without controversy. Old issues and themes continued to resurface. The hoary questions that deal with the nature and balance of activities on the exhibition site and the PNE's relationship with the local community would suggest that, given the nature of the institution and the complex, varied, and changing character of its urban setting, such tensions are simply inherent. Still, the P.N.E.'s continued search for identity and definition after 1973 is particularly important. Hindsight may eventually reveal that these years were ones of critical transition.

The directors appointed by the provincial government in 1973 to replace the deposed administration were charged with setting to rest the growing animosity between the exhibition and local residents and with providing direction and purpose for what was expected to be a new chapter in the history of the exhibition. To achieve these goals and armed with preceptions about the "country club" character of earlier governing bodies, the provincial government appointed a Board of Directors that it thought was more broadly representative. This sixteen-person board included seven provincial appointees to represent agriculture, mining, forestry, fishing, manufacturing, business, commercial, cultural, ethnic, artistic, sports, recreational, and trade union interests, and three persons resident within a one mile radius of the exhibition site; five Vancouver aldermen, nominated by the Council of the Corporation of the City of Vancouver; and one person appointed by the City of Vancouver Board of Parks and Recreation. It was expected that such a group would manage the fair in a more open manner and quickly earn, through participation, the goodwill of all groups represented. In the process the fair would be brought closer to the people.

With enthusiasm, if limited experience, the directors commenced the task of creating a "new" Pacific National Exhibition. Following the suggestion of the architect of the P.N.E. takeover, Resource Minister Bob Williams, studies were undertaken to consider the possibility and advisability of reviewing all existing P.N.E. leases. Arguing that the agreements negotiated by the old board seemed mainly to benefit the owners of Vancouver's professional sports franchises, it was suggested that renegotiations were in order. Similarly, exhibition directors decided to re-examine the relationship between the B.C. Jockey Club and the exhibition. Under the existing lease, the Jockey Club was slated to occupy the racetrack and its accompanying facilities (built at the club's expense) until 1994, an arrangement several board members found objectionable. The uproar which attended the lease review issue matched the furore that surrounded the 1973 takeover. Some columnists and public commentators wondered if the proposals were an indication of the new NDP government's commitment to existing legal contracts. In the end the directors were forced to recognize that their ability to reshape the system and structure of Exhibition Park was constrained by the existence of long-term binding contracts. With the Jockey Club, Burrard Amusements (operators of the amusement park), B.C. Lions Football Club, and the Vancouver Canucks hockey team all tied to existing contracts, the directors' manoeuvrability was sharply restricted.

There was really only one area of lease renegotiations where the directors could move ahead and this was with the City of Vancouver. One of Williams' key arguments in 1973 had been that the P.N.E. was not paying its way. Despite the existence here also of a long-term lease, and the diminishing likelihood of increasing revenues from P.N.E. leaseholders, the new board was directed to open negotiations with the city that would lead to a more substantial yearly payment. While it was initially suggested that the yearly rental fee for the grounds might be raised to at least $500,000, the directors were swept from office before agreement could be reached.

By tying or identifying the Board of Directors so closely with the party in power in Victoria, the 1973 reorganization assured that with any change of government, a new body of P.N.E. directors would shortly follow. When the Social Credit party returned to power in December 1975, the existing board, which had been in office for less than eighteen months, was soon removed and a new slate announced. Perhaps the most important of the new government's eventual board appointments was that of Erwin Swangard, well-known sportsman and former editor of the Vancouver *Sun*. Elected president shortly afterwards by his board colleagues, Swangard has remained in office from 1977 to the present. After four presidents in four years, Swangard's incumbency brought a measure of stability and strength to the president's office that had not been characteristic for many years.

During the 1973 debate over reorganization of the P.N.E., Social Credit party spokesmen had supported the P.N.E.'s old guard, arguing in defence of the tradition of voluntary commitment by interested people. Back in power, however, they showed no sign of wishing a return to the former system. With a less interventionist government, the new Board of Directors were left largely to themselves to define a character and direction for the fair. What emerged was a reflection of the new board. Cut of a somewhat different stripe, its vision was not modelled on the "community centre" concept and hence was less focused upon social restructuring. When the new board thought about restructuring or rebuilding, it thought mainly in terms of the P.N.E.'s physical and economic assets. The vision that distinguished the new board was particularly that of one man, the dynamic and single-minded president. Perhaps more than any other, Swangard was able to see and face the fact that the P.N.E. was at the crossroads. It had to vastly rebuild and modernize its deteriorating and inadequate physical plant or collapse as a fair, and as a convention and sports facility of national and international stature.

By the fall of 1976 preliminary proposals calling for a major overhaul of the P.N.E. physical plant as well as a substantial re-orientation of the fair itself were presented for public discussion. Within this early redevelopment plan the construction of a "multiplex" was suggested. A term Vancouverites would come to hear a lot of, it referred to a multiple-use facility incorporating stadium, convention display space, and livestock exhibit components. Soon presented to the P.N.E. board in a more comprehensive form, the "Action '78" redevelopment plan of a consortium of architectural, engineering, economic, and traffic consultants called for a complete revamping of the fair grounds. The emphasis was to be on year-round activities, with amenities to include an outdoor amphitheatre, a children's world, assorted restaurants, specialty attractions, and a pioneer village. The centrepiece was a 50,000-seat stadium complex.

In keeping with the pattern of the past, when the redevelopment plans were made public, a storm of controversy developed. The P.N.E. nonetheless stayed with the plan, and in August 1978 President Swangard announced the association's formal endorsement of Multiplex, a stadium now expanded to 60,000 seats, 227,000 square feet of exhibit space, and a 239,000 square foot capacity for agricultural events. While the concept had supporters, critics lined up to protest its cost and what they saw as deficiencies in design and purpose. Some sports fans questioned the failure to include the capacity for baseball in the covered stadium, certain local residents articulated the old concern about the impact of increased parking and traffic on their neighbourhoods, and some local politicians complained about the manner in which the plan was developed and presented.

A formidable array of opponents emerged, but this was hardly a new phenomenon to the P.N.E. The real problem at this juncture was the competition of some other grand visions to which powerful interests were attached. First, there was the proposed downtown trade and convention centre with its spectacular waterfront setting known as "Pier BC," which already had first-level government commitment. Then early in 1979 a group favouring a covered stadium at False Creek in downtown Vancouver came forward with a competing proposal. The ensuing battle was curiously familiar to that waged in the 1950's over the location of a proposed arena for professional hockey. Ultimately, the provincial government intervened with the appointment of a third party, Paul Manning, to study the contending proposals and offer a recommendation on the appropriate location and design. In April 1980, Manning announced that he had decided in favour of a domed stadium on the north shore of False Creek that would be the anchor piece of the larger B.C. Place Redevelopment Project. The decision marked the end of Multiplex as the grand design that was to take the P.N.E. into the twenty-first century.

It was back to square one. About to lose its position as the centre of professional sport in Vancouver and soon to be in competition with Pier BC, yet only able to offer second-rate exhibition space, the now bleak task of establishing a raison d'être was at once more difficult and more urgent. Without a future plan the immediate problems of crumbling facilities and uneasy community relations could only be dealt with in an ad hoc and temporary fashion.

A clear manifestation of the difficulty in which the P.N.E. now finds itself is apparent in the most recent minor hockey controversy to confront the P.N.E. In the summer of 1981 P.N.E. officials decided that one of their old exhibition facilities, the Showmart building built in 1912, had to come down. The building no longer met municipal fire and safety standards and for some years special permits had been required for its use. Moreover, the general condition of the building did not seem to warrant the cost of extensive renovation. To accommodate events already scheduled for the building, the directors decided to shift Showmart space bookings to the Forum. To clear dates in the latter facility, the Hastings Park Minor Hockey Association and other skating groups were asked to accept reduced ice time. Local and political reaction was immediate and bitter, as area residents protested what they saw to be the breach of a contract and the alienation of a valued community facility. The mayor of Vancouver and several aldermen assailed the P.N.E. for allegedly mistreating east-end youngsters. Caught by the need to replace the Showmart and the existence of number of contracts requiring it to provide exhibit space, the P.N.E. found itself in the awkward position of doing public battle with minor hockey. While the court to which the matter was eventually taken decided in the exhibition's favour, Vancouver City Council exercised its authority to prevent the demolition of the Showmart. Eventually the P.N.E. and the council agreed that the facility be renovated.

For the P.N.E. it was a no-win situation. With the expenditure of $410,000 the life-span of one of the exhibition's aging structures was to be extended for five years. But doing so did not address the fundamental question that cannot be postponed much longer. What is to be the future role of the Pacific National Exhibition?

The 1981 P.N.E. Board asked the provincial government to underwrite a $20 million loan to upgrade all the facilities to meet modern exhibition requirements. Instead the government set up a three-person steering committee to probe these requirements and subsequently in 1982, it set up another committee, this time of seven members, to study the future of the P.N.E. on a long-range basis and the potential of continued provincial government involvement. At this point it is not yet clear whether it is the end or a new beginning that is looming.

Appendix 1

PRESIDENTS AND MANAGERS, V.E.A. AND P.N.E., 1907-1981

Year	President	Manager
1910	J. J. Miller, Realtor	J. Roy
1911	J. J. Miller, Realtor	J. Roy
1912	J. J. Miller, Realtor	H. S. Rolston
1913	J. J. Miller, Realtor	H. S. Rolston
1914	J. J. Miller, Realtor	H. S. Rolston
1915	J. J. Miller, Realtor	H. S. Rolston
1916	J. J. Miller, Realtor	H. S. Rolston
1917	J. J. Miller, Realtor	H. S. Rolston
1918	J. J. Miller, Realtor	H. S. Rolston
1919	J. J. Miller, Realtor	H. S. Rolston
1920	J. J. Miller, Realtor	H. S. Rolston
1921	J. J. Miller, Realtor	H. S. Rolston
1922	H. T. Lockyer, General Manager, Hudson's Bay Company	H. S. Rolston
1923	H. T. Lockyer, General Manager, Hudson's Bay Company	H. S. Rolston
1924	W. C. Brown, Lawyer	H. S. Rolston
1925	W. C. Brown, Lawyer	J. K. Matheson
1926	R. P. McLennan	J. K. Matheson
1927	W. Leek, Contractor	J. K. Matheson
1928	W. Leek, Contractor	J. K. Matheson
1929	W. Leek, Contractor	J. K. Matheson
1930	W. Leek, Contractor	J. K. Matheson
1931	W. Leek, Contractor	J. K. Matheson
1932	W. Leek, Contractor	J. K. Matheson
1933	W. Leek, Contractor	J. K. Matheson
1934	W. Leek, Contractor	J. K. Matheson
1935	W. Leek, Contractor	J. K. Matheson
1936	W. Leek, Contractor	J. K. Matheson
1937	W. Leek, Contractor	J. K. Matheson
1938	W. Leek, Contractor	S. C. McLennan
1939	J. Dunsmuir, Automobile Dealer	S. C. McLennan
1940	J. Dunsmuir, Automobile Dealer	S. C. McLennan

1941	J. Dunsmuir, Automobile Dealer	S. C. McLennan
1942	J. Dunsmuir, Automobile Dealer	S. C. McLennan
1943	J. Dunsmuir, Automobile Dealer	S. C. McLennan
1944	J. Dunsmuir, Automobile Dealer	S. C. McLennan
1945	M. Bowell, Automobile Dealer	Ida Rae
1946	M. Bowell, Automobile Dealer	V. B. Williams
1947	M. Bowell, Automobile Dealer	V. B. Williams
1948	H. M. King, U.B.C. Professor, Faculty of Agriculture	V. B. Williams
1949	H. M. King, U.B.C. Professor, Faculty of Agriculture	V. B. Williams
1950	H. M. King, U.B.C. Professor, Faculty of Agriculture	V. B. Williams
1951	G. M. Ferguson, Comptroller, B.C. Packers	V. B. Williams
1952	G. M. Ferguson, Comptroller, B.C. Packers	V. B. Williams
1953	J. S. C. Moffitt, Kaufman Rubber Co., Agent	V. B. Williams
1954	J. S. C. Moffitt, Kaufman Rubber Co., Agent	V. B. Williams
1955	J. S. C. Moffitt, Kaufman Rubber Co., Agent	V. B. Williams
1956	W. J. Borrie, President, Pemberton Securities	V. B. Williams
1957	W. J. Borrie, President, Pemberton Securities	H. M. King
1958	J. F. Brown, President, Brown Bros. Florists	A. P. Morrow
1959	J. F. Brown, President, Brown Bros. Florists	A. P. Morrow
1960	Dr. J. C. Berry, U.B.C. Professor, Faculty of Agriculture	A. P. Morrow
1961	Dr. J. C. Berry, U.B.C. Professor, Faculty Agriculture	A. P. Morrow
1962	T. R. Fyfe, General Manager, Black Bros.	A. P. Morrow
1963	T. R. Fyfe, General Manager, Black Bros.	A. P. Morrow
1964	H. W. Mulholland, Director, Carling Brewery	A. P. Morrow

1965	Captain H. Terry, President, Northland Shipping	A. P. Morrow
1966	Captain H. Terry, President, Northland Shipping	A. P. Morrow
1967	Captain H. Terry, President, Northland Shipping	A. P. Morrow
1968	H. Fairbank, Business Manager	D. Dauphinee
1969	H. Fairbank, Business Manager	D. Dauphinee
1970	C. W. Jaggs, General Manager, Simpson Sears, Catalogue Division	D. Dauphinee
1971	C. W. Jaggs, General Manager, Simpson Sears, Catalogue Division	J. D. Rennie
1972	W. M. Anderson	J. D. Rennie
1973	A. Phillips, Mayor of Vancouver	J. D. Rennie
1974	A. Phillips, Mayor of Vancouver	J. D. Rennie
1975	P. Brennan, Mayor of Squamish	J. D. Rennie
1976	E. C. Sweeney, Vancouver Alderman	J. D. Rennie
1977	E. M. Swangard, Newspaper Executive	D. Town
1978	E. M. Swangard, Newspaper Executive	D. Town
1979	E. M. Swangard, Newspaper Executive	D. Town
1980	E. M. Swangard, Newspaper Executive	D. Town
1981	E. M. Swangard, Newspaper Executive	W. Goddard

Appendix 2

EXHIBITION ATTENDANCE, 1910-1981

1910	68000	1934	(290000)	1958	925000
1911	78000	1935	(310000)	1959	880000
1912	91000	1936	377000	1960	963000
1913	92000	1937	(350000)	1961	922000
1914	46000	1938	(340000)	1962	976000
1915	44000	1939	320000	1963	1018000
1916	61000	1940	372000	1964	1034000
1917	81000	1941	(390000)	1965	1099000
1918	95000	1942	no fair held	1966	1092000
1919	121000	1943	no fair held	1967	1035000
1920	90000	1944	no fair held	1968	1039000
1921	96000	1945	no fair held	1969	1149000
1922	111000	1946	no fair held	1970	1167000
1923	108000	1947	587000	1971	1105000
1924	100000	1948	644000	1972	1193000
1925	198000	1949	(600000)	1973	1290000
1926	275000	1950	614000	1974	1302000
1927	275000	1951	666000	1975	1287000
1928	283000	1952	717000	1976	1271000
1929	288000	1953	835000	1977	1280000
1930	290000	1954	871000	1978	1219000
1931	300000	1955	751000	1979	1278000
1932	(305000)	1956	735000	1980	1287000
1933	267000	1957	820000	1981	1197000

Source: V.E.A. *Bulletins;* P.N.E. *Annual Reports.* Estimated figures (marked in brackets) are drawn from comments in Bulletins, Directors' Minutes, and local newspapers.

Appendix 3

FAIR ATTENDANCE AND AREA POPULATION

Reported attendance as a percentage of local and regional population, 1910-1980

	Exhibition Attendance	Vancouver Population (%)	Metropolitan Area Population (%)	British Columbia Population (%)
1910	68,000	120,800 (56)	142,200 (48)	392,000 (17)
1920	90,000	163,200 (55)	226,500 (40)	524,000 (17)
1930	290,000	246,600 (118)	334,400 (87)	694,000 (42)
1940	371,000	275,400 (135)	388,700 (95)	818,000 (45)
1950	614,000	344,800 (178)	554,200 (111)	1,165,000 (53)
1960	963,000	384,500 (250)	769,000 (125)	1,629,000 (59)
1970	1,167,000	426,300 (274)	985,700 (118)	2,184,000 (53)
1980	1,287,000	410,200 (314)	1,159,500 (111)	2,687,000 (48)

Source: *Census of Canada; Canada Yearbook;* Vancouver Exhibition Association, *Bulletin;* Pacific National Exhibition, *Annual Report*.

Appendix 4

BY-LAW SUBMISSIONS BY THE P.N.E.

Year	Request	Outcome	Favourable Vote
1908	$50,000	Lost	(58%)
1909	$50,000	Carried	(61%)
1910	$85,000	Carried	(76%)
1911	$115,000	Carried	(75%)
1912	$85,000	Lost	(58%)
1913	$165,000	Carried	(65%)
1925	$25,000	Lost	(36%)
1927	$130,000	Lost	(41%)
1930	$300,000	Carried	(68%)
1952	$1,000,000	Carried	(73%)
1956	$1,000,000	Lost	(42%)

Appendix 5

REVENUE FROM FAIR AND YEAR ROUND OPERATIONS 1910-1969

	Fair Revenue[1] / Total Revenue	Fair Expenditure / Total Expenditure
1910-1914	95%	93%
1915-1919	79%	71%
1920-1924	79%	70%
1925-1929	75%	64%
1930-1934	68%	60%
1935-1939	67%	41%
1940-1944[2]	64%	32%
1945-1949[3]	67%	55%
1950-1954	70%	61%
1955-1959	60%	53%
1960-1964	53%	54%
1965-1969	49%	49%

[1] Figures are percentages and five year averages.
[2] Only two years, 1940 and 1941.
[3] Only three years, 1947-1949.

Appendix 6

GRANTS, FAIR PROFITS, AND MEMBERSHIP REVENUES, 1910-1969

	Provincial Grant[3]	Federal Grant[3]	Profit (Fair)	Profit (Year)	Revenue from Member- ships[6]
1910-1914	$6,200	0	$2,550	$2,240	$1,890
1915-1919	$1,000[1]	$2,900	$11,200	$8,400	$980
1920-1924	$6,200	$4,100	$8,200	$4,800	$1,770
1925-1929	$5,900	$3,900	$24,400	$13,700	$1,800
1930-1934	$6,400[2]	$3,500	$22,200	$16,700	$930
1935-1939	$17,500	$4,200	$47,500	$9,500	$650
1940-1944	$14,600[4]	0	$62,200[4]	$42,100	$340
1945-1949	$23,333[5]	$1,500[5]	$115,500[5]	$60,000[5]	$880
1950-1954	$25,000	$1,500	$179,900	$158,000	$1,500
1955-1959	$25,000	$1,500	$181,100	$146,000	$1,690
1960-1964	no figures available		$134,300	$304,000	$2,180
1965-1969			$144,300	$100,400	$2,600

Figures are in dollars and represent five year averages.
[1] No grants between 1915-1918, $5,000 in 1919.
[2] In 1933, the provincial government began granting the association a percentage of pari-mutuel taxes.
[3] Figures are exclusive of building grants.
[4] Only two years are covered, 1940 and 1941.
[5] Only three years are covered, 1947-1949.
[6] Annual memberships only until 1948. Both annual and life memberships included thereafter.

Notes

CHAPTER 1: FAIRS AND EXHIBITIONS: AN HISTORICAL BACKGROUND

1. Wayne Neely, *The Agricultural Fair* (New York: Columbia University Press, 1935), pp. 3-26.
2. Ibid., pp. 27-40.
3. Ibid., pp. 41-70.
4. Ontario Association of Agricultural Societies, *The Story of Ontario Agricultural Fairs and Exhibitions, 1792-1967* (Toronto: O.A.A.S., 1967), pp. 1, 15-17, 23.
5. Grant MacEwan, *Agriculture on Parade* (Toronto: Thomas Nelson and Sons, 1950), passim. For the best discussion of prairie fairs, see David C. Jones, *Judges, Midways, and Sharp-Tongued Fakirs* (Saskatoon: Prairie Producer, in press).
6. MacEwan.
7. Neely, pp. 14-20; John Allwood, *The Great Exhibitions* (London: Studio Vista, 1977).
8. MacEwan, pp. 97-101.
9. Neely, p. 16.
10. The major studies are all by popular historians. G. MacEwan, *Agriculture on Parade* and T. Cashman, *Edmonton Exhibition: The First Hundred Years* (Edmonton: Edmonton Exhibition Association, 1979). Cashman's study is unabashedly partisan and ends with an open appeal to Edmontonians to rally around their exhibition. See also Central Canada Exhibition, *History of the Central Canada Exhibition from 1888* (Ottawa: Central Canada Exhibition, 1976). James Lorimer, *The Ex: A Picture History of the Canadian National Exhibition* (Toronto: James, Lewis and Samuel, 1973). For a more serious analysis of the role of fairs, see David C. Jones, *Judges, Midways, and Sharp-Tongued Fakirs*, D. C. Jones, "From Babies to Buttonholes," *Alberta History* 29 (Autumn 1981): 26-32; B. Osborne, "Trading on a Frontier: The Function of Peddlars, Markets and Fairs in 19th Century Ontario," *Canadian Papers in Rural History II* (1979).

Another work which deals exclusively with fairs, looking this time at Canada's participation at world class exhibitions, is D. Newell, "Canada at World's Fairs, 1851-1876," *Canadian Collector*, vol. II, no. 4 (July/August 1976). Fairs and exhibitions receive minor mention in a wide variety of studies. For instance, see the discussion in J. Spelt, *Urban Development in South-Central Ontario* (Toronto: McClelland and Stewart, 1977) which uses fairs as a means of defining an urban centre's evolving service function; M. Foran, *Calgary: An Illustrated History* (Toronto: Lorimer, 1978) sees the Calgary Stampede as indicative of the city's attempt to hold on to its ranching past and as a reflection of continuing American influences: G. Tulchinsky, *The River Barons: Montreal Businessmen and the Growth of Industry and Transportation, 1837-53* (Toronto: University of Toronto Press, 1977) and L. F. S. Upton, *Micmacs and Colonists: Indian-White Relations in the Maritimes, 1713-1867* (Vancouver: University of British Columbia Press, 1979) discuss, in different contexts, how colonial displays at the Great Exhibition of 1851 in London reflect Colonial values and aspirations; H. M. Troper, *Only Farmers Need Apply* (Toronto: Griffin House, 1972) shows how the Canadian government used American fairs to contact prospective immigrants; K. Kelly, "The Development of Farm Produce Marketing Agencies . . . in Western Simcoe County, 1850-1875," *Canadian Papers in Rural History I* (1978) briefly discusses the marketing value of fairs; R. Ankli et al, "The Adoption of the Gasoline Tractor in Western Canada," *Canadian Papers in Rural History II* (1979) describes how fairs were used to spread technological knowledge; one area where greater analysis of exhibitions was expected was that increasingly shop-worn topic of urban boosterism. Somewhat surprisingly, historians dealing with this subject have offered little discussion of fairs. Three notable examples, P. Roy, *Vancouver: An Illustrated History* (Toronto: Lorimer, 1980), A. Artibise, *Winnipeg: An Illustrated History* (Toronto: Lorimer, 1977) and Artibise, *Winnipeg: A Social History of Urban Growth, 1879-1914* (Montreal: McGill-Queens, 1975) do not deal with fairs even though all the works discuss extensively the booster ethos of the early Twentieth Century, of which exhibitions were a highly visible example. As well, in a recently published

collection of essays focusing largely on boosterism in Western Canada, A. Artibise, ed., *Town and City: Aspects of Western Canadian Urban Development* (Regina: Canadian Plains Research Center, 1981) fairs are discussed, and here only briefly, only in P. Voisey, "Boosting the Small Prairie Town, 1904-1931," and C. Betke, "The Original City of Edmonton: A Derivative Prairie Urban Community." This list of studies dealing with fairs makes no pretentions of being complete but is designed to indicate the range and diversity of works which discuss, if only briefly, exhibitions and fairs.

CHAPTER 2: ORIGINS OF THE VANCOUVER EXHIBITION ASSOCIATION, 1907-1910

1. For an analysis of Vancouver's expansion in this period, see P. Roy, *Vancouver: An Illustrated History* (Toronto: Lorimer, 1980); N. MacDonald, "A Critical Growth Cycle for Vancouver, 1900-1914," *B.C. Studies* No. 17 (Spring 1973): 26-45; R. McDonald, "Victoria, Vancouver and the Evolution of British Columbia's Economic System, 1886-1914," in Artibise, *Town and City*.

2. Minutes of the Jockey Club Committee, 3 October 1890, RG 2 B 2, vol. 66, f. 32, VCA. The original clearing of the grounds was undertaken with a view to its use as an exhibition site, Minutes of Council Meeting, RG 2 B 1, vol. 3, VCA.

3. Vancouver *Daily Province*, 26 May 1902.

4. B.C. Agricultural Fairs Association, First Annual Convention, 1910, *B.C. Sessional Papers 1910*, p. N28. There were 33 fairs held in the province that year.

5. J. S. Matthews, comp., *Early History of the Vancouver Exhibition Association* (Vancouver: City Archives, 1953), p. 37; Memorandum of Conversation with H. S. Rolston and Major Matthews, 3 April 1934, Add. Mss. 281 (hereafter cited as PNE), vol. 179, VCA.

6. Matthews, *Early History*, pp. 3, 37.

7. Minutes of Preliminary Meeting, 31 May 1907, PNE, vol. 1, f. 1, VCA.

8. List of Members in Vancouver Club, 1 July 1908, Add. Mss. 309, vol. 5, f. 30-45, VCA.

9. R. A. J. McDonald, "Business Leaders in Early Vancouver" (unpublished Ph.D. dissertation, University of British Columbia, 1972). Appendix B lists all the major busi-

ness leaders in the city and their primary occupations and commercial interests; *Henderson's British Columbia Directory, 1908* (Vancouver: Henderson, 1908), passim.

10. Matthews, *Early History*, pp. 8-9.

11. Minutes of an Emergency Meeting, 27 November 1907, PNE, vol. 1, f. 16-17, VCA; Minutes of Committee Meeting, 14 June 1907, PNE, vol. 1, f. 6-8, VCA.

12. Minutes of an Emergency Meeting, 27 November 1907, PNE, vol. 1, f. 16, VCA; Minutes of Council Meeting, 30 December 1909, PNE, vol. 1, f. 99, VCA; Minutes of Directors Meeting, 27 December 1910, PNE, vol. 1, VCA.

13. Minutes of Executive Council, 29 July 1910, PNE, vol. 1, f. 122-124, VCA.

14. Minutes of Executive Council, 5 March 1909, PNE, vol. 1, f. 46-47, VCA; Minutes of Executive Council, 7 July 1909, PNE, vol. 1, f. 67-68, VCA.

15. Minutes of Executive Council, 24 August 1909, 4 February 1910, PNE, vol. 1, f. 75 , vol. 1, f. 75 and 109, VCA.

16. Minutes of Executive Council, 4 February 1910, 12 August 1910, PNE, vol. 1, f. 109 and 133, VCA.

17. Minutes of Extraordinary General Meeting, 19 July 1907, PNE, vol. 1, f. 12-23, VCA.

18. Vancouver *Daily News Advertiser*, 8 January 1908, p. 4.

19. Record of 1908 elections, 9 January 1908, RG 2 D 1, vol. 1, f. 219, VCA.

20. Minutes of Committee Meeting, 16 January 1908, PNE, vol. 1, f. 19, VCA.

21. Minutes of Executive Council, 3 July 1908, PNE, vol. 1, f. 32, VCA.
22. Ibid.
23. Minutes of Vancouver City Council, 8 January 1909, RG 2 B 1, vol. 16, f. 17, VCA.
24. Record of 1909 elections, 14 January 1909, RG 2 D 1, vol. 1, f. 233, VCA.
25. Minutes of Executive Council, 25 June 1909, PNE, vol. 1, f. 66, VCA.
26. Minutes of Executive Council, 24 October 1909, PNE, vol. 1, f. 86, VCA; Minutes of Executive Council, 12 November 1909, PNE, vol. 1, f. 97, VCA; Minutes of Vancouver City Council, 7 December 1909, 17 January 1910, RG 2 B 1, vol. 16, f. 518 and 579, VCA; Record of 1910 elections, 13 January 1910, RG 2 D 1, vol. 1, f. 240, VCA.
27. V.E.A. Report, 16 December 1910, PNE, vol. 1, f. 166-178, VCA.
28. Minutes of Committee, 5 July 1907, PNE, vol. 1, f. 10-11, VCA; W. McKee, "The Vancouver Parks System" (unpublished M.A. thesis, University of Victoria, 1976). McKee's reading of the evidence appears incorrect. The argument advanced here is based on Vernon to City of Vancouver, 20 November 1888, RG 2, Series A1, vol. 1, VCA; Gore to Oppenheimer, 10 August 1889, RG 2, Series A1, vol. 2, VCA.
29. Unattributed history of the exhibition, nd, PNE, vol. 179, History, VCA.
30. McKee, "Vancouver Parks System"; Minutes of Jockey Club Committee, 3 October 1890, RG 2 B 2, vol. 66, f. 32, VCA.
31. Minutes of General Meeting, B.C. Jockey Club, 2 June 1892, Add. Mss. 244, VCA; Ibid., 1 April 1893.
32. Minutes of Vancouver City Council, 22 July 1907, RG 2 B 1, vol. 14, f. 635, VCA; Minutes of Annual General Meeting, 21 December 1908, PNE, vol. 1, f. 40-41, VCA.

33. Minutes of Committee Meeting, 19 July 1907, PNE, vol. 1, f. 12-13, VCA; Minutes of Vancouver City Council, 15 June 1908, 27 July 1908, RG 2 B 1, vol. 15, f. 401 and 459, VCA; Minutes of Executive Council, 1 May 1908, PNE, vol. 1, f. 29, VCA; Minutes of Vancouver City Council, 30 November 1908, RG 2 B 1, vol. 15, f. 621, VCA; Minutes of Executive Council, 25 September 1908, PNE, vol. 1, f. 33-34, VCA.
34. Minutes of Vancouver Parks Board, 19 December 1908, RG 7 A 1, vol. 3, f. 18, VCA.
35. Minutes of Vancouver City Council, 14 December 1908, RG 2 B 1, vol. 15, f. 660, VCA; Ibid., 5 October 1909, f. 556.
36. Minutes of Executive Council, 7 April 1909, PNE, vol. 1, f. 55-57, VCA.
37. Ibid., 15 June 1909, PNE, vol. 1, f. 65, VCA; Ibid., 13 October 1909, f. 83-84; Minutes of V.E.A. Grounds and Works Committee, 27 May 1909, RG 2, vol. 33, Exhibition Association and Buildings, VCA; Ramsay, Hepburn and Macpherson to Finance Committee, n.d., RG 2, vol. 25, Exhibition Association, 1909-10, VCA; J. E. Bird to Comptroller, 12 July 1910, RG 2, vol. 33, Exhibition Association and Buildings, VCA; Bird to Comptroller, 12 July 1910, RG 2, vol. 33, Exhibition Association and Buildings, VCA.
38. Alderman McSpadden was a particularly valued proponent of the V.E.A. cause, especially in the debate over the Hastings Park lease. Minutes of the Executive Council, 19 March 1909, PNE, vol. 1, f. 50-54, VCA.
39. Minutes of Vancouver City Council, 28 February 1910, RG 2 B 1, vol. 16, f. 673, VCA.
40. Minutes of Executive Council, 10 April 1908, PNE, vol. 1 f. 28, VCA.
41. Ibid., 23 July 1909, f. 70; Minutes of Council, 13 October 1909, PNE, vol. 1, f. 83, VCA.

CHAPTER 3: FIRST YEARS, 1910-1914

1. B.C. Agricultural Fairs Association, First Annual Convention, *B.C. Sessional Papers*, 1910, p. N17.
2. Ibid., p. N28.
3. Minutes of Council, 29 April 1910, PNE, vol. 1, f. 117-119, VCA; V.E.A. Report, 16 December 1910, PNE, vol. 1, f. 166-178, VCA.

4. *Vancouver Daily Province*, 5 August 1910, p. 16; See V.E.A. advertisments in the local press for usage of "Industrial Exhibition."
5. Ibid.
6. *Vancouver Daily Province*, 13 August 1910, p. 17.
7. Minutes of Council, 5 August 1910, PNE, vol. 1, f. 128, VCA; Vancouver *Daily News*

Advertiser, Second Section, 14 August 1910, p. 1.

8. *Vancouver Daily Province*, 11 August 1910, p. 6.

9. Matthews, *Early History of the V.E.A.*, p. 42.

10. Vancouver *Daily News Advertiser*, 17 August 1910.

11. *Vancouver Daily Province*, 5 August 1910, p. 16; Vancouver *Daily News Advertiser*, 16 August 1910, p. 2.

12. Ibid.; Vancouver *Daily News Advertiser*, Second Section, 14 August 1910, p. 1.

13. V.E.A. Report, 16 December 1910, PNE, vol. 1, f. 166-178, VCA.

14. Ibid.; Vancouver *Daily News Advertiser*, 16 August 1910, p. 4.

15. Minutes of Council, 12 August 1910, PNE, vol. 1, f. 133, VCA; Statement of Receipts and Expenditures, 1910 Exhibition, PNE, vol. 1, f. 178, VCA.

16. Vancouver *Daily News Advertiser*, 16 August 1910, p. 4.

17. *Vancouver Daily Province*, 22 August 1910, p. 3.

18. V.E.A. Report, 16 December 1910, PNE, vol. 1, f. 166-178, VCA; Minutes of Council, 8 November 1910, PNE, vol. 1, f. 151-153, VCA; Ibid., 25 November 1910, PNE, vol. 1, f. 154-155, VCA.

19. V.E.A. Report, 10 November 1911, PNE, vol. 1, f. 206-208, VCA; V.E.A., *Bulletin #4* (1913).

20. Ibid.

21. Ibid.

22. Minutes of Board of Directors, 17 August 1912, PNE, vol. 1, f. 246, VCA; V.E.A., *Bulletin #4* (1913), Comparative Statement, p. 21.

23. Ibid.

24. Ibid., p. 11; Minutes of Board of Directors, 4 April 1913, PNE, vol. 1, f. 267, VCA.

25. Vancouver *Daily News Advertiser*, 2 August 1910, p. 3; V.E.A. Report, 16 December 1910, PNE, vol. 1, f. 166-178, VCA; Minutes of Vancouver City Council Exhibition Committee, 10 August 1911, RG2 B2, vol. 53, f. 16, VCA.

26. Minutes of Vancouver City Council, 1 August 1910, RG2 B1, vol. 17, f. 255, VCA.

27. Ibid., 10 October 1910, RG2 B1, vol. 17, f. 375, VCA; Minutes of Board of Park Commissioners, 12 October 1910, RG7 A1, vol. 3, f. 151, VCA; Minutes of Vancouver City Council, 24 October 1910, RG2 B1, vol. 17, f. 408-409, VCA; Minutes of Board of Park Commissioners, 14 December 1910, RG7 A1, vol. 3, f. 169, VCA.

28. For a sketchy outline of this conflict, see W. McKee, "The Vancouver Parks System."

29. Minutes of Board of Park Commissioners, 12 February 1913, RG7 A1, vol. 3, f. 458, VCA; Minutes of Vancouver City Council, 24 February 1913, vol. 19, f. 298, VCA; Minutes of Vancouver City Council Exhibition Committee, 21 February 1913, RG2 B2, vol. 53, f. 25, VCA.

30. Minutes of Board of Directors, 26 February 1913, PNE, vol. 1, f. 262-263, VCA. Some minor adjustments were made the following year. Minutes of Board of Control, 25 February 1914, PNE, vol. 2, VCA; Minutes of Special Meeting with Council and the Parks Board, 7 May 1914, PNE, vol. 2, VCA. The Board of Park Commissioners remained a vocal critic, but as the by-law results show the ratepayers generally supported Council's action.

31. V.E.A., *Bulletin #4* (1913).

32. Record of 1911 Election, 12 January 1911, RG2 D1, vol. 1, f. 265, VCA; Record of 1912 Election, 11 January 1912, RG2 D1, vol. 1, f. 293, VCA.

33. Ibid.

34. Record of 1913 Election, 9 January 1913, RG2 D1, vol. 1, f. 306, VCA.

35. V.E.A., *Bulletin #4* (1913), Comparative Statement, p. 21.

36. Minutes of Directors' Meeting, 8 May 1912, PNE, vol. 1, f. 233, VCA.

37. V.E.A. Report, 16 November 1911, PNE, vol. 1, f. 206-208, VCA; V.E.A., *Bulletin #4* (1913), Comparative Statement, p. 21.

38. V.E.A., *Bulletin #3* (1912), p. 15.

39. New Westminster did not even send a representative to the first meeting of the B.C.A.F.A. in 1910. B.C. Agricultural Fairs Association, First Annual Convention, *B.C. Sessional Papers, 1910*; V.E.A., *Bulletin #3* (1912).

40. V.E.A., *Bulletin #4* (1913).

41. V.E.A., *Bulletin #3* (1912), pp. 32-43.

42. V.E.A., *Bulletin #4* (1913).

CHAPTER 4: THE WAR YEARS, 1914-1918

1. V.E.A. *Bulletin #5* (1914).
2. Minutes of the Vancouver Board of Trade, 31 January 1914, Add. Mss. 300, vol. 3, f. 197, VCA. On this date the Board of Control finally accepted the V.E.A.'s long standing offer to place a representative of the V.B.C. on the exhibition Board of Directors; Ibid., 7 February 1918, Add. Mss. 300, vol. 3, f. 431, VCA.
3. Vancouver *Daily Province*, 3 September 1914, p. 6. See also Vancouver *Sun*, 2 September 1914, p. 3; Vancouver *Daily News Advertiser*, 14 August 1915, 4 September 1914, p. 1.
4. V.E.A. *Bulletin #5* (1914).
5. Ibid., p. 22.
6. Ibid., p. 15.
7. Minutes of the Board of Directors, 14 October 1914, PNE, vol. 132, f. 33-34, VCA; Ibid., 13 November 1914, f. 38.
8. Minutes of the Exhibition Committee, 5 July 1918, RG 2 B 2, vol. 53, f. 70, VCA.
9. Ibid., 15 July 1918, f. 71.
10. V.E.A. *Bulletin #8* (1917); Minutes of the Vancouver Board of Trade, 6 September 1918, Add. Mss. 300, vol. 96, f. 10, VCA; Ibid., 25 November 1918, f. 11.
11. Ratepayers' Central Association Petition, 1917, PNE, vol. 3, VCA; Minutes of the Board of Control, 11 March 1918, PNE, vol. 4, f. 25-27, VCA.
12. Exhibition Association to the Ratepayers' Central Executive, 23 October 1917, PNE, vol. 3, VCA.
13. V.E.A. *Bulletin #9* (1918).
14. Report of the Board of Control, 11 January 1918, PNE, vol. 3, VCA.
15. Ibid., 20 March 1918; Minutes of the Vancouver Board of Trade, 18 February 1918, Add. Mss. 300, vol. 144, f. 60-62, VCA.
16. Ibid., 8 March 1918, f. 62.
17. Grisdale to Cowan, 28 April 1928, RG 17 (Department of Agriculture), vol. 3197, file 150(2), PAC; V.E.A. *Bulletin #6-#9* (1915-1917); See also, Minutes of the Vancouver Board of Trade, 8 March 1918, Add. Mss. 300, vol. 144, f. 62, VCA.
18. Report on the North Pacific Fairs Association Convention, 20 December 1916, PNE, vol. 3, VCA; Minutes of the Board of Control, 11 January 1918, PNE, vol. 4, VCA; Report on Fair Convention, 20 February 1918, PNE, vol. 4, VCA.
19. V.E.A. *Bulletin #8* (1917); Minutes of the Board of Control, 11 January 1918, PNE, vol. 4, VCA.
20. See for example Manager's Report, 19 June 1918, PNE, vol. 3, VCA.
21. V.E.A. *Bulletin #5* (1914); V.E.A. *Bulletin #6* (1915).
22. Exhibition Association to Officer Commanding, 23rd Infantry, 11 October 1917, PNE, vol. 3, VCA: Mathews, *Early History*, pp. 24-26.
23. Manager's Report, 15 January 1919, PNE, vol. 3, VCA.
24. V.E.A. *Bulletin #9* (1918), p. 37.
25. V.E.A. *Bulletin #7* (1916), p. 6; V.E.A. *Bulletin #8* (1917) p. 9.
26. V.E.A. *Bulletin #8* (1917), pp. 53-55; V.E.A. *Bulletin #9* (1918), pp. 38-39.
27. V.E.A. *Bulletin #9* (1918).

CHAPTER 5: CONTROVERSY, DEFIANCE AND EXPANSION, 1919-1930

1. V.E.A., *Bulletin #10* (1919), p. 19.
2. V.E.A., *Bulletin #10* (1919), p. 21.
3. Ibid., p. 25.
4. Minutes of Board of Control, 30 July 1919, PNE, vol. 4, f. 70-72, VCA; Ibid., 17 April 1919, PNE, vol. 3; Ibid., 30 July 1919, PNE, vol. 4, f. 70-72, VCA.
5. V.E.A., *Bulletin #10* (1919), p. 15, 76.
6. Minutes of Board of Control, 23 June 1919, PNE, vol. 4, f. 66-67, VCA.
7. Ibid., 22 October 1919, PNE, vol. 4, f. 78-79, VCA.
8. V.E.A., *Bulletin #11* (1920), pp. 9-10.
9. V.E.A., *Bulletin #12* (1921). Relative Importance of B.C. Fairs, 1923, PNE, vol. 1A, f. 173-177, VCA.
10. Minutes of Board of Control, 2 March 1923, PNE, vol. 8, VCA. For reports of this meeting, see Vancouver *Sun*, 3 March 1923 and 20 March 1923.

11. Minutes of Board of Park Commissioners, 13 March 1923, RG 7 A1, vol. 7, f. 5, VCA; Ibid., 12 June 1923, f. 98.

12. Minutes of Board of Control, 25 April 1923, PNE, vol. 8, VCA.; Rolston to Board of Directors, (1923), PNE, vol. 1A, f. 182, VCA.

13. V.E.A., *Bulletin #12* (1921); Rolston to Board of Directors, (1923), PNE, vol. 1A, f. 182.

14. Minutes of Board of Control, 8 June 1923, PNE, vol. 8, VCA.

15. Ibid., 18 August 1924.

16. Minutes of Vancouver City Council, 1 December 1924, RG 2 B 1, vol. 25, f. 394; Vancouver *Sun*, 18 December 1924, p. 1.

17. See copies of civic correspondence dated 10 January 1925 between Pilkington and McQueen, RG 2, vol. 107, Special Committee on V.E.A., VCA.

18. McQueen to Manager, Vancouver Daily Province, 10 January 1925, McQueen to Pilkington, 10 January 1925, McQueen to Bird, 10 January 1925, McQueen to Rolston, 10 January 1925, McQueen to Carmichael, 10 January 1925, McQueen to Williams, 10 January 1925, RG 2, vol. 107, Special Committee on V.E.A., VCA.

19. McLean, Matheson, Baynes, Horie and Craddock to Executive Committee, Associated Property Owners of Vancouver, 17 March 1925, RG 2, vol. 107, Special Committee on V.E.A., VCA.

20. Vancouver *Sun*, 19 January 1925, T. B. Gray letter to the editor; 22 January 1925, E. Bougoin letter to the editor; 27 January 1925, A. R. Miller letter to the editor; 31 January 1925, C. J. Fothergill letter to the editor; 20 March 1925, I. Bailey letter to the editor; 25 April 1925, A Lover of a Clean Exhibition letter to the editor.

21. Minutes of Special Committee on V.E.A., 5 January 1925, RG 2 B 1, vol. 25 f. 505, VCA; Ibid., 4 March 1925, f. 557.

22. Ibid., 5 January 1925.

23. Things the Public Should Know Regarding the Vancouver Exhibition, 21 March 1925, RG 2, vol. 107, Special Committee on V.E.A., VCA. Manager's Report, 18 March 1925, Ibid.; Results of Questionnaire Mailed Out by the Vancouver Exhibition, 19 March 1925, Ibid. The association received considerable criticism, led by Alderman Bennett, for what was seen as a blatant attempt to manufacture public support. Vancouver *Sun*, 31 January 1925.

24. Rolston to Exhibition Committee of City Council, 28 January 1925, Ibid.

25. Minutes of Special Committee on V.E.A., 5 January 1925, RG 2 B 1, vol. 25, f. 505, VCA.

26. Vancouver *Daily Province*, 26 April 1925.

27. Minutes of Board of Control, 24 April 1925, PNE, vol. 11, VCA.

28. Minutes of Vancouver City Council, 13 May 1925, RG 2 B 1, vol. 25, f. 674, VCA; Minutes of the Board of Control, 1 May 1925, PNE, vol. 11, VCA. The press generally supported the V.E.A.'s attempt to retain control. See Vancouver *Daily Province*, 11 April 1925, 25 April 1925.

29. Record of 1925 Elections, RG 2 D 1, vol. 2, f. 43-44, VCA.

30. See in particular two editorials, Vancouver *Sun*, 18 April 1925 and Vancouver *Daily Province*, 18 April 1925. Rolston's rebuttal and a further comment by the editor can be found in Vancouver *Daily Province*, 21 April 1925.

31. Minutes of the Board of Control, 11 May 1925, PNE, vol. 11, VCA.

32. Ibid., 23 October 1925; Draft letter re: Proposed Amalgamation of New Westminster and Vancouver Exhibitions, February 1926, RG 17, vol. 3207, file 150-23(1), PAC.

33. Ibid.

34. Minutes of Executive Meeting, 9 February 1927, PNE, vol. 14, VCA; Minutes of the Board of Control, 10 February 1927, PNE, vol. 14, VCA.

35. E. S. Archibald to Dr. Grisdale, 4 April 1929, RG 17, vol. 3208, file 150-23(2), PAC.

36. Minutes of the Board of Control, 21 September 1928, PNE, vol. 15, VCA. Vancouver *Daily Province*, 7 December 1928.

37. Mackenzie to Arkell, 17 October 1929, RG 17, vol. 3212, file 150-57(1), PAC.

38. Mackenzie to Motherwell, Minister of Agriculture, 27 December 1929, Ibid.

39. Minutes of the District of Burnaby Council, 10 December 1928, 21 December 1928, 19 August 1929, 30 September 1929, November 19, 1928 to December 30, 1929, RG 61, Simon Fraser University Archives; Mackenzie to Motherwell, 27 December 1929, Reeve W. L. Burdick to W. L. Mackenzie King, 7 November 1929, RG 17, vol. 3212, file 150-57(1), PAC; Walter Leek, "Vancouver's Position with Regard to its Exhibition Site," Vancouver *Sunday Province*, 2 March 1930.

40. Grisdale to Mackenzie, 9 January 1930, RG 17, vol. 3212, file 150-57(1), PAC.
41. Privy Council Minute 2417, 15 September 1930, RG 17, vol. 3208, file 150-23(2), PAC.
42. Rolston to Board of Control, 15 June 1922, PNE, vol. 1A, f. 56-57, VCA; Minutes of the Board of Control, 28 March 1930, PNE, vol. 16, VCA.
43. Exhibition Policies of the Federal Deparment of Agriculture, (c. 1922), RG 17, vol. 3198, file 150-1(1), PAC.; Motherwell to D. W. Warner, M.P., 4 April 1922, RG 17, vol. 3198, file 150-1(1), PAC.
44. Protests were primarily directed through Members of Parliament. Ladner to Motherwell, 1 May 1922, Ibid; Motherwell to Ladner, 3 May 1922, Ibid.; Rolston to Board of Control, (1922), PNE, vol. 1A, f. 51-52, VCA.
45. Federal Aid to Exhibition Associations, 26 March 1923, RG 17, vol. 3198, file 150-1(1), PAC; Memorandum re: Grants to Class "A" Fairs, (1923), RG 17, vol. 3198, file 150(3), PAC; Grisdale to Cowan, 28 April 1928, RG 17, vol. 3197, file 150(2), PAC.
46. Relative Importance of British Columbian Fairs, 1923, PNE, vol. 1A, f. 173-177, VCA.
47. King to Motherwell, 14 May 1923, RG 17, vol. 3198, file 150(3), PAC.
48. Motherwell to King, 23 May 1923, Ibid.; Arkell to Grisdale, 17 May 1923, RG 17, vol. 3198, file 150-1-1, PAC. Grisdale to Cowan, 28 April 1928, RG 17, vol. 3197, file 150(2), PAC.; Privy Council Minute 2147, 15 September 1930, RG 17, vol. 3208, file 150-23(2), PAC.
49. Archibald to Grisdale, 4 April 1929, Ibid.
50. V.E.A. to Motherwell, 1 November 1926, RG 17, vol. 3207, file 150-23(1), PAC.
51. Record of 1928 Elections, RG 2 D 1, vol. 2, f. 71-72, VCA.
52. Record of 1925, 1928, 1930 Elections, RG 2 D 1, vol. 2, VCA.
53. Minutes of the Board of Control, 3 November 1929, PNE, vol. 15, VCA.
54. Ibid., 7 November 1930, 26 November 1930, PNE, vol. 16, VCA.
55. Record of 1930 Elections, RG 2 D 1, vol. 2, f. 154-157, VCA.
56. V.E.A., *Bulletin #15* (1924); Minutes of the Building, Markets and Exhibition Committee, 6 April 1925, RG 2 B 2, vol. 52, f. 441, VCA; Matheson to McQueen, 2 October 1925, RG 2, vol. 107, V.E.A., VCA;

V.E.A., *Bulletin #12* (1921); V.E.A., *Bulletin #15* (1924); Walter Leek, "Vancouver's Position with Regard to its Exhibition Site," Vancouver *Sunday Province*, 2 March 1930; V.E.A., *Bulletin #21* (1930).
57. Relative Importance of B.C. Fairs, 1923, PNE, vol. 1A, f. 173-177, VCA; Minutes of the Board of Control, 23 June 1925, PNE, vol. 11, VCA; Draft letter re: Proposed Amalgamation of New Westminster and Vancouver Exhibitions, February 1921, RG 19, vol. 3207, file 150-23(1); Minutes of the Board of Control, 22 January 1930, PNE, vol. 16, VCA.
58. Minutes of the Board of Control, 11 December 1929, PNE, vol. 15, VCA; V.E.A., *Bulletin #11* (1920).
59. Grisdale to Matheson, 20 October 1925, RG 17, vol. 3207, file 150-23(1), PAC.
60. V.E.A. to Motherwell, January 1927, Ibid.
61. Arkell to Grisdale, 4 May 1926, Ibid.
62. V.E.A. to Motherwell, January 1927, Ibid; Matheson to Motherwell, 16 May 1928, Ibid; Privy Council Minute 1915. 2 October 1929, RG 17, vol. 3208, file 150-23(2), PAC; Grisdale to Motherwell, 12 September 1930, Ibid.
63. Minutes of the Board of Control, 13 November 1922, PNE, vol. 8, VCA; Ibid., 1 October 1923. 19 June 1924, PNE, vol. 8, VCA; Ibid., 12 October 1927, PNE, vol. 14, VCA; V.E.A., *Bulletin #14* (1923); V.E.A., *Bulletin #17* (1926).
64. Minutes of Market and Exhibition Committee, 8 November 1920, RG 2 B 2, vol. 52, f. 321, VCA; Ibid., 23 January 1922, 20 February 1922, f. 348, 350, VCA; Minutes of the Board of Control, 4 September 1922, PNE, vol. 4, f. 159, VCA; Ibid, 8 June 1923, vol. 8, VCA; Ibid., 1 June 1923, PNE, vol. 8, VCA; Ibid., 23 October 1925, PNE, vol. 11, VCA; Minutes of the Market and Exhibition Committee, 26 October 1925, RG 2 B 2, vol. 26, f. 74, VCA; Minutes of the Board of Control, 1 June 1923, PNE, vol. 8, VCA.
65. Ibid., 19 September 1930, PNE, vol. 16, VCA.
66. Ibid., 28 April 1926, PNE, vol. 13, VCA. Ibid., 17 June 1927, 22 June 1927, PNE, vol. 14, VCA.
67. Ibid., 25 April 1922, 29 June 1922, PNE, vol. 4, f. 136-138, 148-149; Manager's Report, 15 January 1919, PNE, vol. 1A, f. 13-14, VCA. V.E.A., *Bulletin #12* (1921); Rolston to Board of Control, (c. 1923), PNE, vol. 1A, f. 13-14, VCA.

68. V.E.A., *Bulletin #11* (1920), p. 16.
69. V.E.A. letterhead retained the heading "Vancouver Exhibition Association," but a sidebar reminded the observer that the or-

ganization operated "Canada's Pacific Exhibition." V.E.A., *Bulletin #16* (1925), p. 16.

CHAPTER 6: PROSPERITY IN TIMES OF TROUBLE, 1930-1939

1. Open letter to President and members of the V.E.A. Board of Control, 15 July 1930, PNE, vol. 23, VCA; General Manager to Woodlord, City Clerk, 17 July 1935, PNE, vol. 23, VCA; Minutes of the Board of Control, 31 July 1938, PNE, vol. 24, VCA; Minutes of the Parade Committee, 26 July 1935, PNE, vol. 24 VCA; Ibid., 30 July 1938, 23 August 1938.
2. Minutes of the Board of Control, 21 July 1930, PNE, vol. 16, VCA.
3. Ibid., 9 January 1931, PNE, vol. 17, VCA; V.E.A. *Bulletin #22* (1931); Minutes of the Board of Control, 14 September 1931, PNE, vol. 17, VCA; Ibid., 11 March 1932, vol. 18; Minutes of the Board of Control, 11 March 1932, PNE, vol. 18, VCA; Ibid., 9 January 1931, vol. 17.
4. Regarding the use of relief gangs for building projects, see Correspondence with City of Vancouver, 1930-1932, PNE, vol. 170, VCA. See also Minutes of the Board of Control, 19 December 1938, PNE, vol. 141, VCA; Leek and Matheson to Hon. Nels Lougheed, 7 September 1930, RG 17, vol. 3208, file 150-23(2), PAC; Leek to Robert Weir, 12 January 1935, RG 17, vol. 3208, file 150-23(3), PAC.
5. Leek to Weir, 12 January 1935, RG 17, vol. 3208, file 150-23(3), PAC.
6. Minutes of the Board of Control, 11 March 1931, PNE, vol. 17, VCA; Memo from President Leek, 8 October 1935, PNE, vol. 23, VCA; V.E.A. *Bulletin #29* (1938); Minutes of the Board of Control, 22 May 1935, PNE, vol. 23, VCA.
7. VCA Clipping file, 20 October 1932, V.E.A. doc. I, VCA; V.E.A. *Bulletin #23* (1932). V.E.A. *Bulletin #24* (1933).
8. See for example President Walter Leek's message to the members of the Board of Control, 15 October 1934, PNE, vol. 170, VCA. Minutes of the Board of Control, 16 December 1931, PNE, vol. 17, VCA; Manager to Finance Committee, n.d. (1933), PNE, vol. 19, VCA; Minutes of the Board of

Control, 8 June 1934, PNE, vol. 21, VCA; 31 October 1934; 22 May 1935, vol. 23; 12 June 1935.
9. Ibid., 11 July 1930, vol. 16; 29 April 1931, vol. 17; 13 May 1931, 25 September 1931, 14 October 1931, vol. 17; 23 October 1931, 26 November 1931. 6 April 1932, vol. 18.
10. See Minutes of B.C. Amusement Co. (volume is improperly named), 1932-1937, PNE, vol. 138, passim. for evidence of the P.C.A.C.'s efforts; Minutes of the Board of Control, 4 March 1930, PNE, vol. 26, VCA; 6 April 1936, 13 May 1936, vol. 26. See also Mathers to Banfield, 21 May 1935 and Banfield to V.E.A., 27 May 1935, Pacific Coast Amusement Co. Ltd., #1, PNE, vol. 184, VCA. V.E.A. *Bulletin #29* (1938), pp. 16-18; P.C. Amusement Co. Ltd. To Gross, Acting General Manager, V.E.A., 7 March 1938, P.C. Amusement Co. Ltd., #2, PNE, vol. 184, VCA; Minutes of the Board of Control, 2 December 1936, PNE, vol. 26, VCA; Old Exhibition Contracts, PNE, vol. 184, passim., VCA.
11. Minutes of the Board of Control, 27 March 1935, PNE, vol. 23, VCA; Ibid.; 8 January 1936, 16 January 1936, 6 May 1936, 22 July 1936, 1 August 1936, 11 September 1936, vol. 26, 25 November 1936.
12. Ibid., 2 December 1936, 7 December 1936.
13. Vancouver *Daily Province*, 3 December 1936.
14. Ibid., 16 December 1936, 18 December 1936; Leek to City Council, 17 December 1936, Leek to Mayor McGeer, 21 December 1936, RG 3, vol. 16, Exhibition Association, VCA. See also Auditors 1936, re: White, n.d., PNE, vol. 170, VCA.
15. Minutes of the Board of Control, 17 December 1936, PNE, vol. 26, VCA.
16. Ibid., 23 December 1936; V.E.A. *Bulletin #27* (1936). This entire issue is extremely well documented. See City Audit and Auditors, PNE, vol. 170, VCA; Correspondence with Price, Waterhouse and Co., 1934, 1936, PNE, vol. 171, VCA; V.E.A. Audit

Inquiry, 3 April 1937, PNE, vol. 171, VCA; Embezzlement, 1936-1937, PNE, vol. 132, VCA.

17. Vancouver *Sun*, 31 March 1937.
18. Minutes of the Board of Control, 27 January 1937, PNE, vol. 29, VCA; For a text of the Hockley inquiry see V.E.A. Audit Inquiry, 3 April 1937, PNE, vol. 171, VCA.
19. Minutes of the Board of Control, 19 March 1937, PNE, vol. 29, VCA.
20. Ibid., 23 April 1937, 28 April 1937.
21. Ibid., 19 March 1937.
22. Ibid., 23 April 1937.
23. Leek to Matheson, 6 May 1937, PNE, vol. 29, VCA. For Leek's public pronouncements on the same issue, see president Walter Leek's message to the V.E.A., August 1937, PNE, vol. 171, VCA.
24. Minutes of the Board of Control, 16 February 1938, PNE, vol. 139, VCA. There were a total of 146 applications including, somewhat surprisingly, G. S. Hockley, the recently dismissed Assistant General Manager; Minutes of the Markets, Exhibition and Tourist Development Committee, 21 February 1938, RG 2 B2, vol. 54, f. 549, VCA.
25. Minutes of the Board of Control, 26 February 1932, PNE, vol. 18, VCA.
26. V.E.A. *Bulletin #30* (1939); Constitution of the Vancouver Exhibition Association, 1 February 1939, RG 17, vol. 3208, file 150-23(3), PAC; Minutes of the Board of Control, 11 May 1938, PNE, vol. 139, VCA.
27. V.E.A. *Bulletin #24* (1933); Pacific Press clipping file, 29 October 1933, PNE, doc. 12, VCA.
28. Leek to members, Vancouver Exhibition Association, n.d. (1937), RG 3, vol. 23, Exhibition Association, VCA. See also V.E.A. *Bulletin #29* (1938).
29. V.E.A. *Bulletin #28* (1937).
30. V.E.A. *Bulletin #22* (1931).
31. Leek and Matheson to Hon. Nels Lougheed, RG 17, vol. 3208, file 150-23(2), PAC; Memorandum with respect to the application of the Vancouver Exhibition Association for grant of $150,000, 25 February 1931, RG 17, vol. 3208, file 150-23(2), PAC; V.E.A. to Hon. Robert Weir, 6 February 1931, V.E.A. to Hon. H. H. Stevens, 1931, V.E.A. to Hon. Robert Weir, 12 January 1935, RG 17, vol. 3208, file 150-23(3), PAC.
32. For an indication of the V.E.A.-Liberal connection see V.E.A. to Motherwell, 1 November 1926, RG 17, vol. 3207, file 150-23(1),

PAC; V.E.A. to Mackenzie King, 28 October 1935, RG 17, vol. 3208, file 150-23(2), PAC.
33. Minutes of the Board of Control, 4 November 1936, PNE, vol. 26, VCA, 26 January 1937, vol. 29; V.E.A. *Bulletin #30* (1939); Minutes of the Board of Control, 9 August 1939, PNE, vol. 34, VCA; Ibid., 31 May 1939, vol. 33, See also Government Grants, PNE, vol. 174, for details on negotiations involved in this transaction; Minutes of the Board of Control, 13 October 1939, PNE, vol. 33, VCA.
34. Minutes of the Board of Control, 16 December 1931, PNE, vol. 17, VCA; 22 May 1934, vol. 21; 12 February 1936, vol. 26.
35. Ibid., 23 January 1935, 13 February 1935. For a complete documentation of the engineering and financial aspects of the reconstruction of the Forum building, see Forum Reconstruction, 1935 and Forum Roof Collapse, January 1935, PNE, vol. 170, VCA; Minutes of the Board of Control, 17 April 1935, PNE, vol. 23, VCA.
36. Ibid., 3 July 1935, vol. 23.
37. Ibid., 1 December 1935, 13 December 1937, vol. 30.
38. Ibid., 6 July 1932, vol. 18; Ibid., 8 September 1933, vol. 19; Ibid., 5 December 1934, vol. 21. See also the various contracts in Forum Contracts, PNE, vol. 184, passim., VCA.
39. Minutes of the Board of Control, 8 November 1933, PNE, vol. 19, VCA; Matheson to Hon. Robert Weir, 15 August 1932, RG 17, vol. 3208, file 150-23(2), PAC; Letter from Vancouver Exhibition Association, 6 August 1936, RG 3, vol. 16, Exhibition Association, VCA. Minutes of the Board of Control, 2 October 1935, PNE, vol. 23, VCA; Ibid., 8 October 1933, vol. 19; Sundry Grounds Revenue Contracts, Lease Agreement between Vancouver Exhibition Association and Vancouver Indoor Tennis Club and A. Stuart Milne, October 1936, PNE, vol. 184, VCA. The arrangement saw the tennis club agree to pay $150.00 per month plus expenses for the use of the Horse Show Building.
40. Minutes of the Board of Control, 14 October 1936, PNE, vol. 26, VCA; Ibid., 15 December 1937, vol. 30.
41. Ibid., 14 October 1936, vol. 26; Ibid., 15 December 1937, vol. 30.
42. Ibid., 11 January 1939, 29 January 1939, vol. 33; 15 December 1937, vol. 30; 23 January 1938, vol. 144; 2 October 1935, vol. 23; 25 January 1939, vol. 33.

CHAPTER 7: THE V.E.A. AND WORLD WAR II, 1939-1946

1. V.E.A., *Bulletin #31* (1940); Article prepared by federal Department of Agriculture staff, submitted over the signature of Hon. James Gardiner for publication in *Billboard Magazine*, 1941, RG 17, vol. 3198, file 150(3), PAC; V.E.A., *Bulletin #31* (1940). Dunsmuir to Breeders of Livestock, Poultry and Pet Stock, 24 March 1941, PNE, vol. 140, VCA; General Manager to editor, 26 March 1941, Ibid.

2. Minutes of the Board of Control, 4 June 1941, PNE, vol. 36, VCA.; Ibid., 20 June 1941.

3. Minutes of the Executive Committee, 10 February 1941, PNE, vol. 35, VCA. V.E.A., *Bulletin #32* (1941). Minutes of the Executive Committee, 18 February 1942, PNE, vol. 38, VCA; Minutes of the Board of Control, 4 March 1942, 18 March 1942, Ibid.

4. Minutes of the Board of Control, 4 June 1941, PNE, vol. 36, VCA; 20 June 1941.

5. Ibid., 11 February 1942, PNE, vol. 38, VCA.

6. V.E.A., *Bulletin #31* (1940); Minutes of the Annual General Meeting, 20 January 1941, PNE, vol. 37, VCA; See also material in PNE, vols. 172-173, Exhibition Gardens, 1939-1941, VCA.

7. Dunsmuir to Gardiner, 3 October 1939, RG 17, vol. 3208, file 150-23(3), PAC.

8. Ibid. The same arrangement was made available to all winter fair organizations across Canada. Gardiner to Dunsmuir, 11 October 1939, RG 17, vol. 3208, file 150-23(3), PAC.

9. Minutes of the Board of Control, 12 September 1939, 13 September 1939, PNE, vol. 34, VCA; Dunsmuir to C. V. Dawson, 8 September 1939, PNE, vol. 184, Government-Military Occupation, VCA. Interestingly, this agreement was reached before Canada was officially at war. Minutes of the Board of Control, 13 August 1941, PNE, vol. 36, VCA; Minutes of the Executive Committee, 22 October 1941, ibid.

10. Minutes of the Board of Control, 26 November 1941, PNE, vol. 37, VCA.

11. The best study of the racial tensions in British Columbia is W. P. Ward, *White Canada Forever: Popular Attitudes and Public Policy Towards Orientals in British Columbia* (Montreal: McGill-Queens, 1978).

12. Quoted in ibid., p. 149.

13. Ibid., pp. 149-155.

14. B.C. Security Commission, *Report of the B.C. Security Commission, March 4, 1942 to October 31, 1942* (Vancouver: B.C.S.C., 1942). For a critical assessment of this organization, see K. Adachi, *The Enemy That Never Was* (Toronto: McClelland and Stewart, 1976), pp. 199-277; A. Sunahara, *The Politics of Racism* (Toronto: Lorimer, 1981).

15. Minutes of the Board of Directors, 28 January 1942, PNE, vol. 38, VCA; Gibson to McLennan, 23 January 1942, PNE, vol. 173, Occupation of Grounds, VCA; Minutes of the Executive Committee, 10 March 1942, PNE, vol. 38, VCA.

16. MacNamara to Taylor, 13 March 1942, RG 27, vol. 655, file 23-2-9-1 pt. 1, PAC.

17. Minutes of the Board of Directors, 25 March 1942, PNE, vol. 38, VCA; Mitchell to Gibson, 27 March 1942, RG 27, vol. 655, file 23-2-9-1 pt. 1, PAC; Mackenzie to Mitchell, 31 March 1942, ibid; Privy Council Minutes 2972, 14 April 1942, ibid.; Minutes of the Board of Control, 6 June 1942, PNE, vol. 38, VCA.

18. Privy Council Minute, 2 July 1942, RG 27, vol. 655, file 23-2-9-1 pt. 1, PAC, Minutes of the Board of Control, 6 June 1942, PNE, vol. 38, VCA. For additional detail on the lease negotiations, see PNE, vol. 174, Military lease of Hastings Park, 1942-1943, VCA.

19. Muriel Fujiwara Kitagawa to Wesley Kitagawa, 20 April 1942, Kitagawa Papers, MG 31 E26, PAC.

20. Adachi, *The Enemy That Never Was*, pp. 246-249; *Report of the B.C. Security Commission*, pp. 7-8, Sunahara, *The Politics of Racism*.

21. *Report of the B.C.S.C.*, p. 8.

22. Adachi, p. 247.

23. *Report of the B.C.S.C.*, p. 8.

24. H. H. Wrong to Consul General of Spain, 6 October 1942, RG 27, vol. 655, file 23-2-9-1, pt. 1, PAC; Hodgins to MacNamara, 26 September 1942, ibid.

25. Mayor Cornett to Hon. H. Mitchell, 29 April 1942, ibid.

26. Adachi, p. 246; *Report of the B.C.S.C.*, p. 8.

27. V.E.A., *Bulletin #32* (1942); V.E.A., *Bulletin #34* (1943); V.E.A., *Bulletin #35* (1944); Minutes of the Executive Committee, 21 October 1943, PNE, vol. 40, f. 100,

VCA; Ibid, 10 November 1943, f. 112; For greater detail on the administration of the park and financial dealings between the V.E.A. and the B.C.S.C. and the Department of National Defence, see PNE, vol. 172-173, select files.

28. Minutes of the Executive Committee, 15 November 1944, PNE, vol. 42, f. 33, VCA.

29. V.E.A., *Bulletin #36* (1945); Minutes of the Board of Directors, 11 March 1948, PNE, vol. 45, f. 37, VCA; Minutes of the Executive Committee, 14 May 1946, 12 July 1946, ibid., f. 87, 128; Dunsmuir to Deputy Minister, Department of National Defence, 18 October 1946, PNE, vol. 44, f. 37, VCA; Minutes of the Board of Directors, 29 October 1946, PNE, vol. 46, f. 89, VCA; Privy Council Minute 4857, 26 November 1946, RG 27, vol. 655, file 23-2-9-1 pt. 1, PAC.

30. Minutes of the Boys' and Girls' Competitions Committee, 28 August 1942, PNE, vol. 39, f. 1, VCA; Minutes of the Board of Control, 1 April 1942, PNE, vol. 38, VCA; Ibid., 10 October 1945, PNE, vol. 43, f. 125, VCA.

31. Minutes of the Post-War Planning Committee, 3 October 1945, PNE, vol. 43, f. 128, VCA; Minutes of the Board of Directors, 1 March 1945, PNE, vol. 47, f. 79, VCA.

32. Minutes of the B.C. Products Committee, 12 April 1945, PNE, vol. 47, f. 117, VCA. For examples of events staged see PNE, vol. 184, Forum Contracts, passim, and ibid., Box Lacrosse: Inter-City League, passim.

33. Dunsmuir to V.E.A., 27 February 1941, PNE, vol. 172, Lipsett Museum, VCA; McLennan to Frank Jones, City Comptroller, 17 June 1941, ibid.; Edward and Mary Lipsett to Fred Howlett, City Clerk, April 1941, ibid.

34. Minutes of the Board of Control, 18 March 1942, PNE, vol. 38, VCA. Minutes of the Callister Exhibition Park Committee, 18 October 1945, PNE, vol. 43, f. 137, VCA.

35. Minutes of the Board of Control, 15 October 1943, PNE, vol. 40, VCA. Ibid., 27 January 1944, PNE, vol. 41, f. 11-14, VCA; Dunsmuir to City Council, 25 January 1944, ibid.

36. Minutes of the Park Extension Committee, 12 February 1945, PNE, vol. 47, f. 57, VCA.

37. Report re: Extension, 26 March 1945, PNE, vol. 47, f. 85-87, VCA. V.E.A., *Bulletin #37* (1946); The complex expansion process is well documented in PNE, vol. 174, Golf Course Extension, 1933-44, VCA.

38. V.E.A., *Bulletin #33* (1942); Minutes of the Board of Control, 10 July 1945, PNE, vol. 43, f. 62-3, VCA; V.E.A., *Bulletin #34* (1943); Minutes of the Board of Control, 25 November 1942, PNE, vol. 39, f. 49, VCA; Minutes of the Executive Committee, 12 July 1946, PNE, vol. 45, f. 128, VCA.

39. Minutes of the Executive Committee, 12 July 1946, PNE, vol. 45, f. 128, VCA; Minutes of the Board of Control, 4 June 1941, PNE, vol. 36, VCA; Minutes of the Executive Committee, 30 March 1942, PNE, vol. 38, VCA; Meeting of the Vancouver Exhibition Association, 1943, PNE, vol. 40, f. 35, VCA.

40. Minutes of the Board of Directors, 29 July 1943, PNE, vol. 38, f. 137, VCA.

41. Minutes of the Board of Control, 26 April 1944, PNE, vol. 41, VCA; Vancouver *Sun*, 30 May 1945.

42. Minutes of the Board of Control, 2 May 1946, PNE, vol. 45, VCA; PNE, vol. 169, General Manager Competitions, 1937-1946, VCA.

43. Minutes of the Executive Committee, 22 November 1944, PNE, vol. 42, f. 34-36, VCA; Ibid., 8 October 1943, PNE, vol. 40, f. 98, VCA. VCA Clipping File, 27 January 1945, V.E.A. Doc. II.

44. *Western Business and Industry*, vol. 27, no. 8 (August 1953), p. 42; Minutes of the Post-War Planning Committee, 1943, PNE, vol. 40, f. 37, VCA.

45. For examples of the committee's discussions and deliberations, see PNE, vol. 169, Post-War Planning Committee Correspondence, 1944-1947, VCA.

46. Minutes of the Board of Control, 1 November 1944, PNE, vol. 42, f. 27, VCA; Ibid., 21 June 1944, 28 June 1944, PNE, vol. 41, f. 104, 115-117, VCA.

47. Report upon the General Development [of] Exhibition Park, December 1948, PNE, vol. 179, Planning, VCA. There is mention made of a similar though less extensive plan being drawn up in 1939, but it was never adopted. Dunsmuir to A. M. James, 17 April 1944, PNE, vol. 169, Post-War Planning Committee Correspondence, 1944-1947, VCA.

48. V.E.A., *Bulletin #34* (1943).

49. P.N.E., *Bulletin #37* (1946). Minutes of the Market, Exhibition, Industry and Tourist Development Committee, 10 July 1939, RG 2 B2, vol. 54, f. 283, VCA.

CHAPTER 8: THE PACIFIC NATIONAL EXHIBITION: THE "NEW" FAIR AND THE BRITISH
EMPIRE GAMES, 1946-1954

1. Minutes of the Board of Control, 9 April 1947, PNE, vol. 49, f. 58, VCA; Minutes of the Attractions and Concessions Committee, 25 February 1947, PNE, vol. 48, f. 52, VCA; Minutes of the Board of Control, 9 April 1947, PNE, vol. 49, f. 58, VCA.
2. Ibid., 13 March 1947, PNE, vol. 49, f. 8, VCA.
3. Ibid., 23 April 1947, PNE, vol. 49, f. 77, VCA.
4. Ibid., 14 April 1948, PNE, vol. 53, f. 52, VCA; Minutes of the Attractions and Concessions Committee, 26 May 1948, PNE, vol. 53, f. 92, VCA; Minutes of the Board of Control, 2 June 1948, vol. 53, f. 102, VCA; Minutes of the Board of Control, 1 June 1949, PNE, vol. 56, f. 111, VCA; P.N.E. *Bulletin #41* (1950); Minutes of the Attractions Committee, 12 September 1950, PNE, vol. 61, f. 37, VCA.
5. Minutes of the Executive Committee, 20 January 1947, PNE, vol. 48, f. 3 VCA; Minutes of the Board of Control, 2 April 1947, PNE, vol. 49, f. 57, VCA.
6. Ibid., 16 April 1947, vol. 49, f. 64; Minutes of the Board of Directors, 29 December 1942, PNE, vol. 51, f. 62, VCA.
7. Minutes of a Special Meeting, 11 March 1948, PNE, vol. 52, f. 92-93, VCA; P.N.E. *Bulletin #42* (1951).
8. Minutes of the Board of Control, 7 November 1947, PNE, vol. 51, f. 21, VCA; Minutes of the Board of Directors, 12 November 1947, vol. 51, f. 26, VCA.
9. Minutes of the Development Committee, 3 January 1949, PNE, vol. 55, f. 44, VCA; Minutes of the Board of Control, 31 May 1950, PNE, vol. 60, f. 42, VCA; Minutes of the Board of Directors, 29 December 1947, PNE, vol. 51, f. 59, VCA; Minutes of the Market Exhibition, Industry and Tourist Development Committee, 9 February 1948, RG 2 B 2, vol. 5, f. 83, PAC. The new holes allowed the PNE to close nine holes of the golf course located west of Windermere Street, making that space available for the exhibition, P.N.E. *Bulletin #43* (1952). Minutes of the Board of Control, 18 July 1951, PNE, vol. 64, f. 44, VCA; P.N.E. *Bulletin #43* (1952).
10. P.N.E. *Bulletin #42* (1951); Public letter

from President Ferguson, November 1952, PNE, vol. 67, f. 8-9, VCA; Minutes of the Board of Control, 11 February 1953, PNE, vol. 67, f. 107, VCA; Ibid., n.d. (1953), vol. 70, f. 1; Ibid., 12 August 1953, vol. 71, f. 73.
11. Minutes of the Development Committee, 3 April 1951, PNE, vol. 63, f. 48, VCA; Minutes of the Board of Control, 11 April 1951, PNE, vol. 63, f. 74, VCA; Minutes of the Board of Control, 30 July 1952, PNE, vol. 68, f. 17, VCA; Public letter from President Ferguson, November 1952, PNE, vol. 67, f. 8-9, VCA; Minutes of the Board of Control, 11 February 1953, PNE, vol. 67, f. 107, VCA.
12. Minutes of the Board of Directors, 27 April 1949, PNE, vol. 56, f. 42, VCA; Minutes of the Development Committee, 11 January 1952, PNE, vol. 65, f. 90, VCA; Minutes of the Board of Control, 30 September 1953, PNE, vol. 71, f. 129, VCA; Minutes of the Board of Control, 6 June 1951, PNE, vol. 64, f. 3-4, VCA. 28 February 1951, PNE, vol. 63, f. 27, VCA; *Burnaby Advertiser*, 9 October 1952.
13. P.N.E. *Bulletin #44* (1953); Minutes of the Board of Control, 30 November 1952, PNE, vol. 72, f. 30-31, VCA; Minutes of the Board of Control, 13 January 1954, PNE, vol. 72, f. 101, VCA; Report of the Technical Planning Board, March 1954, Board of Administration, Series I, vol. 10, loc. 111-C-2, VCA; Treatise on Convention-Hall Arena vs. Exhibition Park Coliseum, PNE, vol. 73, f. 126-127, VCA.
14. VCA clipping file, 5 January 1954, V.E.A. doc. III, VCA; Minutes of the Public Relations Committee, 19 May 1954, PNE, vol. 74, f. 67, VCA.
15. Minutes of the Board of Control, 8 February 1950, PNE, vol. 58, f. 139, VCA; Minutes of the Development Committee, 11 January 1952, PNE, vol. 65, f. 90, VCA.
16. Vancouver *Province*, 25 March 1952; See newspaper clipping collection in Add. Mss. 172, British Empire and Commonwealth Games Canada (1954) Society, VCA; Vancouver *Province*, 26 March 1952, 27 March 1952, 22 April 1952; Vancouver *Sun*, 24 April 1952; Vancouver *Province*, 5 April

1952; Vancouver *Sun*, 24 April 1952; Victoria *Times*, 27 March 1952; Vancouver *Sun*, 12 June 1952, 20 September 1952.

17. Vancouver *Sun*, 20 September 1952; Vancouver *Province*, 29 October 1952; Vancouver *Province*, 30 October 1952; Vancouver *Province*, 31 October 1952.

18. General Manager to City Council, 14 November 1952, PNE, vol. 67, f. 52-53, VCA.

19. Vancouver *Sun*, 15 November 1952; Public letter from President Ferguson, November 1952, PNE, vol. 67, f. 8-9, VCA; Vancouver *News-Herald*, 12 November 1952, 19 November 1952.

20. Vancouver *Sun*, 11 December 1952; Voters Records, Money By-Laws, December 1952, MCR-19, Record of Elections, 1950-1976, VCA.

21. Minutes of the Board of Control, 26 November 1952, PNE, vol. 67, f. 62, VCA; Add. Mss. 172-8, 16 January 1953, VCA; President to City Council, 3 September 1953, PNE, vol. 71, f. 103-106, VCA; Minutes of the Board of Control, 4 September 1953, vol. 71, VCA; Welsh to P.N.E., 3 September 1953, PNE, vol. 71, VCA.

22. Minutes of the Board of Control, 6 October 1954, PNE, vol. 76, f. 4, VCA; Ibid., 17 March 1954, vol. 73, f. 97.

23. Minutes of the Board of Directors, 26 May 1954, PNE, vol. 74, f. 83, VCA; Ibid., 7 July 1954, vol. 74, f. 134.

24. Minutes of the Board of Control, 11 August 1954, PNE, vol. 75, f. 50, VCA.

25. Ibid., 1 August 1951, PNE, vol. 64, f. 62-63, VCA, 5 October 1951, PNE, vol. 65, f. 5, VCA.

26. Ibid., 6 October 1954, PNE, vol. 76, f. 5, VCA; P.N.E. *Bulletin #45* (1954).

27. Minutes of the Board of Control, 4 August 1954, PNE, vol. 75, f. 42, VCA.

28. Minutes of the Racing Committee, 4 March 1947, PNE, vol. 48, f. 60, VCA.

29. Vancouver *Sun*, 26 June 1952, 21 August 1952; Minutes of the Board of Control, 8 October 1952, PNE, vol. 67, f. 4, VCA.; Ibid., 3 September 1953, PNE, vol. 71, f. 101-102, VCA; Ibid., 3 March 1954, vol. 73, f. 75.

30. Minutes of the Executive Committee, 20 January 1947, PNE, vol. 48, f. 3, VCA.

31. Minutes of Elected Directors, 25 January 1948, PNE, vol. 52, f. 30, VCA.

32. Minutes of the Board of Control, 30 August 1948, PNE, vol. 54, f. 101, VCA.

33. Ibid., 28 June 1950, PNE, vol. 60, f. 82, VCA.

CHAPTER 9: FALL FROM FAVOUR, 1954-1960

1. Minutes of the Executive Committee, 16 June 1959, PNE, vol. 98, f. 30, VCA; 10 April 1959, PNE, vol. 97, f. 70, VCA; Minutes of the Board of Directors, 17 April 1959, Ibid; Minutes of the Executive Committee, 12 February 1959, PNE, vol. 96, f. 89, VCA; Ibid., 22 July 1959; Minutes of the Theme Committee, 1960, PNE, vol. 105, f. 38, VCA.

2. Minutes of the Board of Control, 23 August 1954, PNE, vol. 75, f. 73, VCA.

3. Ibid.: Pacific Press clipping file, 17 August 1954, PNE Doc. 10, VCA; Ibid., 3 September 1954.

4. VCA clipping file, 24 August 1959, PNE Doc. 1, VCA.

5. Minutes of the Board of Directors, 12 October 1955, PNE, vol. 81, f. 10, VCA; Ibid., 17 April 1957, PNE, vol. 88, f. 39-40, VCA; Public Relations Report, 23 October 1958, PNE, vol. 95, f. 122, VCA.

6. Minutes of the Board of Directors, 24 October 1956, PNE, vol. 86, f. 29-30, VCA.

7. Ibid., 5 September 1955, PNE, vol. 80, f. 22, VCA; VCA clipping file, 10 April 1958, PNE Doc 1, VCA.

8. Minutes of the Board of Directors, 15 January 1958, PNE, vol. 91, f. 129, VCA; Minutes of the Executive Committee, 20 January 1958, PNE, vol. 92, f. 132, VCA; Ibid., 5 February 1958, PNE, vol. 92, VCA; Ibid., 27 May 1958, PNE, vol. 93, f. 120, VCA; Minutes of the Board of Directors, 2 July 1958, PNE, vol. 94, f. 71-72, VCA.

9. Minutes of the Project "X" Committee, 1 August 1958, PNE, vol. 94, f. 111-113, VCA; Minutes of the Executive Committee, 9 September 1958, PNE, vol. 95, f. 44, VCA; Minutes of the Board of Directors, 8 October 1958, PNE, vol. 95, f. 65-66, VCA.

10. Minutes of the Executive Committee, 1 October 1958, PNE, vol. 95, f. 56, VCA.

11. Minutes of the Board of Directors, 8 October 1958, PNE, vol. 95, f. 66, VCA.
12. Ibid.; PNE, *Annual Report 1959*.
13. Minutes of the Board of Directors, 8 April 1960, PNE, vol. 103, f. 101-103, VCA; 18 May 1960, PNE, vol. 104, f. 17-18, VCA.
14. Pacific Press clipping file, 28 June 1960, PNE Doc. 6, VCA.
15. Minutes of the Board of Directors, 27 June 1960, PNE, vol. 104, f. 60, VCA; Minutes of the Sub-Committee on New Brighton Park, 30 June 1960, PNE, vol. 104, f. 61, VCA.
16. Pacific Press clipping file, 10 August 1960, PNE Doc. 6, VCA.
17. P.N.E., *Annual Report 1961*.
18. VCA clipping file, 20 January 1955, PNE Doc 1, VCA; Press-radio release 45/58 (n.d.), PNE, vol. 178, Advance Sale, 1954-1961, VCA; P.N.E., *Bulletin #46* (1955); Minutes of the Board of Directors, 29 June 1955, PNE, vol. 79, f. 44, VCA; Minutes of the Board of Control, 2 March 1955, PNE, vol. 77, f. 56-57, VCA. For a complete summary of the debate and the issues surrounding the advance sale controversy, see PNE, vol. 178, Advance Sale, 1954-1957, VCA and PNE, vol. 178, Advance Sale, 1954-1961, VCA; Minutes of the Board of Directors, 16 December 1959, PNE, vol. 100, f. 76, VCA; VCA clipping file, 14 January 1955, PNE Doc. 1, VCA.
19. Minutes of the Board of Directors, 16 December 1959, PNE, vol. 100, f. 76; VCA; VCA clipping file, 14 January 1955, PNE Doc. 1, VCA. For documentation of the discussion over the constitution, see PNE, vol. 168, Constitution and By-Law Revision, 1954-1955 and vol. 169, Constitution, VCA.
20. Vancouver *Sun*, 12 January 1955, VCA clipping file, 26 January 1955, PNE Doc. 1, VCA; Ibid., 17 January 1955.
21. Vancouver *Sun*, 2 February 1955; Vancouver *Province*, 2 February 1955.
22. PNE, vol. 168, Constitution and By-Law Revision, 1954-1955, VCA.
23. PNE Incorporation Act, *B.C. Statutes*, Chapter 107, p. 531.
24. Ibid., p. 526.
25. Minutes of Annual General Meeting, 12 December 1957, PNE, vol. 106, f. 3, VCA.
26. Minutes of the Board of Directors, 5 June 1957, PNE, vol. 88, f. 121, VCA.
27. Ibid., 12 March 1958, PNE, vol. 93, f. 32, VCA; Ibid., 20 January 1958, PNE, vol. 91,

f. 134, VCA; Public Relations Report, 30 October 1958, PNE, vol. 95, f. 123-124, VCA.
28. VCA clipping file, 30 August 1961, PNE Doc. 2, VCA; Coleman Hull to PNE, 16 November 1956, PNE to Hull, 23 November 1956, PNE, vol. 86, f. 64-66, VCA; Minutes of the Board of Directors, 16 December 1959, PNE, vol. 100, f. 76, VCA; Pacific Press clipping file, 17 November 1961, PNE, Doc. 9, VCA.
29. VCA clipping file, 3 September 1957, PNE Doc. 1; Vancouver *Province*, 3 September 1957.
30. Minutes of the Executive Commitee, 29 May 1958, PNE, vol. 93, f. 139, VCA.
31. Minutes of the Board of Directors, 23 May 1956, PNE, vol. 83, f. 97, VCA; 19 June 1957, 17 July 1957, PNE, vol. 89, f. 7, 47, VCA; Ibid., 5 January 1961, PNE, vol. 105, f. 113-114, VCA. See also New Proposals Re: Police Training Academy, PNE, vol. 176, New Livestock Building #2, VCA, and PNE, vol. 180, City of Vancouver-Police, 1962-1966, VCA.
32. Minutes of the Board of Directors, 22 August 1957, PNE, vol. 89, f. 109, VCA; Ibid., 8 October 1957, PNE, vol. 91, f. 22-23, VCA.
33. Minutes of the Executive Committee, 10 July 1958, PNE, vol. 94, f. 100, VCA.
34. VCA clipping file, 30 April 1958, PNE Doc. 1, VCA.
35. Minutes of the Executive Committee, 17 February 1959, PNE, vol. 96, f. 88, VCA; Minutes of the Board of Directors, 5 August 1959, PNE, vol. 98, f. 102, VCA.
36. VCA clipping file, 7 December 1956, PNE Doc. 1, VCA; Minutes of the Board of Directors, 12 April 1961, PNE, vol. 106, f. 135, VCA.
37. VCA clipping file, 7 December 1956, PNE Doc. 1, VCA; Ibid., 30 August 1961, PNE Doc. 2, VCA.
38. Minutes of the Board of Directors, 3 February 1960, PNE, vol. 100, f. 114, VCA. Ibid., 12 September 1958, 18 September 1958, 19 September 1958, PNE, vol. 95, f. 49, 52-53, 56, VCA; VCA clipping file, 14 September 1960, PNE Doc. 1, VCA; Minutes of the Stadium Negotiating Committee, 7 September 1960, PNE, vol. 105, f. 18, VCA.
39. Pacific Press clipping file, 14 December 1960, Ascot Jockey Club; Minutes of the Board of Directors, 12 April 1961, PNE,

vol. 106, f. 134-135, VCA; PNE, *Annual Report 1961*.

40. PNE, *Annual Report 1961*.

41. Minutes of the Executive Committee, 19 October 1961, PNE, vol. 109, f. 25, VCA; 29 May 1958, PNE, vol. 93, f. 139, VCA.

42. Minutes of the Board of Directors, 15 June 1955, 10 August 1955, PNE, vol. 79, f. 4, 116, VCA; P.N.E., *Bulletin #47* (1956).

43. Minutes of the Board of Directors, 1 June 1955, PNE, vol. 78, f. 119, VCA.

44. Ibid., 20 March 1957, PNE, vol. 87, f. 120, VCA.

45. Ibid., 3 April 1957, 3 July 1957, PNE, vol. 89, f. 14, 43, VCA; 11 December 1957, PNE, vol. 91, f. 107, VCA; Minutes of the Annual General Meeting, 12 December 1957, PNE, vol. 166, VCA.

46. Minutes of the Board of Directors, 21 May 1958, PNE, vol. 93, f. 124, VCA.

47. VCA clipping file, 13 July 1961, PNE Doc. 1, VCA.

48. Minutes of the Board of Directors, 11 September 1957, PNE, vol. 90, f. 30-37, VCA; Pacific Press clipping file, 9 July 1958, PNE Doc. 12, VCA; Minutes of the Board of Directors, 18 July 1956, PNE, vol. 84, f. 57-59, VCA.

49. Ibid., 5 December 1956, PNE, vol. 86, f. 102-103, VCA.

50. Ibid., 19 December 1956, PNE, vol. 86, f. 108-109, VCA. Dorwin Baird personally entered the fray, making a number of broadcasts on local radio to back the P.N.E.'s stance. Copy of a commentary broadcast on CKNW, 16 July 1959, PNE, vol. 176, New Livestock Building #2, VCA.

51. Voters' Records, 1956, Livestock Coliseum, MCR-19, Record of Elections, 1950-1956, VCA; VCA clipping file, 6 March 1957, PNE Doc. 1.

52. Downtown Convention Hall-Sports Arena, 1954-1961, Appendix A, Report of Technical Planning Board, 21 September 1956, Historical Summary, Board of Administration, series I, vol. 16, Loc. 111-c-2, VCA.

53. Minutes of the Board of Directors, 20 March 1957, PNE, vol. 87, f. 121, VCA.

54. PNE Agricultural Building, 1962, "Factual Summary of Proposed PNE Livestock Arena," 10 February 1960, Board of Administration, series 1, vol. 20, Loc. 111-c-6, VCA; Minutes of the Executive Committee, 2 December 1958, PNE, vol. 96, f. 7-8, VCA.

55. Minutes of the Board of Directors, 28 October 1958, 11 February 1960, PNE, vol. 100, f. 28, 137, VCA.

56. See "Factual Summary of Proposed PNE Livestock Arena" 10 February 1960, for a statement of the proposals as of that date; Ferguson to Bowell, 11 December 1959, PNE, vol. 100, f. 69-72, VCA.

57. Berry to Council, 6 March 1961, PNE, vol. 106, f. 91, VCA.

58. VCA clipping file, 11 February 1961, PNE Doc. 2, VCA.

59. Vancouver *Province*, 5 May 1961, 6 May 1961.

60. VCA clipping file, 6 June 1961, PNE Doc. 2, VCA; City Council Minutes, 16 May 1961, RG 2 B 2, vol. 77, f. 24, VCA.

61. Minutes of the Board of Directors, 13 September 1961, PNE, vol. 108, f. 93, VCA; VCA clipping file, 14 September 1961, PNE Doc. 2, VCA.

62. Minutes of the Sub-Committee on the Livestock Arena, 22 September 1961, PNE, vol. 109, f. 1, VCA; P.N.E., *Annual Report 1961*; Minutes of the Board of Directors, 2 May 1961, PNE, vol. 107, f. 33-34, VCA.

63. The debate over the coliseum is exhaustively documented in PNE, vol. 176, New Livestock Building #2, 1956-1963; PNE, vol. 177, Downtown Stadium Controversy, 1950-1961 and New Livestock Building #3, 1958-1960; PNE, vol. 178, New Livestock Building, 1955-1957, VCA.

Included in these extended files are relevant correspondence with civic, federal and provincial officials, House of Commons debates, transcripts of radio broadcasts, a few newspaper clippings and submissions by the PNE, Downtown Business Association and the Technical Planning Board on this controversial issue. VCA clipping file, 1 November 1961, PNE Doc. 2, VCA; City Council Minutes, 31 October 1961, 6 November 1961, RG 2 B 1, vol. 78, f. 490-491, 551-552, VCA; Minutes of the Board of Directors, 8 December 1961, PNE, vol. 109, f. 40-41, VCA.

64. Vancouver *Province*, 23 May 1961.

65. Pacific Press clipping file, 2 March 1961, PNE Doc. 7, VCA.

66. VCA clipping file, 16 November 1961, PNE Doc. 2, VCA.

67. Ibid., 7 December 1961, PNE Doc. 2, VCA.

CHAPTER 10: POLITICS OF CHANGE, 1960-1973

1. VCA clipping file, 10 November 1966, PNE doc. III, VCA. Minutes of the Board of Directors, 16 February 1967, PNE, vol. 122, f. 91, VCA.
2. Minutes of the Special Committee on Stadium Shows, 21 December 1965, PNE, vol. 121, f. 33, VCA; Minutes of the Board of Directors, 13 December 1967, PNE, vol. 123, f. 91, VCA; Ibid., 3 January 1968, PNE, vol. 123, f. 100, VCA; Vancouver *Sun*, 8 September 1969; Minutes of the Board of Directors, 16 June 1971, PNE, vol. 128, f. 31, VCA; Ibid., 18 May 1971, vol. 128, f. 18.
3. Minutes of the Attractions Committee, 11 January 1963, PNE, vol. 113, f. 46-47, VCA; Minutes of the Executive Committee, 17 December 1964, vol. 118, f. 117, VCA; Minutes of the Board of Directors, 20 January 1965, PNE, vol. 118, f. 135, VCA; Minutes of the Board of Directors, 12 July 1967, PNE, vol. 123, f. 35, VCA.
4. Vancouver *Sun*, 5 September 1968, 3 October 1968, 4 October 1968; Vancouver *Province*, 1 November 1968; In 1971, there appeared to be a slight chance that the old advance sale would be re-established. Inquiries to the federal government generated a decidedly negative response and the idea was soon dropped. See Minutes of the Finance Committee, 8 February 1971, PNE, vol. 127, f. 77, VCA; Minutes of the Executive Committee, 23 February 1971, PNE, vol. 127, f. 85, VCA.
5. Minutes of the Executive Committee, 26 June 1963, PNE, vol. 114, f. 85-86, VCA; Minutes of the Canadian Confederation Centennial Committee — PNE Sub-Committee, 30 September 1964, PNE, vol. 118, vol. 118, f. 46-48, VCA; Minutes of the Centennial Committee, 2 July 1965, PNE, vol. 120, f. 5-6, VCA; 14 November 1967, PNE, vol. 123, f. 83, VCA; Minutes of the Board of Directors, 11 January 1967, PNE, vol. 122, f. 78, VCA.
6. VCA clipping file, 23 August 1965, PNE doc. III, VCA; Vancouver *Province*, 12 June 1968; Minutes of the Board of Directors, 29 July 1968, PNE, vol. 124, f. 81, VCA; 7 August 1968, PNE, vol. 124, f. 83, VCA; Vancouver *Province*, 9 August 1968, 16 August 1968; Minutes of the Executive Committee, 9 April 1969, PNE, vol. 125, f. 58, VCA; Vancouver *Province*, 2 June 1969.
7. VCA clipping file, 14 November 1963, PNE doc. II, VCA; Minutes of the Board of Directors, 22 August 1968, PNE, vol. 124, f. 86, VCA; 29 August 1968, vol. 124, f. 90; 11 December 1968, vol. 125, f. 22.
8. Minutes of the Executive Committee, 24 February 1965, PNE, vol. 119, f. 38, VCA. 27 October 1965, vol. 121, f. 8; Minutes of the Board of Directors, 2 February 1966, vol. 121, f. 49; Ibid., 10 August 1966, vol. 122, f. 27. For a report recommending the admission increase and discussion of how other fairs made similar advances see Material re: Raising Ticket Prices, n.d., PNE, vol. 175, VCA. Minutes of the Board of Directors, 23 February 1971, PNE, vol. 127, f. 86, VCA. 31 August 1971, vol. 128, f. 58.
9. PNE *Annual Report 1967*.
10. Acres of Food, PNE, n.d., B.C. Federation of Agriculture Papers, vol. 3, file 3/6, Add. Mss. 365, Public Archives of British Columbia.
11. Minutes of the Livestock Sub-Committee, 22 September 1971, PNE, vol. 128, f. 68, VCA; Minutes of the Agricultural and Development and Coordinating Committee, 24 March 1972, PNE, vol. 129, f. 26, VCA; Minutes of the Elected and Advisory Directors, 29 September 1971, PNE, vol. 128, f. 66, VCA.
12. VCA clipping file, 10 March 1962, PNE doc. II, VCA; Minutes of the Board of Directors, 15 March 1962, PNE, vol. 110, f. 65-66, VCA; Minutes of the Executive Committee, 10 April 1962, vol. 110, f. 108, VCA; P.N.E. *Annual Report 1962*; Pacific Press clipping file, 10 June 1964, PNE doc. 7, VCA; Minutes of the Executive Committee, 11 September 1963, PNE, vol. 114, f. 2, VCA.
13. Minutes of the Board of Directors, 17 March 1965, PNE, vol. 119, f. 75, VCA.
14. Vancouver Civic Action Association Brief re: Sports Coliseum, 19 March 1965, Coliseum — Multi purpose 1962-1967, Board of Administration, Series I, vol. 16, VCA; Minutes of the Executive Committee, 28 July 1965, PNE, vol. 120, f. 34, VCA; Minutes of the Board of Directors, PNE, vol.

120, f. 9, VCA; Minutes of the Board of Directors, 28 July 1965, PNE, vol. 120, f. 36, VCA; Report of John Dunsmuir, 14 July 1965, vol. 120, f. 12-14, VCA.

15. R. G. Robertson to Ida Rae, 30 September 1965, Exhibition and Sports Building, PNE, vol. 176. Details of lobbying are noted throughout this file. See also Interview with Erwin Swangard, 3 June 1981; Misc. Material re: Exhibition and Sports Building, 1965, PNE, vol. 168, VCA; Harry Hays, Minister of Agriculture, to H. J. C. Terry, 26 May 1965, PNE, vol. 168, VCA; Minutes of the Sports Building Special Committee, 18 August 1965, PNE, vol. 168, VCA; Terry and Dunsmuir to W. A. C. Bennett, 25 August 1965, Exhibition and Sports Building, PNE, vol. 176, VCA; Minutes of the Board of Directors, 6 September 1965, PNE, vol. 120, f. 83-84, VCA; Ibid., 13 October 1965, vol. 121, f. 2-3. Negotiations for the various government grants can be followed in Misc. Material re: Exhibition and Sports Building, 1965, PNE, vol. 168, VCA; 27 August 1965, vol. 120, f. 71; 17 December 1965, vol. 121, f. 34.

16. VCA clipping file, 4 April 1966, PNE doc. III, VCA; 6 April 1966; Minutes of the Board of Directors, 17 June 1966, PNE, vol. 122, f. 1, VCA; 8 November 1967, vol. 123, f. 79; Ibid., 3 January 1968, vol. 123, f. 100.

17. Minutes of Planning Meeting, 29 October 1962, PNE, vol. 113, f. 18-20, VCA; Minutes of the Board of Directors, 19 December 1962, PNE, vol. 113, f. 38-39, VCA. Minutes of the Board of Directors, 7 December 1966, PNE, vol. 122, f. 66, VCA; Minutes of the Planning and Development Committee, 15 December 1969, PNE, vol. 126, f. 40, VCA.

18. Pacific Press clipping file, 20 February 1965, PNE doc. 12, VCA; Minutes of the Board of Directors, 15 April 1970, PNE, vol. 126, f. 84, VCA; 27 March 1965, PNE, vol. 119, f. 74, VCA; VCA clipping file, 18 March 1965, PNE doc. III, VCA; Minutes of the Executive Committee, 17 May 1965, PNE, vol. 119, f. 104, VCA; Minutes of the Board of Directors, 12 October 1966, PNE, vol. 122, f. 45, VCA.

19. Minutes of the Elected and Advisory Directors, 20 October 1971, PNE, vol. 128, f. 68, VCA; Minutes of the Planning and Development Sub-Committee (Livestock), 12 May 1971, PNE, vol. 128, f. 11, VCA.

20. Minutes of the Executive Committee, 9 May 1966, PNE, vol. 121, f. 93, VCA; Ibid., 3 January 1969, vol. 125, f. 24; Minutes of the Board of Directors, 19 March 1969, PNE, vol. 125, f. 50, VCA; Vancouver *Province*, 20 February 1971; Minutes of the Board of Directors, 23 February 1971, PNE, vol. 127, f. 86, VCA; Ibid., 28 April 1971, vol. 128, f. 7.

21. Minutes of the Board of Directors, 17 July 1968, PNE, vol. 124, f. 76, VCA; Vancouver *Sun*, 23 July 1968. The PNE's decision was backed up by the association's legal counsel. See Campbell to Puckstone, 10 May 1968, PNE, vol. 172, Lipsett Museum; Minutes of the Lipsett Indian Collection Sub-Committee, 9 February 1970, PNE, vol. 126, f. 61, VCA; Ibid., PNE, vol. 172, Lipsett Museum; Minutes of the Board of Directors, 21 May 1970, PNE, vol. 126, f. 94, VCA; Extracts from Vancouver City Council meeting, 28 February 1970, PNE, vol. 172, Lipsett Museum; PNE news press release, 28 July 1971, PNE, vol. 172, Lipsett Museum.

22. Minutes of the Board of Directors, 6 September 1971, PNE, vol. 128, f. 61, VCA; Ibid., 16 June 1971, vol. 128, f. 31.

23. Minutes of the B.C. Pavilion Committee, 12 July 1971, PNE, vol. 172, Lipsett Museum.

24. VCA clipping file, 20 September 1962, PNE doc. II; Pacific Press clipping file, 27 May 1964, B.C. Jockey Club, VCA; Minutes of the Board of Directors, 24 August 1964, PNE, vol. 118, f. 24, VCA; Minutes of the Board of Directors, 4 September 1972, PNE, vol. 129, f. 95, VCA; Minutes of the Executive Committee, 23 February 1966, PNE, vol. 121, f. 63, VCA; Minutes of the Executive Committee, 5 February 1964, PNE, vol. 116, f. 89-90, VCA; Minutes of the Board of Directors, 2 July 1969, PNE, vol. 125, f. 87, VCA; Vancouver *Province*, 21 January 1971.

25. Minutes of the Executive Committee, 8 May 1968, PNE, vol. 124, f. 52, VCA; Minutes of the Board of Directors, 1 November 1968, PNE, vol. 125, f. 7 VCA; 29 October 1969, vol. 126, f. 13; Ibid., 19 November 1969, vol. 126, f. 24. Tartan Turf was installed at a cost of $796,000. See Ibid., 19 July 1969, vol. 125, f. 90.

26. PNE *Annual Report 1962;* Minutes of the Board of Directors, 14 February 1962, PNE, vol. 109, f. 115-116, VCA; Minutes of the Board of Directors, 15 March 1962, PNE, vol. 110, f. 64, VCA; Ibid., 22 May 1962,

vol. 111, f. 31-32; Minutes of the Executive Committee, 28 May 1962, PNE, vol. 111, f. 38, VCA.

27. Minutes of the Board of Directors, 27 August 1965, PNE, vol. 120, f. 75, VCA; 19 November 1969, PNE, vol. 126, f. 24, VCA; Pacific Press clipping file, 19 November 1969, PNE doc. 12, VCA; Minutes of the Board of Directors, 26 November 1969, PNE, vol. 126, f. 30, VCA.

28. For changes in P.N.E. committee structure see Minutes of the Executive Committee, 22 November 1962, PNE, vol. 113, f. 30-31, VCA; Minutes of the Board of Directors, 12 October 1967, PNE, vol. 122, f. 46, VCA; Minutes of the Executive Committee, 13 October 1971, PNE, vol. 128, f. 67, VCA. Minutes of Elected and Advisory Directors, 29 September 1971, PNE, vol. 128, f. 68, VCA; Ibid., 13 November 1964, vol. 118, f. 100; Minutes of the Board of Directors, 18 November 1964, PNE, vol. 118, f. 67, VCA; Minutes of the Board of Directors, 8 December 1971, PNE, vol. 128, f. 88, VCA.

29. Minutes of the Elected and Advisory Directors, 29 September 1971, PNE, vol. 128, f. 66, VCA; Minutes of the Executive Committee, 20 January 1965, PNE, vol. 118, f. 131, VCA.

30. Minutes of the Elected and Advisory Directors, 20 October 1971, PNE, vol. 128, f. 68 VCA; Vancouver *Province*, 6 July 1962; Minutes of the Executive Committee, 27 May 1963, PNE, vol. 114 f. 47, VCA; Minutes of the Board of Directors, 8 August 1963, PNE, vol. 114, f. 120, VCA; Lease Agreement between the City of Vancouver and the Pacific National Exhibition, August 1963. Copy in the possession of the P.N.E.

31. Minutes of the Board of Directors, 19 September 1962, PNE, vol. 112, f. 12, VCA.

32. Ibid., 20 March 1968, vol. 124, f. 31; 16 April 1969, vol. 125, f. 61; 19 March 1969, vol. 125, f. 50.

33. Minutes of the Vancouver City Council, 6, 13, 20, 27 February 1973, RG 2 B 2, vol. 112, f. 189, 202, 312, 386, VCA.

34. Ibid., 20 February 1973, vol. 112, f. 312, The P.N.E. side of the debacle is described in Committee Minutes, October 1972–21 November 1973, PNE, vol. 182, VCA. The fight in City Council was led by Ald. Harry Rankin who, like Williams, was a long time opponent of the P.N.E. For a rebuttal to many of Rankin's charges see Takeover 1973 — Misc. Material, Rebuttal Points for Press Conference, n.d., PNE, vol. 182, VCA. For almost daily reports of the controversy see PNE, vol. 182, clipping book, PNE takeover.

35. *Western News*, 8 February 1973.

36. Vancouver *Province*, 19 February 1973; Pacific Press clipping file, 23 February 1973, PNE doc. 1, VCA.

37. British Columbia *Debates of the Legislative Assembly of B.C.*, 2nd Session, 30th Parliament, vol. 1, no. 1, p. 630.

38. Ibid., p. 631.

39. Ibid.

40. Vancouver *Province*, 24 February 1973.

41. Vancouver *Sun*, 24 February 1973.

42. *Debates*, vol. 1, no. 3, p. 2614.

43. Pacific Press clipping file, 2 March 1973, PNE doc. 1, VCA; Minutes of Vancouver City Council, 6 March 1973, RG 2 B 2, vol. 112, f. 428, VCA. For the certificate of surrender see Takeover 1973 — Misc., 28 February 1973, PNE, vol. 182, VCA.

44. Pacific National Exhibition Incorporation Act, 18 April 1973, British Columbia Statutes, chapter 66.

Bibliography

PRIMARY

VANCOUVER CITY ARCHIVES
1) *Additional Manuscripts*
   B.C. Jockey Club
   British Empire and Commonwealth Games
        Canada (1954) Society
   Pacific National Exhibition
   Terminal City Club
   Vancouver Board of Trade
   Vancouver Club
2) *City Records*
   Board of Administration
   City Clerk's Correspondence
   City Council Committee Minutes
        Jockey Club Committee
        Exhibition Committee
        Building, Markets, and Exhibition Committee
        Market and Exhibition Committee
        Market, Exhibition, and Tourist Development Committee
        Market, Exhibition, Industry, and Tourist Development Committee
   City Council Minutes
   Mayor's Correspondence
   Parks Board (a.k.a. Board of Park Commissioners)
   Record of Elections
PUBLIC ARCHIVES OF BRITISH COLUMBIA
        B.C. Federation of Agriculture Papers
PUBLIC ARCHIVES OF CANADA
        B.C. Security Commission
        Department of Agriculture
        Department of Labour
        Kitagawa Papers
SIMON FRASER UNIVERSITY ARCHIVES
        District of Burnaby Council Minutes

SECONDARY

Adachi, Ken. *The Enemy That Never Was*. Toronto: McClelland and Stewart, 1976.

Allwood, John. *The Great Exhibitions*. London: Studio Vista, 1977.

British Columbia Security Commission. *Report of the B.C. Security Commission, March 4, 1942-October 31, 1942*. Vancouver: B.C.S.C., 1942.

Cashman, Tony. *Edmonton Exhibition: The First Hundred Years*. Edmonton: Exhibition Association, 1979.

Central Canada Exhibition. *History of the Central Canada Exhibition from 1888*. Ottawa: Central Canada Exhibition, 1976.

Jones, David C. "Agriculture, The Land and Education." Ph.D. diss., University of British Columbia, 1978.

_____. "From Babies to Buttonholes." *Alberta History* 29 (Autumn 1981): 26-32.

_____. *Midways, Judges and Smooth Tongued Fakirs. The Illustrated Story of Country Fairs and the Prairie West*. Saskatoon: Prairie Producer, in press.

_____. "We cannot allow it to be run by those who do not understand education." *B.C. Studies* 39 (Autumn 1978): 30-60.

Lorimer, James. *The Ex: A Pictorial History of the Canadian National Exhibition*. Toronto: James, Lewis and Samuel, 1973.

MacDonald, Norbert. "A Critical Growth Cycle for Vancouver, 1900-1914." *B.C. Studies* 17 (Spring 1973): 26-45.

McDonald, R. A. J. "Business Leaders in Early Vancouver." Ph.D. diss., University of British Columbia, 1977.

_____. "Victoria, Vancouver, and the Evolution of British Columbia's Economic System, 1886-1914," in Alan Artibise, ed. *Town and City: Aspects of Western Canadian Urban Development*. Regina: Canadian Plains Research Center, 1981.

MacEwan, Grant. *Agriculture on Parade*. Toronto: Thomas Nelson and Sons, 1950.

McKee, William "The Vancouver Parks System." M.A. thesis, University of Victoria, 1976.

Matthews, James S., comp. *Early History of the Vancouver Exhibition Association*. Vancouver: Vancouver City Archives, 1953.

Neely, Wayne. *The Agricultural Fair*. New York: Columbia University Press, 1935.

Newell, Diane. "Canada at World's Fairs, 1851-1876." *Canadian Collector* 11, no. 4 (1976).

Ontario Association of Agricultural Societies. *The Story of Ontario Agricultural Fairs and Exhibitions, 1792-1967*. Toronto: O.A.A.S., 1967.

Osbourne, B. "Trading on a Frontier: The Function of Pedlars, Markets, and Fairs in 19th Century Ontario." *Canadian Papers in Rural History* II (1979).

Roy, Patricia. *Vancouver: An Illustrated History*. Toronto: Lorimer, 1980.

Sunahara, Ann G. *The Politics of Racism*. Toronto: James Lorimer, 1981.

Ward, W. Peter. *White Canada Forever: Popular Attitudes and Public Policy Towards Orientals in British Columbia*. Montreal: McGill-Queens, 1978.

Index